## DATE DUE

| | |
|---|---|
| 3430919 | 10/30/04 |
| 9796905 | NOV 2 4 1996 |
| JAN 1 3 1998 | |
| MAR 29 2002 | |
| MAR 28 2002 | |
| | |
| | |
| | |
| | |
| | |
| | |
| | |
| | |
| | |
| | |
| | |

# PORTRAITS OF SPIRITUALITY
# IN RECOVERY

## ABOUT THE AUTHOR

Nancy Barrett Chickerneo is currently a full-time art therapist and Director of Educational Services for the Central DuPage Pastoral Counseling Center in Wheaton, Illinois. She also facilitates workshops and retreats on local, state, and national levels. She formerly worked as an art therapist at an inpatient treatment center for chemical dependency.

She received her Doctor of Philosophy degree in Art Therapy from The Union Institute in Cincinnati, Ohio. Her Substance Abuse Certification was earned through the Alfred Adler Institute in Chicago. She received her M.A. in Religious Studies from Mundelein College in Chicago.

Doctor Chickerneo is also a working artist, living in the Chicago area with her husband and children.

# PORTRAITS OF SPIRITUALITY IN RECOVERY

## The Use of Art in Recovery from Co-Dependency and/or Chemical Dependency

*By*

NANCY BARRETT CHICKERNEO, Ph.D., A.T.R., CADC

*Director of Educational Services*
*Central DuPage Pastoral Counseling Center*
*Wheaton, Illinois*

CHARLES C THOMAS • PUBLISHER
*Springfield • Illinois • U.S.A.*

*Published and Distributed Throughout the World by*

CHARLES C THOMAS • PUBLISHER
2600 South First Street
Springfield, Illinois 62794-9265

© *1993 by* CHARLES C THOMAS • PUBLISHER

ISBN 0-398-05845-8

Library of Congress Catalog Card Number: 92-42194

*With* THOMAS BOOKS *careful attention is given to all details of manufacturing
and design. It is the Publisher's desire to present books that are satisfactory as to
their physical qualities and artistic possibilities and appropriate for their particular
use.* THOMAS BOOKS *will be true to those laws of quality that assure a good
name and good will.*

*Printed in the United States of America*
*SC-R-3*

**Library of Congress Cataloging-in-Publication Data**

Chickerneo, Nancy Barrett.
    Portraits of spirituality in recovery / the use of art in recovery
from co-dependency and/or chemical dependency / by Nancy Barrett
Chickerneo.
        p.      cm.
    Includes bibliographical references.
    ISBN 0-398-05845-8
    1. Substance abuse—Patients—Rehabilitation.   2. Substance abuse—
Patients—Rehabilitation—Case histories.   3. Codependents—
Rehabilitation.   4. Codependents—Rehabilitation—Case histories.
5. Art therapy.   6. Recovering addicts—Religious life.      I. Title.
RC564.C493     1993
616.86'065156—dc20
                                                                           92-42194
                                                                           CIP

*To my husband, Leon, and my children, Lindsey and Jay, for teaching me about love, God, and being free . . . to the people who have allowed me to share their lives and their stories on every level including the spiritual . . . and mostly to God who has provided the foundation of encouragement and love without which this project would never have been started.*

# PREFACE

My personal life journey is interwoven with art, spirituality, and recovery. It is as though I was living and preparing for this book for many years previous to considering it at a conscious level. Working with clients and students over the years, I kept hearing bits and pieces of stories which echoed my own experience. I became increasingly interested in and curious about a more formal exploration of the experience of the contribution of art to spirituality in recovery from co-dependency and/or chemical dependency. That exploration resulted in gathering together ten personal stories which are woven with many common themes, creating the powerful portrait of recovery presented in this book.

Since much of the previous work in these combined areas is theoretical, there is a need for research which highlights the essence of the experience of recovery including the spiritual dimension as experienced through art and art therapy. Very little research is currently available which interfaces these areas, and spirituality is an important component in the process of recovery. Therefore, knowledge about the contribution of art to recovery is valuable. Addiction is exterior attachment, whereas recovery is finding healing and wholeness through an interior journey. This book, about the interior experience, attempts to add clarity to the literature on the recovery process.

The ten co-researchers who are part of the study, both men and women, span a significant age range. Their stories, told in their own words, involve co-dependency and/or chemical dependency recovery. The themes which emerged from the data can be of use to art therapists or counselors who are currently working with recovering addicts, as well as to individuals who are recovering or interested in recovery.

Awareness of spirituality in recovery, as well as an awareness of the role that art can play in spiritual growth, is heightened by this book. Because art allows the one who creates it to be more visible to others, this work gives a deeper understanding of the disease of addiction, more comprehension of the recovery process, and more compassion for the individuals who suffer with the disease and have joy in recovery.

The book is designed to be enjoyed by general readers, professionals, and/or researchers in the fields of study. For example, the stories in Chapters 3–12 can be read separately from the rest of the text for the general reader. Chapter 1 provides some background information, and insight into the method of study is offered in Chapter 2. The common themes which emerged would be of general interest and are uncovered in Chapter 13. If a reader desires more background information about the literature in areas studied, it is found in Chapter 14. A realization of the broader deeper vision for the information in this book is detailed in Chapter 15.

*New Images, Ancient Paradigm: A Study of the Contribution of Art to Spirituality in Addiction Recovery* (Chickerneo, 1990) is the study from which this book has evolved and can be found through the reference section. The original study contains further information which might be useful such as additional literature reviews, specific procedures for conducting the study, limitations, etc.

I would be interested in reading your response to this work as well as your own experience of art and spirituality in recovery and I invite you to write, although I am unable to reply to each letter. Meanwhile, I continue to be amazed and delighted as I hear personal stories of art and spiritual journey through my work. It is my hope that this book and its stories will be useful as well as inspiring to all who read it.

NANCY BARRETT CHICKERNEO, PH.D., A.T.R., CADC
*Central DuPage Pastoral Counseling Center*
*714 Ellis Avenue*
*Wheaton, Illinois 60187*

# ACKNOWLEDGMENTS

I wish to thank The Share Program and the College of DuPage for providing the kind of open environment where stories such as the ones found in this book can be told. I also wish to thank The Union Institute which allows and encourages qualitative research, honoring to the subjective nature of art.

Carol Barrett, Ph.D.; Bruce Douglass, Ph.D.; Carol Frances Jegen, BVM, Ph.D.; Evadne McNeil, Ph.D., A.T.R., Dominic Fontaine, FSC, Ph.D., and Virginia Shaver, Ph.D. Cand., A.T.R., cooperated and worked hard in helping me refine the original study from which this book was created. For that I am grateful.

Thanks to John Crouch for all of his hard work with the photography. I also wish to thank Chilton Knudsen, Keena Cole, Elise Hamilton, Juanita Seavoy, Sandy Alcorn, Judy Sutherland, Lee Van Ham, Marty Painter, and Anne Utterback for their insightful suggestions and feedback in the making of this book.

# CONTENTS

# PORTRAITS OF SPIRITUALITY
# IN RECOVERY

Part I
# INTRODUCTION TO THE PROBLEM
# AND THE METHOD OF STUDY

# Chapter 1

# ADDICTION, SPIRITUALITY, AND ART

### Introduction

Addiction is a problem of enormous proportion in our culture. It is a problem which hurts people physically, emotionally, and spiritually. Therefore, recovery from the devastation of addiction includes all of the affected areas. Often the spiritual part of the recovery from addiction is either ignored or treated ineffectually. There is a need to deal with spirituality in order to provide a holistic treatment of addiction. Both spiritual growth and art making require an openness to the creative process, and art making and art therapy have been a conscious part of the recovery process for a number of recovering people, including myself.

With the problem of addiction permeating our society, each avenue of recovery must be thoroughly researched. Incredible numbers of lives are being lost or not lived to potential because of this disease. As an artist, I have personally experienced both spiritual growth and healing through art making. As an art therapist, I have been privileged to share in many amazing stories of transformation. Having first noticed the spiritual pathway created by art making in my own recovery, I later observed similarities in the recovery processes of others. My interest in further study developed. This book has evolved out of that study. It contains the documented stories and artwork of myself and nine others who have found art to be a powerful door to a personal spirituality in recovery.

The question of art's contribution to the spiritual part of recovery has evolved for me out of my own experience of recovery from co-dependence. My method of study, Heuristic Inquiry, required a personal immersion in the question as the first step in the research process. Although this is a book about recovery, it addresses the addictive process of each co-researcher so that the reader will have a context for the stories of recovery.

I believe my own addictive process began when I was a small child. My family was filled with tension and problems which eventually resulted in the divorce of my parents. During one period of upheaval, I lived

5

with an aunt for a year until things were settled between my parents. My childlike response to the painful situation in my family was to judge myself at fault, believing that I had in some way contributed to it. There was a great deal of verbal denial about the family problems and even the divorce. I was not even told of the divorce by my parents, but rather found out on the school bus from another child whose mother had read about it in our small town newspaper.

Divorce was much more rare when I was a child than it is now. That fact, coupled with the controlling denial of my family, caused me to feel great shame and I spoke of the situation to no one. As a result of this and other circumstances, I began to withhold much of my true self, including my fear and anger. I worked very hard at being good and not making waves in order to "fix" my family. Eventually, I even forgot my painful feelings as I directed most of my attention outwardly as a co-dependent pleaser of others. For the past fifteen years, I have been in the process of letting go of my codependent, people-pleasing, perfectionist behaviors and recovering my true self.

Spiritual growth and art have been an important part of the recovery process for each personal story in this book, including mine. The question that each recovering co-dependent and or chemical dependent answered was, "How has art contributed to the spiritual part of your recovery?" This book describes the effect art making has had on the experience of spirituality in these ten people. The word *art* was defined as graphic art but included other expressive art forms that grew out of this experience for the co-researcher. The word *spiritual* in this study was defined as the co-researchers defined it personally, in order to encourage freedom for each person to define this as it emerged individually. The word *recovery* was defined in this study as the process of restoration to health and wholeness in which what has been lost or missing for the co-researchers is recouped. The recovery process from addiction will be emphasized in this study; however, before recovery is considered, addiction itself will be discussed by each participant.

Next, for the reader's clarity, addiction will be defined for the purposes of this book. Chemical dependence and co-dependence are described in the sections immediately following the section on addiction. This will be followed by a clarification of the role that spirituality plays in the recovery process from addiction. A section on the use of art therapy in the treatment of chemical dependence will complete this chapter.

## Addiction

Addiction is defined in *The American Heritage Dictionary* as devoting or giving "(oneself) habitually or compulsively" to something. The word "slave" is used later in the definition (Morris, 1976). In this book the word *addiction* will be used to mean the continuous, compulsive enslavement to anything which is harmful for the person. Addiction happens when attachments to behaviors, things, or people become obsessive.

The cycle of addiction, as described by Charles Whitfield, in *Healing the Child Within* (1987), goes from a repression of feelings, to a tension buildup, to the compulsive behavior, to painful feelings about the compulsion, and a consequential denial of feelings. There is a healthy alternative offered through addictions counseling, the meetings of Alcoholics Anonymous, and many other 12-step programs: express your feelings, share your story, experience your own reality. The difficulty often comes because the feelings and stories that need to be expressed are deeply painful, and escape to addiction seems to be more tolerable than encountering the truth.

During the course of the addictive process, addicted people find themselves compulsively repeating once pleasurable activities which now bring despair and isolation. The addictive process may involve a chemical (referred to as chemical dependence) or certain relationship dynamics (co-dependence). The symptoms of chemical dependence and co-dependence are very similar, apart from the physical effect of the chemical (Johnson, 1980). All addiction is attachment, and the recovery process from all addiction requires breaking the attachment.

## Chemical Dependence

Chemical dependence is a devastating problem in our culture, destroying people physically, mentally, emotionally, and spiritually. In the United States, alcoholism is the third leading cause of death. Alcohol-related crime costs over $3 billion a year according to Kinney and Leaton (1987). They state that the projected cost of alcohol misuse in the United States for 1983 was $116.7 billion, and the problem has increased.

In 1957 the American Medical Association accepted alcoholism as a disease. Chemical dependency is considered by many to be a disease in which addicts become dependent on a substance outside of themselves in an attempt to secure internal serentiy. Alcoholism is often thought of as a spiritual disease. In the case of an alcoholic, alcohol can be "used" to deal with stress, problems, or lack of inner peace.

Relapse is a problem for recovering substance abusers. Involvement in a program based on the 12 steps of Alcoholics Anonymous or long-term treatment have been found to aid in the attainment of long-term sobriety (Farris-Kurtz, 1981).

Denial and dishonesty are cornerstone characteristics of the disease of chemical dependency. As a result, addicts continue to believe they can "solve" this problem while continuing to relapse into their destructive dependency behavior. Clients who felt very powerless when entering treatment often begin to forget this as they feel better and thus sow the seed for relapse once more because the disease of alcoholism is chronic and progressive.

## Co-Dependence

Also a devastating problem in our culture, co-dependence destroys people physically, mentally, emotionally, and spiritually. The word *co-dependence* was first used to describe the family members of an alcoholic who react as though they are controlled by the behavior of the alcoholic. Co-dependents frequently repress their feelings and reactions about the alcoholism and deny that there is a problem. For instance, if the alcoholic is drinking, other family members might alter their lives and take over the alcoholic's responsibilities. In effect, they are enabling the alcoholic to continue drinking. If the alcoholic is angry, the family might respond by trying to make the situation better by being nicer. This action very possibly covers their true feelings of disgust and anger over the situation. The co-dependents, eventually, lose touch with their own feelings, reacting, instead, to the feelings or behavior of another. The chemically dependent person is addicted to a chemical. Co-dependents become addicted to the chemical dependents as they increasingly react to the situations set up by the behavior of the chemical dependents. Eventually the co-dependent's feelings and behavior are no longer inner controlled but, rather, are controlled from the exterior by the chemical dependent. It has been reported that co-dependents are sometimes more dysfunctional than chemical dependents, exhibiting the many stress-filled symptoms associated with the denial of their true self (Whitfield, 1984; Woititz, 1984). Repressed feelings, delusions, low self-esteem, denial, extreme dependence and compulsiveness characterize the co-dependent

(Wegscheider, 1985). Co-dependence can best be described as a progressive and debilitating disease entity (Cermak, 1986).

In recent years the addictive process has been seen to apply to much more than chemical dependence. Co-dependence is now much more generally defined as the behavior pattern of reacting to or being controlled by forces or people outside of oneself rather than responding out of one's own self and feelings.

These co-dependent patterns can occur as a result of being in any family system or situation where there are oppressive rules which cause people to deny part of their true selves. In this progressive debilitating addictive process, the connection to one's true self is gradually lost until one's life revolves around controlling, manipulating and/or pleasing others. The co-dependent often wears a mask of strength, covering the pain, fear, confusion and loneliness underneath. This disease process is a progressively non-living condition (Schaef, 1986). Co-dependence is not simply a restatement of another personality disorder; rather it is a complex psychological concept referring to both intrapsychic and interpersonal dynamics (Cermak, 1986). Intrapsychic refers to what is happening within the mind or self, while interpersonal refers to relations between persons.

Many addiction counseling professionals, myself included, believe that the addictive process is the addictive process whether one is addicted to people or chemicals (May, 1988; Schaef, 1987). The diseases of chemical dependency and co-dependency greatly overlap, as do the recovery processes (Cermak, 1986). Some professionals think that co-dependency often precedes the alcoholic experience, in that oppressive rules which bring denial of self open the door to other compulsive addictive behavior (Friel and Friel, 1988; Subby, 1984). The 12 steps of the Alcoholics Anonymous Program have now been used successfully to help people deal with a wide variety of addictive behaviors including co-dependence.

## 12-Step Spirituality and Recovery from Addiction

Alcoholics Anonymous was the first 12-step program for recovery from an addiction, and many other recovery programs have been developed using that model. The 12 steps of Alcoholics Anonymous have a spiritual base which affirms May's (1988) assertion that growing spiritually is necessary for recovery from addiction. Active internal involvement in a spiritually based 12-step program is one way to grow spiritually. The 12-

step programs which are available for substance abuse and co-dependency have almost identical steps with only the object of attachment differing. The following discussion uses the 12-step model of Alcoholics Anonymous which is the most researched and oldest 12-step group.

Once dependence has become destructive, the addict has usually tried repeatedly and unsuccessfully to stop the dependence before coming to a 12-step program and so enters treatment with little self-esteem or idea about what will make a difference (Johnson, 1980). Much of the job of treatment for people in early recovery from chemical dependence is to educate them about the disease and about the need for active involvement in AA as well as other recommended aftercare (Kinney and Leaton, 1987). The problem is that the client's pattern is to try to solve his/her own problems, believing that with one more attempt it will be possible. For a client in this stage, a spirituality-based 12-step program seems to make little logical sense.

The person who has been looking to the "higher power" of drugs and/or alcohol is now being asked to give up control when the chaos of the disease increases the desire for control. The first step of AA requires an admission of powerlessness and unmanageability. The second step of AA states that belief in a higher or greater power could restore sanity. For people in early recovery who have been experiencing powerlessness over most of their life, the idea of turning their life over to someone/ something else is often more frightening than the mess they have made on their own. The third step of AA makes another leap by calling for a decision to turn one's life and will over to the care of one's higher power.

Entry into an active personal involvement in a 12-step program that leads to beginning or deepening a personal spiritual journey is a difficult and problematic task during early recovery. Denial, dishonesty, and the desire for control create barriers. Without involvement in a 12-step program, the chance of relapse is great.

In the ensuing section, further terms will be defined as they are used in this book. Any other definitions of additional terms and words will be included later in the book as it becomes necessary.

## Further Definitions

(1) ALCOHOLICS ANONYMOUS 12 STEPS. The 12 steps of Alcoholics Anonymous are as follows (The same basic steps are used in other 12-step programs with the addictive substance changed.):

1. We admitted we were powerless over alcohol—that our lives had become unmanageable.
2. Came to believe that a Power greater than ourselves could restore us to sanity.
3. Made a decision to turn our will and our lives over to the care of God as we understood Him.
4. Made a searching and fearless moral inventory of ourselves.
5. Admitted to God, to ourselves, and to another human being the exact nature of our wrongs.
6. Were entirely ready to have God remove all these defects of character.
7. Humbly asked Him to remove our shortcomings.
8. Made a list of all persons we had harmed, and became willing to make amends to them all.
9. Made direct amends to such people wherever possible, except when to do so would injure them or others.
10. Continued to take personal inventory and when we were wrong promptly admitted it.
11. Sought through prayer and meditation to improve our conscious contact with God as we understood him, praying only for knowledge of His will for us and the power to carry that out.
12. Having had a spiritual awakening as the result of these steps, we tried to carry this message to alcoholics, and to practice these principles in all our affairs.
    (*Alcoholics Anonymous*, 1976, pp. 59–60)

(2) CO-RESEARCHERS. The subjects of this study including myself are referred to as co-researchers.

(3) WORKING THE STEPS. In this study, working the steps means involving oneself on a personal journey of discovery, using the 12-step framework, to find one's own unique path for living. Addicts who are used to looking to the exterior for such things as comfort, approval and satisfaction, begin to look to the inside to find their own feelings, opinions, ideas, and beliefs. The steps may be experienced in order or "worked" in any order which is appropriate for one's current situation.

(4) SPIRITUALITY. Spirituality in this study is defined as the co-researchers define it personally, with special attention paid to personal experience of any of the 12 steps of a 12-step program through art, meditation, writing and/or discussion.

(5) SPIRITUAL GROWTH. Spiritual growth will be defined as the co-researchers define it personally, with special attention paid to increasing and ongoing personal experience of any of the 12 steps of a 12-step program through art, meditation, writing, and/or discussion.

## The Use of Art with Recovering Chemically Dependent Adults

Art uses abilities that include both the intuitive, timeless, image-oriented, creative, open, and holistic behaviors of a human being as well as functions which are more analytical, logical, linear, verbal, structured, and time oriented. Because creativity is a threat to society's status quo, May (1985) has suggested that courage and decisiveness are required in the creative process. Activities which use the abilities of the language-oriented left brain hemisphere, as well as the spatially oriented right brain hemisphere (Gardner, 1982), bring a balanced approach to living. The creative process in graphic art opens opportunity for holistic involvement, along the continuum from the chaotic encounter with something new through feelings, imagery, product, and the resulting conceptual insights (McNeil, 1984).

Addiction promotes overly passive behavior with little activity. Art making calls for movement in the alternation between activity and passivity as the creator bonds and separates from the work during the process (McNeil, 1984). This involvement encourages a powerful experience outside the deadly passivity of the client recovering from addiction. Addiction promotes the expectation that a substance from outside will bring answers and serenity. Art making finds the images and resulting concepts, ideas, and gifts on the inside of the maker. In this way personal power is reclaimed for the creator of the art.

As we encourage our logic-driven adult side at the expense of our open, creative childlike side, we deny our own wholeness and lose part of our own reality. The denial of part of one's true self leaves a lonely painful hole which invites addictive behavior.

Graphic art bypasses words with its images, and very often the image is on the paper before the analytical side of the artist has a chance to judge and deny. Once the image is on the paper, it can be processed in the context of art therapy for greater conscious understanding. Denial, one of the cornerstones of addiction, is difficult when a concrete expression of your feelings is sitting right in front of you, and discussion with the picture buffer is often less threatening than without it (Albert-Puleo and Osha, 1976–77; Donnenberg 1978).

Art is a way to bring out unconscious feelings (Foulke and Keller, 1976; Marinow, 1980), providing a way to "see" what is inside of oneself instead of constantly looking outside of oneself for answers. It is a therapeutic experience to honor that yet "uncivilized" part of oneself, that does not cover up what it perceives as truth, but is willing to express it.

Meeting deadlines and completing responsibilities in our fast-paced world is very wearing. Through creative activity, we can enter into a timeless space where there is rest. There is a Greek word, *kairos*, which means timelessness and is used in the Bible to describe the kind of time zone God lives in. Children seem to live very comfortably in this timeless space, appearing unaware of time as they play and create, involved in the moment. The chronic fast-paced time in which our Western culture lives can create unbalanced prisoners of the clock. Nurturing the creative, free, open part of us, we can once again become more fully present to ourselves. The idea of living "one day at a time" or in the moment is central to the philosophy of recovery in Alcoholics Anonymous.

Recovery from addictive behavior requires the balance of carrying necessary responsibility as well as experiencing the freedom of *kairos*. Art is a way to enter into *kairos*, to be refreshed, to reenter responsibility, to find unconscious images and feelings, and to connect with ourself on a deeper level. Art is a way to relearn just being, to respond once again to your inner child, and to feel the peace and sanity of a balanced life.

The next chapter details the passionate and personal method used for studying the experience of spiritual journey through art in recovery.

# Chapter 2

# A PASSIONATE AND PERSONAL
# METHOD OF STUDY

Heuristic Inquiry was the method of study used for obtaining and comprehending the information in this book. Heuristic research is autobiographical, with passionate, discerning, personal involvement, using the researcher's wealth of experience. The emphasis is on originality with a reverence for the individual's experience. One's own experience is the most important component. The researcher needs to become totally immersed in this research process with a deep commitment to discover meaning in human experience. The process remains fluid while different parts overlap. Heuristic inquiry is an attempt to understand the meaning and essence of some part of life through inner self processes, and it affirms imagination, intuition, and spontaneity.

I decided on heuristic inquiry as a method of study, partially because I, as a recovering co-dependent, have had and am having personal experience with the areas being studied. When I speak of recovery, in a very real sense I am referring to the holistic recovery of oneself and so the holistic approach of heuristics is also appropriate. The recovery process from an addiction requires an honoring of the individuality of each person, as does heuristics. Heuristic inquiry and its existential and humanistic roots open to the possibility of transcendent and alive spirituality, which is necessary to a healthy and full recovery from an addictive process. Heuristic inquiry is also open to the validity of art and aesthetics as a part of human experience.

The step-by-step growing awareness in my own life of the phenomenon being studied developed gradually into a great curiosity about what this experience might mean to others. I desired to find the essence of the experience and heuristics was an excellent vehicle for this exploration.

Heuristic inquiry is a qualitative model for research. Qualitative research is a newer paradigm in psychological research than the quantitative "scientific method" which perceives science as objective, linear, and reductive. Qualitative research offers opportunities to study both subjective and objective data in a deductive manner, thus obtaining a holistic view of what is being studied.

Scientific credibility comes through the disciplined commitment which accompanies the passionate search for meaning. The search starts with internal immersion in the question, with eventual consultation of others regarding their experience. This process requires an urgency for new insight and takes into account subtle meanings. In heuristic inquiry, one can learn the essence of people's experience while honoring and encouraging them to be who they are. There is an emphasis on self-disclosure in order to help facilitate disclosure from others. The scientist aims at finding what is already there in reality. In this type of research, the people studied remain visible and are treated as whole people.

The steps of heuristic inquiry include first an *Immersion,* which is a personal self-searching exploration of the question. The second phase is *Acquisition,* during which further data is collected that adds to what is known of the phenomenon. The final phase is a *Realization* synthesis, which calls the researcher to generate a new, more full, conscious reality of the topic (Douglass and Moustakas, 1985).

The idea that we know more than we are able to speak about, which we can't necessarily explain, refers to what Michael Polanyi (1967) called the "tacit dimension." Intuition rises out of this dimension. Heuristic researchers might get a "clue" in the outside world which connects with something inside of them and gets them closer to the Gestalt of something. One experiences this dimension when one can "almost glimpse" what is happening, but can't quite get it on a conscious level. Through reading, talking to others, self-dialogue, and indwelling, the researcher begins to see in new ways, in effect making the unconscious conscious.

The writing in heuristic research is usually very descriptive, creating a vivid experience which we can live. When accurate, it yields agreement from the reader, cutting through the complexity of the subject with clear simplicity.

In interviews for heuristic studies, the researcher can both write and interact, including personal thoughts and ideas. The topic chosen is something one wants to understand for oneself. It is not contaminating to mention personal ideas to the interviewed person if it helps the flow of the interview. Respect is given to the co-researcher as the source of data. Heuristics uses the most spontaneous and natural interview.

This type of research is valid when themes and patterns form a whole that communicates essential or ultimate meanings. There is constant internal testing in both the immersion and the withdrawal. The researcher acquires the data from people who have a common experience such as growing spiritually through art making in the recovery process, which is the experience examined in this book. As the stories are told, common themes emerge and reveal the shared essence of the experience. The synthesis period rides on the "waves" of the common themes into a realization of the broader implications of the experience studied. Through dissemination others experience the significance of the findings. Because of the subjective nature of both art and spirituality, heuristics was an excellent method for this study.

### Existentialism and Humanistic Psychology are Foundations of Heuristics

Heuristic inquiry is rooted in the ideas of both existentialism and humanistic psychology. It is also related to phenomenology. In this section, existentialism, humanistic psychology, and phenomenology will be examined because they are foundational to heuristics.

### Existentialism

Existentialism seeks to depict the human condition and look for possible ways to respond to it. The writings of existentialist philosophers are expressive of the intense experience lived out in their own lives (Capaldi, Kelly, and Navia, 1981). Existential philosophy was originated by Kierkegaard who believed we are spiritually impoverished

> for we have neglected our own existence while constructing the marvelous edifice of science—which, in the end, cannot tell me who I am, or what I ought to be about, or what it means to die . . . But of course! Only I, not science and philosophy, can tell me who I am, and what I am to believe in! (Capaldi et al., p. 242)

We learn from Kierkegaard that although objectivity helps us understand the world, it is not all we need to understand our lives. Through Kierkegaard, modern philosophy opened again to a desire to understand what humans have inside. Most existentialists turned away from nihilism, looking instead for salvation and meaning in life, believing that each human being could create his or her own values to live by (Capaldi et al., 1981).

Phenomenology was a component of twentieth-century existentialism.

It was established as a school in Germany by Edmund Husserl who wanted to see how human beings experience the world (Capaldi et al., 1981). Phenomenologists look for the essence of what is studied as it naturally occurs in everyday life. The researchers who are doing the studies bracket out their personal opinion focusing only on what is studied.

Martin Heidegger, a young colleague of Husserl's, thought of phenomenology not only as the study of how humans experience the world but also of how they exist in the world. He did not think of himself as an existentialist thinker, but he offered a very comprehensive analysis of the human condition (Capaldi et al., 1981). Heidegger is interested in leaving the consciousness of the past and the future and concentrating on the ontology of "being" in the present (Heidegger, 1972).

The existentialism of Jean-Paul Sartre centered around the idea that only a human can be his or her own object and conscious of selfhood (Capaldi et al., 1981). Sartre said there is a divergence between the dreams and potentials of a human being which in a sense cause us to want to be our own God (Capaldi et al., 1981).

Existentialist thought promotes the freedom and dignity of each person. People who are living authentic lives are responsible for their own lives and deal with the problems of existence, according to the existentialists (Capaldi et al., 1981).

The Jewish existentialist thinker Martin Buber considered the spiritual part of life. He promoted the idea that we could make even the secular sacred. In the process of looking for our gratification through things, we have lost ourselves and become lonely (Buber, 1970). Buber says that when one enters into a relationship with God, everything in life is included in the relationship, while nothing has particular importance.

## Humanistic Psychology

Humanistic psychology is rooted in existentialist philosophy. The importance of and respect for each person's being, experience, holism, and potential is stressed in this branch of psychology. In the context of humanistic psychology, each person is perceived as a unique and complex human being with distinct potential. Humanistic psychology developed through the work of such psychologists as Maslow, Moustakas, Rogers, and May.

Abraham Maslow described himself as Freudian, behavioristic, humanistic and transcendent (Maslow, 1978). He studied and promoted the concept of a person becoming self-actualized which he described as "experiencing fully, vividly, selflessly, with full concentration and total absorption" (p. 44). He encouraged living in the moment, being honest, and taking responsibility for oneself as a part of becoming self-actualized. Maslow said that good therapists do not impose themselves on clients but would rather help clients break through their defenses to reclaim or know themselves more fully. He said that "sick" people are those who are defensive and not fully themselves.

May (1967) says that human beings need to affirm their being in order not to lose it. He also states that in our culture, we have become such an outer-directed people that we fear the disapproval of others more than the loss of our personal power.

Eugene Gendlin and a group of researchers at the University of Chicago spent many years studying why psychotherapy so often fails (Gendlin, 1978). They found out that the successful patient can be easily identified early in treatment. The therapist's technique made little difference according to their findings. They found that the successful patients had the natural ability to connect with their feelings in their body, feel them, and move on to the next feeling, thus facilitating the process of their own lives. Gendlin and his colleagues have developed a method which helps people learn this natural process, and the results have been very successful. In other words, the way to get healthier is to once again learn what it means to be fully human.

### Humanistic Research

Rollo May (1967) says that it is a predicament that humans can see themselves as both the subject and object of experiments. Because of this we are involved in the whole process, and the experimenter is part of the experiment. May believes that both subjectivity and objectivity are necessary to good therapy, healthy living, and psychological science.

May maintains that in our technological culture, people who succeed give up their individuality to the organization. He says we in Western civilization think we can understand things through a knowledge of their cause, asking "why" rather than knowing "what" the thing, the phenomenon, is. "Why" gains meaning only when one knows "what" one is talking about, according to May (1967).

Sidney Jourard said in his 1968 book, *Disclosing Man to Himself,* that psychology was in the process of being changed via existentialism, phenomenology, and humanism, with the psychologists using their own experience to help in understanding others. He believes scientific inquiry needs to bring to light people as human beings rather than just biological or social beings. Jourard says that if scientists shared with subjects in a more reciprocally disclosing relationship, then the information obtained would be of a more diverse and revealing quality. He believes that subjects who are treated as scientific objects in an experiment rather as than human beings provide poor-quality data. Jourard's students who have researched this hypothesis found that the amount of data was significantly greater when obtained from subjects who had more self-disclosing researchers (Jourard, 1968).

Clark Moustakas's book *Loneliness* (1961) is an example of qualitative scientific research approached heuristically. This study rose out of a crisis in the researcher's own life. Through his own experience, he developed a passionate interest in doing further research on the human experience of loneliness. His deep personal interest in the nature and the meaning of the subjective experience of loneliness motivated not only the immersion in his own experience but also the acquisition of rich data from others who shared the experience. The resulting themes and generalizations about human loneliness present the reader with a deep understanding as well as new ideas for positive associations with this often painful area of human experience. It is as though a thorough examination of this topic and its human meaning disarms it so that the reader might enter into the experience with more willingness and understanding. Heuristic research effectively addressed this highly subjective area of human experience.

## Further Description of the Heuristic Research Model

Michael Polanyi did much of the pioneer work of defining Heuristics as a philosophical approach. He was born in Hungary in 1891 and became a medical doctor, but eventually moved on to a career as a physical chemist in Germany. With the rise of Hitler, Polanyi, who was Jewish, moved on to England. Well-established in the profession of physical chemistry, Polanyi gradually began to publish and shift his academic interests to philosophy. He was critical of the positivist position that sense perceptions are the only acceptable evidence of human knowledge and accurate thinking (Prosch, 1986).

As Western culture put increasing value on what was verified through the scientific method and devalued what was not provable through that method, Polanyi saw the existence of free society as well as verifiable science as being in jeopardy. People didn't realize that a free society

> rested upon freely held beliefs in ideals and principles that not only could not be proved, but could not even be made wholly explicit. It seemed to him that no one saw that the unprovability of these beliefs did not render them intellectually unrespectable or unworthy of being held. It therefore appeared to him necessary to show people, philosophers included, why and how this was so. (Prosch, 1986, p. 5)

Polanyi's value of what he called "personal knowledge" was in a sense a defense for the freedom and wholeness of human beings. He called the deeper knowing that human beings have *tacit knowing*. This tacit knowing comes from the preconscious intuitive part of a human being and cannot be analyzed because of its holistic nature and unconscious operation. Polanyi said, "I shall reconsider human knowledge by starting from the fact that we know more than we can tell" (Polanyi, 1967, p. 4). To illustrate this kind of knowing, Polanyi suggests that although we can recognize a particular human face out of a million, we cannot exactly analyze why this is so. We have found through police methods that we actually recognize separate features of faces. Polanyi suggests that within the tacit dimension, we recognize the separate features and present the conscious mind with the whole. In other words, it is through the tacit knowing of the features that our conscious mind is given a knowledge of the whole. We know the face, but unless the tacit process is made known to us, we cannot tell how we know. As a matter of a fact, when we try to separate the features consciously and then put them together, it causes temporary confusion. It would be like asking a speed typist to explain the process of typing. Tacitly we integrate intricate evidence into a whole which then has meaning for us. Polanyi links this theory of the tacit to Gestalt psychology's idea of knowing the whole without being able to identify the parts. He says,

> I am looking at Gestalt, on the contrary, as the outcome of an active shaping of experience performed in the pursuit of knowledge. This shaping or integrating I hold to be the great and indispensable tacit power by which all knowledge is discovered and once discovered, is held to be true. (p. 6)

Heuristic research expedites studying the holistic experience of human beings. It honors personal immersion and indwelling in the tacit dimension as ways of learning. Indwelling involves an "interiorization" where the parts of a thing are integrated, according to Polanyi. He states that in the process of indwelling, or by dwelling in the data, we come to understand what the meaning of the whole is. Indwelling and tacit knowing acknowledge the value of the internal processes of human beings as ways for new awarenesses to arise.

The work of Gendlin (1978) on the use of focusing in psychotherapy is a

> working illustration of the disciplined use of indwelling and tacit knowing to make new discoveries about the self. The rigorous use of the indwelling and tacit knowing process is the basis of heuristic research. (Clark, 1987)

Because of heuristic research scientists' personal involvement in what is being studied, their bias must be acknowledged. The pluses that come with this bias include passion, commitment, and personal insight. The researchers' personal involvement in heuristics puts them on equal footing with the co-researchers and creates an atmosphere of openness and honesty.

Heuristic research's "ultimate purpose is to cast light on a focused problem, question, or theme" according to Douglass and Moustakas (1985, p. 40). They indicate that heuristic inquiry is powerful because of its capability for revealing what is true.

> Through rigor and disciplined commitment, one follows the subjective past ordinary levels of awareness, living the question internally in sources of being and nonbeing, recording hunches, ideas, and essences as they emerge, and, ultimately, consulting with others regarding the phenomenon or experience. (p. 40)

According to Douglass and Moustakas, the passionate process of discovery involved in heuristics differentiates it from other models of research. They also say that heuristics is an attitude of inquiry involving a series of processes rather than a prescribed method. The scientist is challenged to find what actually is. There is no formal hypothesis in this type of research, and the learning is "self directed, self motivated, and open to spontaneous shift" (p. 44). They say there is freedom in the discovery process as it unfolds.

Douglass and Moustakas have divided the process of heuristic inquiry into three phases: immersion, acquisition and realization. The first of these phases will each be examined next.

### Immersion

In this phase, the researcher is totally involved and centered on the thing to be studied. Douglass and Moustakas say that the awareness of the researcher is at first vague and out of conscious reach, but gradually the meaning and direction of the study become clearer. They indicate that this is a time of searching the self internally and indwelling. In retrospect, the researcher becomes consciously aware that he or she has been incubating and considering what is being studied for quite a length of time previous to the conscious immersion (Clark, 1987).

> In the process, a more definitive awareness is formed. A feeling of lostness and letting go pervades, a kind of being wide open in surrender to the thing itself, a recognition that one must relinquish control and be tumbled about with the newness and drama of a searching focus that is taking over life. (Douglass and Moustakas, 1985, p. 47)

Douglass and Moustakas describe the immersion phase as if it were a meandering time of being in or with the thing rather than a goal-oriented active period (1985). Immersion prepares the researcher for acquisition.

### Acquisition

During this phase, the researcher has come to a point in the study when the direction has been established, and he or she knows tacitly what to do to bring more clarity according to Douglass and Moustakas (1985). They say that heuristics encourages the instinctive creation of methods to bring meaning. As certain parts of an experience become more clear, they have found that these parts are consciously understood and therefore no longer tacit. Tacit knowing, intuition, inference, self-dialogue, self-disclosure and signitive-symbolic-representation are included in this phase. Douglass and Moustakas state that "the tacit is visionary; it incorporates the aesthetic and artistic aspects of consciousness without neglecting the clues of cognition" (p. 49).

Douglass and Moustakas say that the self-disclosure is a way of bringing disclosure from others which comes into play now as this phase includes the exploration of the experiences of others. Jon Clark (1987) says, "The acquisition phase may involve the use of open-ended or semi-structured interviewing, journaling, art, or other methods of data collection."

*Realization*

In the third phase of heuristics, according to Douglass and Moustakas, a synthesis brings the pieces back to a whole. The data is examined "in creative combinations and recombinations, sifting and sorting, moving rhythmically in and out of appearance, looking, listening carefully for the meanings within meanings, attempting to identify the overarching qualities that inhere in the data" (p. 52). They say that the movement in this phase is from the specific to the general.

In this phase, the researcher rigorously and creatively handles the data aiming toward understanding the meaning of what is being studied. There is "the disciplined use of tacit knowing, as in the entire process of heuristic research. The purposeful rhythm between immersion and incubation, active and passive states, is pursued in order to facilitate the natural process of tacit knowing" (Clark, 1987, p. 71).

During this phase, there is an illumination stage says Clark. He calls this the "creative leap" during which a new reality is discovered. He states that an explaining stage follows illumination in which the discoveries are expressed and clarified as "patterns, themes, relationships and meanings" and thus communicated to others to whom the information might be useful (p. 72).

Clark states that in the final creative synthesis, the essence of the experience is captured and revealed, bringing out the meanings at the core. The nature of the experience is descriptively related so that others who may not have had this experience can understand it at a deep level. Douglass and Moustakas (1985) conclude:

> Throughout the investigation, one must openly and energetically accept the way in which knowledge can be most authentically revealed, be it through metaphor, description, poetry, song, dance, art, or dialogue. Heuristics encourages the researcher to go wide open and to pursue an original path that has as its origins within the self and that discovers its direction and meaning within the self. It does not aim to produce experts who learn the rules and mechanics of science; rather, it guides human beings in the process of asking questions about phenomena that disturb and challenge their own existence. (p. 53)

The subjective experience of each co-researcher studied is the basis of this study which explores the contribution of art to the spiritual part of recovery from an addiction. Qualitative research with a humanistic basis is an appropriate choice of methodology because it is suited to the examination of human experience, which is subjective.

The step-by-step growing awareness in my own life of the phenomenon being studied developed gradually into a great curiosity about what this experience might mean to others. In the next chapters, I and the other co-researchers will share our personal experiences of spiritual journey via art making in recovery.

# Part II
# STORIES OF THE CO-RESEARCHERS

# INTRODUCTION TO THE STORIES
# IN CHAPTERS 3 THROUGH 12

Ann, whose life story appears in Chapter 10, wrote the following story about the "box" of her co-dependency and the liberating process of her recovery.

### Experiences and Learnings from Along my Journey

Once upon a time, in a land far, far away, there was a little girl who lived in a box. It wasn't like anyone else's box, for everyone has theirs custom-tailored. Her's was brightly painted in smiles on the outside, though the inside was dark and cluttered, and sometimes the girl's legs got cramped, and sometimes the sharp glass inside poked at her, but all of that was okay because sometimes the box was also a warm and secure place.

She hadn't always lived in this box, although she couldn't remember when it had become home. On sunny days she could look out through the bars of her door, which she knew was locked, and watch small children laugh and play in the poppy-strewn fields. Day after day she watched and dreamed of a time when she could play with them . . . hadn't she once? But for now, she just watched them through her locked bars. And as she watched, a warmth started to grow in her curled body, a warmth that began to thaw out the pain of her aloneness so that it became alive and crowded her small space and pushed her harder against the sharp glass.

One day a man walked by. "Please sit with me" the little girl called out. And he sat down and asked if she would like to come out of her box and sit beside him in the grass, for a clean breeze was blowing and the sun that day was gentle.

"I can't come out," and she looked away and hoped that he couldn't smell the moldiness of her small life. "The door is locked" she said as she pointed to the bars, not touching them, scared to look at their familiarity while he sat so near.

The man was very concerned and inspected the door closely. Then relief and expectation flooded his face. "No! It's not locked!" And to prove it he reached out and gently tugged on the door.

Disbelief and an overwhelming horror filled the little girl as she watched the blue sky and green grass get bigger and bigger in the hole this man was creating in her box!

"STOP!" she screamed.

And he stopped . . . and then he invited her out into the sun's warmth once more.

For a brief second, the girl could see herself walking out and joining all the blue and green, but only for the briefest second. Then, her trembling hand reached out and pulled the door closed. "No, it's locked," her numb words barely audible because her face was buried in shame. "It's locked and I can't open it." And, having disappointed him, she waited for him to leave.

But he didn't leave. For more than two years he sat with her, and they talked, and they cried, and sometimes they laughed. Somehow he saw past the painted smiles. He seemed to really want to know what it was like inside her box. And, most unbelievable of all, when she dared to let him peek in through the bars, he never ever pulled back in disgust, and sometimes he even found beauty there. So little by little, she came to trust this man, and she began to believe what he had told her all along: that the door wasn't locked. Over the years, she would open the door further and further; at first just enough to let the breeze touch her, and on some rare days near the end, she even slipped out once or twice and sat next to the man. And the sun was gentle and the breeze was clean; but the thrill of freedom was a fragile thing and though it filled her mind with the hope and the wildness of possibility, it also filled her with a terror like the fear of death that left her rushing for safety to the dark corners of her box.

And then the man had to leave, and the little girl was very sad. But she had known freedom, and she had felt the sun and tasted the breeze.

One day a woman danced by. Her dance was a dance of joy and freedom, and the little girl recognized in it the play of the children in the poppy fields.

"Please sit with me," the little girl called out.

So the woman sat for a short while and they talked and laughed, and when the woman laughed, she would look right into the little girl's eyes, into her very soul and again . . . there was no disgust, only sharing and joy. This look continued the thaw.

When the woman was done laughing, she got up and left, promising that she would be back—she would be back with others who also lived in and felt trapped by their boxes. Then with a great leap, she danced off into the green and the blue.

Many days passed, and the little girl lived her life caught, as was so often these days, between touching up' the paint job on her house and hiding inside of it, with daring to step out in order to feel the sun. And she waited.

Until one morning, she woke up, sluggish from an especially restless night to find she had new neighbors; some other boxes had crowded in near her right side . . . and then several on her left . . . and more crowded in front—there was a circle of them, and she was a part of it. Sleep completely left her when she realized that the dancing woman was part of the circle too . . . and, how strange; she had a box as well, but she was using it to sit on.

The woman read to all of them. She had opened before her a copy of the Master Craftsman's Box-Maker's Manual, and so explained the intricacies of box making. She described them as shelters, and the girl thought of how safe she felt in her box. Then the woman described them as cages, and the girl thought of the broken glass, and the dirtiness and her shame. When the woman described the boxes as treasure chests, hiding beauty and wealth, the girl remembered the beauty the man had found in her and her joy in sharing it. The words of this book united the circle in a common language. The words became a secret passageway.

The circle held everyone together for the eternity of several days; and during these days, a funny thing began to happen. Where once the circle seemed a crowded place, the center area now opened up, and there was room—safe, contained room. And where they all started out describing their carefully designed exteriors, slowly they began to tell and to show the secret of what it was really like to live inside their boxes.

The little girl drew maps of her world and gathered the smooth and the sharp edges from the inside of her box. She was scared to show these to everyone, until she realized that they were very much like the painful, dark edges of other's lives. So, in her turn she stepped into the space and showed herself to everyone. Somehow, her shame didn't hide her face, and she could see recognition and caring from the eyes of those who surrounded her. As she dropped some of these edges into the grass, the others came out and they joined with her in the rhythm of the tides of each other's pain and joy.

The circle seemed to expand in these moments, as if taking a deep breath, and here they found room for play. Into one of these full breaths the woman danced, arms exploding with brilliant poppies. She flung them into the air, and all of the children escaped from their boxes to dance with her among the falling blossoms.

Then the exhale . . . and tired with play, all the children returned to their boxes. Some sat next to them on the grass, others left their doors ajar. One day, the little girl thought, she would be able to play all day, and one day she would be able to play in the wide-open fields; but she had learned from the woman that it was okay for now that she wanted to return to her old box, and only slowly venture out into the safe spaces. The little girl gathered a handful of poppies and returned to her box to find it a little roomier, and a little lighter.

## STORIES OF OTHER "BOXES"

Stories of other "boxes" and liberating processes are described in Chapters 3 through 12 by the co-researchers, including myself. With the exception of myself, the names and identifying factors for all of the co-researchers have been changed in order to protect their anonymity. The stories are presented, whenever possible, in the words of the co-researchers from transcribed interviews. Each begins with an introduction and history section. The history is a family, spiritual, and addiction history. The second major section in each story is about the co-researcher's art experience. Much of the artwork has been photographed for this book and will appear with a figure and a number. The artwork which does not appear in a photograph will be described in the text in order to give the reader a complete view of each person's story. Each story ends with my summation and reflection.

The co-researchers chosen for this study met the following criteria: (1) they were recovering from chemical dependency and/or co-dependency (at least one year, for long term), (2) they made spontaneous mention to me of their personal experience of their spirituality through art, and (3) they indicated an interest in further exploration of this phenomenon through an interview process with me.

## Data Collection

I wrote my story directly on my computer before interviewing the other co-researchers. The interviews were non-directive and unstructured with the following exceptions. I asked each co-researcher to give me a brief personal and family history including any memory of childhood spirituality as well as an addiction history. I also asked for an answer to the question, "How has art contributed to the spiritual part of your recovery?"

Chapters 3–8 contain the stories of the six newly recovering co-researchers. All of these people were interviewed after the end of their treatment program for chemical dependency. They all participated in an art therapy program for which I was the therapist. These interviews were done over a seven-week period. The high level of therapist involvement required in the early treatment of chemical dependency was reflected in the structured art therapy sessions designed to facilitate the client's experience and understanding of the first three steps of the Alcoholics Anonymous 12-step program. The rest of the treatment program also encouraged active involvement in a 12-step program. There were two exceptions during which the clients used the art therapy group to process their feelings about two holidays.

The early recovery stories are dramatic, possibly because the first steps from addiction into recovery cause radical changes. They are shorter in length than the long-term recovering stories because the length of recovery has been much less.

Chapters 9–12 contain the stories of the four long-term recovering co-researchers, including myself. The long-term co-researchers willingly shared their art, writing, stories, and/or experiences about the topic studied during the interview process. I taught the other three in a college course I designed which was called "Discovering the Inner Child." Ann's story about her "box", "Experiences and Learnings From Along My Journey," was written as a paper for this course. The data was collected for their stories after the completion of the course. They have had years of living in the daily process of recovery and so their stories are deep and thoughtful and slower moving than the stories of the newly recovering people. I include both the newly recovering and the long-term recovering people as co-researchers so that the picture presented of recovery from the disease of addiction is more holistic.

## Data Analysis

The analysis of the vast amount of data collected was an intricate process which began as the data was collected and lasted for several months. During the course of this research, there were active and passive cycles alternating between periods of collection and sifting of data.

The data was refined, removing unnecessary portions with each reading, carefully retaining all that might be useful to the understanding of the experience. With each examination of the data, notes were taken and intuitive thoughts were honored. As possible themes and generalizations emerged, they were noted.

After a thorough immersion in the data, each co-researcher's life seemed to take on a story quality with all of the disparate pieces fitting together to form a picture. The co-researchers' narratives gradually surfaced, revealing interwoven personal, addiction, and recovery histories.

The decision was made to call these holistic descriptions of individuals lives "stories" rather than "case studies." I experienced the recovery stories in this study as encouraging and positive with a sense of movement toward health. To me, the word *story* conveys this sense of health more clearly than the label *case study*. The holistic treatment of the individuals in each chapter, including the historical references, as well as current facts, honored each person's story as is appropriate with heuristic reserach. I presented as much of each story as possible in the person's own words so that there would be little tampering with the person's own meaning.

# Chapter 3

## BETTY'S STORY

### INTRODUCTION AND HISTORY

At first meeting, Betty seems soft spoken, thoughtful and cooperative. She is a slim, attractive caucasian woman with smile lines around her eyes who looks younger than her 41 years. She identifies herself as both chemically dependent and co-dependent. Alcohol is her drug of choice, but she has also used cocaine. She is reflective, open and interested in sharing her history. Growing up, Betty had only one sibling who was seven years younger, a half brother with a different father. Her brother has never had a problem with chemical dependency, and Betty thinks maybe this relates to his "luck" of having a non-alcoholic father, although she never knew her own father who was alcoholic. She speaks wistfully of her biological father.

> He was in the service, and when I was born he wasn't there . . . then he never came back. He decided to take his bottle and wherever and go. So I never knew him.
>
> Oh, sure, come birthdays there was never a card, you know, or you see your friends and what looks to be a normal family, and sure, you just grow up feeling real different, empty, like a part of you isn't there, a real empty feeling. And it's been there all along. I felt it from since I was very small. Always there.

Betty reflects on her mother and her grandmother.

> She [mother] was, I guess I've used the word, weak, because maybe I've grown to be sort of independent, but she depended on whatever job she could get and she had no education. She wasn't equipped for the world. She was fifteen when I was born, but she worked hard. She supported me. She saw that I got through high school. She was always there, supporting us, but emotionally she wasn't complete herself. I see that now, but she was not really there either, so I grew up quite alone, quite alone.
>
> Uh, my grandmother lived with us, so I suppose that maybe she took on, maybe, the woman's role. She stayed home and cooked and cleaned and took care of us, and she was a strong spiritual [person]. I didn't care for my grandmother. She was too protective. She didn't let me go [on] my own, but she . . . died a few years ago and I see now . . . I was her whole life—my brother

33

and me. She really never had a life of her own. Neither one of them did. They were women that were just sort of in a trap that took care of their offsprings but nothing else.

### Betty talks about her experience of taking care of other people.

I've just chosen to do it differently and I feel responsible. I almost feel like sometimes I think I've taken on my shoulders that I was born on Christmas day and I think sometimes I think I am or I did think that I was God, that I was responsible for everything that went on in everyone's life. . . . [Spirituality] means being strong; it means—it's like a rock. It's there.

### Betty believes her recent addiction to alcohol has grown out of her co-dependence. She only began using alcohol.

Two years ago. Well, I'd say on a regular basis. Before that I've tasted it like on a social basis, maybe a couple times a year. Relationships [with men] was probably my primary addiction. They would come into my life and everything would start out okay and, uh, it just seemed like they felt like I was maybe an object that they owned, that they needed control of, over me and I'm very rebellious, you know, I have this feeling that no one will control me, no one will. It would end.

Well, I think it [Betty's chemical addiction] came at a period of time that . . . I just ended the relationship [with] probably the only man that I married that I truly, truly loved. And it was like I was fighting myself. I couldn't be controlled. I couldn't settle for being with someone and being controlled, and yet I lost something that I loved very much. So, I think I started to see that I really didn't want to be in a relationship that maybe it was instinctive time to put on the brakes, and uh, there was again that big emptiness that it was just there every minute of the day.

There was loneliness, and in the last relationship I had become very isolated. I really didn't have any friends. I was quite alone . . . I guess by going into bars and getting into the bar scene, there was always somebody to talk to. I would go in and I was like Cinderella, belle of the ball. I'd enter a room and it was instant party. I got very positive feedback for the first time, even though it was the wrong kind, I really thrived on it.

### The emptiness that Betty talks about finally felt as if it was changing at that time.

It was completely filled. Oh, yes, always looking for people. And, uh, yes, the nights I would go out and party, the emptiness was gone . . . after drinking, I experimented with cocaine. I'd probably use it, maybe once a week, never . . . maybe a gram once a week for about a year. Um, it's just that the alcohol has a tendency to make me sick and I found that I could quit earlier in the evening and use the coke and still achieve the same thing. But, uh, you always woke up the next day and the emptiness was back.

Betty had only recently decided to enter treatment.

> I, uh, my tolerance at one point during the two years I'm sure was high, and it seemed to get less and less. My personality would change on three drinks. They would tease me about it . . . people would tease me about it. I just could not drink. Um, I would go from being a very mellow person, and then next drink I would get happy and by the third drink, I'm just a real bitch. Just did not want to be around anyone. And that was probably just the last few weeks that I was drinking.
>
> One day I was concerned again about my ex-husband that I cared for very much. Although we got divorced, we kept in contact with each other. Um, and I was concerned about how he had treated me during the day and I had called a mutual friend and she had asked me to come down to where she worked to a restaurant that I had never been in before, so she suggested that we go down to the bar, and we're sitting there having a drink and talking. I was in a very good mood . . . very good mood, and uh, someone suggested . . . I think a girl from behind the bar said that she was going to call Chad — that's my ex-husband — and invite him down.
>
> He came down and he sat about two bar stools down, and uh, after he sat down I can remember looking over to him and from then on I had a blackout, I don't remember. The next thing I remember is I'm being handcuffed and arrested because I hit [Chad]. . . . I find out, you know, a week later, but I couldn't remember what happened. And, uh, the next day, I guess I just finally woke up to really what was happening to me. I had lost all control of my life, liquor, I could not drink. I was doing physical damage to someone, that's just not my nature. It scared me. I really thought at the time that I'd lost my mind.

## BETTY'S ART THERAPY EXPERIENCE

Betty talks about her experience before coming to the art therapy group.

> I was very apprehensive, I guess. I don't like to draw. I'm not good! [laughter] And anything I'm not good at I have a tendency not to do! I enjoyed it right away. I think the meditation . . . it gave me the ability to go inside which, um, I'd listened to the music before and just relaxed, but for some reason I could start traveling inside.

Betty shares her experience of imaging her adult self reaching out to her baby self during a meditation in the first session.

> I could not only see myself, but it was like everything was in slow motion. I could just see every little feature. It was beautiful, almost like being born again. It was . . . there are no words . . . just unique. Um, it was warm. It felt warm. Uh, felt like something I wanted to bring close to me. I wanted to hold, wanted to love. And then, when I started bringing it in close to me, um, I guess

I came back to reality. There were tears on my cheek. It sort of woke me up. There were tears on my cheek and the vision of the baby was gone. And I again felt the big emptiness that I've felt all my life.

Picture 1 (Figure 3-1), a pastel drawing, shows a yellow triangle containing a pinkish peach fetus-like shape in the lower left-hand corner. Next to the yellow is an orange stripe, then a grey stripe, and last there is an empty black triangle with the white paper showing through. Betty tells about this picture which she drew as a result of her experience during the meditation, and she shares all of the feelings which accompanied it.

> Of course, now I know that usually I use yellow when I'm referring to my higher power.... My higher power is God. My higher power makes me feel warm. It's warmth to me. And in the little yellow spot is my baby, all pink and new, has hope. And the progression of the colors I guess is the feelings I was having as I brought the baby closer to me.
>
> [Orange is] real deep, real intense warmth like yellow to orange, it's getting closer and closer. And then the grey area is starting right when I got the baby to, like my chin and then the tears came and the blackness and the big empty hole, which is probably the clearest spot. The colors are to represent the feelings.

On the day Betty drew Picture 1 (Figure 3-1), she did not connect her picture with her higher power as she later did. She only felt warmth. She wrote these words on the back of it about the experience.

> Felt good—liked looking at baby—She was Perfect—Soft, Warm—even smelled good. Brand new—I want to hold and love her—But just when she was close to my chest—I lost her—I felt empty.

After that experience, coming to art therapy was, for Betty, "like an invitation. Come back, come back—this is where you belong."

During her second art therapy experience, she drew two pictures. First, she drew Picture 2 (Figure 3-2) which represented her recovery, or transformation process. It is a drawing of a glass which has dark brown mixed with black at the bottom, lighter brown in the middle layer, and pale blue at the top and over the edge of the top. A black line drawing faucet is at the upper left. Picture 3 (Figure 3-3) shows Betty's higher power as a large yellow round "smiley" face shape with rays like the sun. Betty describes these two pictures.

> I guess the glass that's under a faucet (Figure 3-2)—at first, it really consciously was not meant to be a glass, it was a mason jar and uh, I guess I just feel ... like my using or my life was mud. And now it's like water is being poured into a

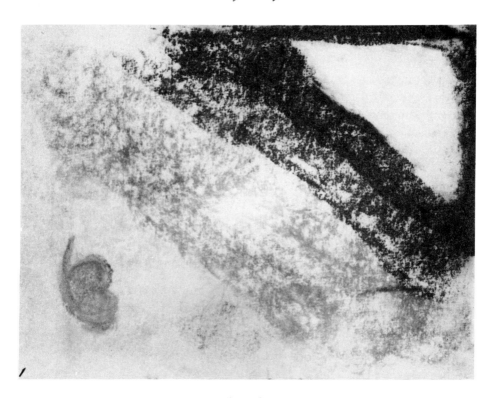

Figure 3-1

vessel and it's washing all the impurities. The end result is very clear, clean water.

And, uh, the other picture (Figure 3-3), that's my higher power. Gosh. When I look at the picture, yeah, I become a child again. I love . . . Well, that little girl [Betty's child self] had a good day that day. Uh, it's simple, it's just everything nice. It makes me smile.

## Betty talks about how her spirituality and her art are related.

. . . it's like being useful again. It's like getting life back again, being clean, whole, just everything good. . . . Well, maybe that picture (Figure 3-3) says it all. Um, art has, I believe that God uses instruments, uses people, situations, uses anything He can to get our attention. Um, He uses ways of opening up eyes, hearts, and mine have been closed for a very long time. And I think He's used art as an instrument to let me go inside without being afraid because it's just a child and some crayons. What damage can I do? It's a very defenseless way of letting me do that. And that's what art has been able to do for me. I can go inside and can journey and can look and see what's there and I can bring it out into consciousness and see it, too. And it's been stepping stones to my recovery, a starting point.

Figure 3-2

You know, my higher power has been with me all my life. . . . I've always believed, I've always talked to my higher power, but at some point and I don't know really what it is or where it was, um, my heart shut and my eyes shut and my ears didn't hear and I was very disconnected with my higher power and myself.

He's always been the one that I prayed to, that I've always had hope, that I remember having hope, so, and I grew up and went to church on my own. No one ever took me or told me. I went because I enjoyed it, and so I grew up learning about God. I grew up Baptist, so, you know, you hear a lot of hell and damnation, but there's also a part of that religion that teaches you that God is love. And I grew up reading that my God was a God of love and I've never been afraid of Him, but He did disappear from me.

Figure 3-3

During the third art therapy session, Betty drew Picture 4 (Figure 3-4) to express her feelings about letting go. This is a picture of a girl with yellow hair with red bows. She is standing on green grass. There is a leafless tree with a red bird on the branch on the left, a black raining cloud to the right of center and a small tree with an oval green top on the right.

Letting go has always been difficult for me. I'm not even sure I knew how to do it. I think this picture actually came right after Thanksgiving. Each of these pictures seems to come at a right time. Amazing! Someone must have been directing my artwork. It came right after Thanksgiving, and my ex-husband had dinner with me.

He came down and took me with him to have a few days. But he is the one thing that I probably have felt that I should let go, but yet cannot do it. So we drew this little picture (Figure 3-4). I ... feel like a little girl in a rainstorm every now and then, and letting go.

Figure 3-4

Noticing the yellow hair on the child in Picture 4 (Figure 3-4), Betty says:

> I think God sort of started coming down at that point. I think, I've shared with you that I guess maybe for a while that God had died and gone to heaven and he wasn't with me. I really believed that and, uh, the more I, uh, draw, I guess the closer I feel to my higher power. And I think at that point He may have just started to come in. So, he was a part of me.
>
> I don't think I've ever had blond hair. I've always had dark hair. . . . When I think of me, I think of me with blonde hair. But He had just started working. I knew He was there. He had to be there or I wouldn't even have had the ability to know that I should be letting go. I'd been holding on tight.

In the next art therapy session, Betty drew Pictures 5 and 6 (not shown). Picture 5 is a pastel drawing indicating how the space in her life felt while she was still using chemicals. It shows a white empty room with a door which is barely cracked open so the blue can be seen outside. Picture 6 is a pastel drawing showing how the space in her life felt on that day in treatment. It is a picture of a pale blue and green earth surrounded by a definite medium blue line, an orange line, and finally a yellow glow. Betty indicated feeling no awareness of her higher power while she was still using chemicals. She discusses these drawings.

> Well, my using I felt like I was in a closed room (Picture 5). Uh, and that's really what the alcohol and the drugs did to me. They made me very isolated. Um, very shut off from the world like almost in a closet or in a room. And just the door is ajar a little bit. I do know there is a world out there.

Betty describes her space on this day.

> Well, it's like the whole world (Picture 6). Uh, He's [God] all over. Well, He's behind. This is like an eclipse [laughter] and the sun is behind. I guess I do feel now that, uh, the world is open to a lot of things . . . just in the circle. . . . Well, I think it's just containing all that's inside . . . this is my world from the inside . . . the fluid. The ring around it is my sun, my higher power. It's like an eclipse. That sun is behind that world. It's keeping it warm. Quite a change from just my little room.

During the next session of art therapy, Betty drew a life line showing the ups and downs in her life and drew Picture 7 (Figure 3-5) to show how the unhealthy repeating pattern of co-dependent relationships with men has felt to her. The black charcoal drawing shows a series of spiral shapes with prickers like barbed wire. Betty talks about this pattern in her life and the picture she drew.

> My . . . repeating habit is relationships with men, definitely. . . . Uh, I picture myself inside this big roll of barbed wire and every time I try to stand up I get pricked really bad (Figure 3-5). So, you really start, I guess, bending over almost like submission type. And I can't crawl, 'cause I get pricked on the bottom. . . . I'm caught between the bottom which I feel is my morals or just what I believe in and the top which are the relationships, and I can't win. Not a good place to be.
> It's real black and white. No, there is no higher power that would permit that to happen. No, this was during the time that I felt His absence.

Betty expresses her feelings about vulnerability in Picture 8 (Figure 3-6). The pastel picture has a black leafless tree on the left with a yellow balloon snagged on the branches. The grass is green with yellow flecks and the other balloons are orange, red, and blue. The sky is a pale blue. Betty tells about her picture and her feelings.

> Well, back to my childhood Picture 8 (Figure 3-6). I love balloons! Uh, I feel like I run into a snag like a balloon [that] is caught on a dead branch and it just

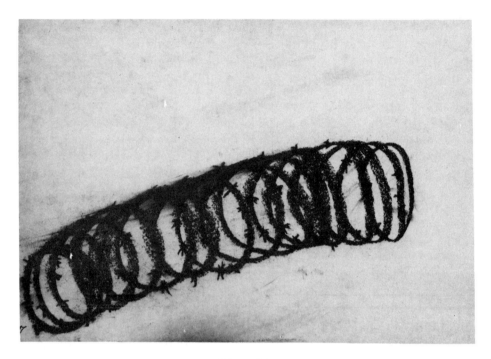

Figure 3-5

can't float free. All my other balloons are floating free and, uh, the sky is the limit. They're just going to go to heights unknown.

That vulnerability, that sort of keeps me attached to the past, like the dead tree, and uh, I think I tried to put a nice breeze in that picture so that, uh, just possibly that balloon could be worked loose. . . . God is now, very much a part of me. He's in all of me in there [Betty is yellow balloon]. I'm aware every day that He's there.

Betty was in art therapy an extra day and so repeated the meditation about imaging her baby self that she had done the first day. This final pastel drawing is Picture 9 (Figure 3-7). There is a yellow-haired woman on the beach with lively medium blue water, a white sky with light blue clouds and a yellow and orange sun in the background. Betty describes the meditation experience and the picture she drew.

Well, during meditation I couldn't pick up the image of a baby. All I could pick up was an image of myself, um in a nice bikini of course, on a sandy beach, warm, relaxing, and felt very comfortable. Very comfortable with myself just being there and enjoying nature, a part of it . . . there isn't any emptiness. . . . Oh, gee, it must be all of that crayon yellow! It's definitely my higher power, um, if you were to paint me a color it would be yellow.

I feel very complete, not all the answers are there, but I am comfortable. I

Figure 3-6

guess I feel complete enough as a human being that I can handle a little bit of emptiness that's left with my own ideas and ways. Um, for the first time in my life I feel more complete. I'm almost there, not quite, but almost and I have a direction.... I couldn't see the baby in the last picture because [now] she is inside.

Before Betty left the treatment program, she shared some keepsakes with me which were meaningful to her in her recovery.

I just want to share with you these keepsakes from Share. The shell I got from one of your first art classes and that probably will remind me I'm just a part of creation. That He [God] created me just like He did the sea and the shells and all the little creatures.

The sand dollar inside reminds me that I am very fragile. Matter of fact, it wasn't broken 'til I came down here today.... It's very fragile and even though we're very fragile, inside [the sand dollar] there are birds to fly free, sort of like our soul or our spirit. No matter how broken we get it's always in there.

And then, of course, I have my sobriety medal for one month and so I guess I feel I got what was inside of me. I got my sobriety. And J. gave me this cross.

Figure 3-7

So, I guess I feel like I had to travel through hell but . . . I came out with my life complete, I came out with my sobriety and I came out with my God.

The last words Betty said to me as we parted were:

I've been in a lot of churches, but I've said if anyone really wants to see God working, they should come here.

## SUMMATION AND REFLECTION

### Addiction History

Betty's abandonment by her father and the resulting "emptiness" and the feeling of being different, combined with her mother's modeling of a "weak" and dependent woman, left Betty with an empty yearning and a history of impoverished relationships since early childhood. Her father's chemical dependency supplied a possible genetic connection to that disease for Betty.

The stress caused by this emptiness and the unresolved co-dependent relationships in her family of origin, combined with the knowledge that she was "different" than the other kids, started an unhealthy repeating pattern in her life. She went through a number of marriages and relationships looking for the right man, always managing to choose someone who would leave her abandoned as her father did. The eventual bottom in her co-dependency led her into chemical dependency as a way to medicate her pain and open her up socially. She came to her "bottom" rather rapidly in this addiction, ending in abrupt personality changes and violence. After this, she sought treatment at Share.

### Spiritual History

Betty was involved with a church as a child where she came to believe in a God who was loving. During her active involvement in the disease of addiction, she felt very far away from God and that He had "disappeared." Upon entering treatment, she was very open to the idea of spirituality and a higher power as a part of a 12-step program.

### Art and Spirituality Experience

The simplicity of the art experience helped Betty to put away her defenses and allow her childlike side to "play." As a vulnerable, open childlike person, Betty was able to connect very deeply with both the meditations and the artwork. Picture 1 (Figure 3-1) led her to a deeper understanding of her emptiness and powerlessness to help herself. The making of Picture 2 (Figure 3-2) helped Betty identify the layers of active process required for recovery. Picture 3 (Figure 3-3) reconnected Betty with the playfulness and love of God and a conscious visual connection with yellow as her color association for God. Betty found her own person being connected to God through her yellow hair in Picture 4 (Figure 3-4). The empty isolated Godlessness of her space during her active addiction was visibly apparent to her through Picture 5. Betty felt the sense of being surrounded and backed up by her God of yellow through Picture 6. The barrenness and repeated pain of her co-dependence was made concrete for her through Picture 7 (Figure 3-5). Picture 8 (Figure 3-6) gave Betty a visual connection with her past, present and future and a realization that she was "filled" with her higher power even though she was fearful about being snagged by old patterns. Picture 9 (Figure 3-7) allowed Betty to see her personal and spiritual growth on paper.

Making art allowed Betty to be connected in a very real way with her childlike self and make her relationship with God visible. Through her artwork, she was able to actually see her relationship with God grow. Betty left treatment with a determination to engage in recommended aftercare, deepened hope, and faith in herself and God.

# Chapter 4

## MARCUS'S STORY

### INTRODUCTION AND HISTORY

Marcus appeared to be arrogant, grandiose, cynically humorous, quick-witted, and very guarded when he first came to art therapy. He alternated funny attention-getting tactics, such as wearing wildly patterned, colorful jams-type shorts in the middle of winter, with emotional sensitivity and embarrassment when he was allowing himself to be vulnerable.

He is a 30-year-old caucasian man who is cocaine addicted and co-dependent. He began using marijuana and amphetamines at age 15 or 16. He rapidly moved on to cocaine within twelve to eighteen months and quickly progressed to "constant" daily use.

> I wanted to be accepted, wanted to have friends. . . . I'd go down to the end of the block and hang out with the older kids . . . they're cool, you know, I didn't have any brothers.

Marcus thought he could get clean on his own and had tried many times.

He describes his life just previous to treatment as:

Shit. Very, very unmanageable. If I had money, I'd go get cocaine. So, one of my sisters—it took my sisters, more or less, to talk me in to coming in here, you know. Seventeen years of using, or whatever it is, you know . . . I've lost so many jobs, so many material things that, you know, I had just to get more drugs. It was insanity, definitely.

He describes his feelings about himself at that time as:

Disgust, um, dislike. I couldn't look in the mirror and say I like this person I saw at all. . . . I didn't like myself at all, you know, I didn't want to be here in the beginning, you know, I was doing it, hoping to get the acceptance from my family again. . . . I knew that they loved me, but I knew they didn't like me. So, I told myself, all right, fine, you guys don't think I can quit, I'll go into a rehab for ya, you know, I'll proved this to ya, yeah, and then you guys'll like me again.

He was the second oldest of six children in his family of origin with one older sister and four younger sisters. He describes his father as a "workaholic," although he states that neither parent was chemically dependent. His father's workaholism is called "abuse" by Marcus. He also remembers "slight" physical abuse from his father, which he calls "being beaten."

> I was always worried about when Dad came home. You had to worry about what kind of mood. . . . Well, you don't hit the girls, so when Dad gets mad, you know, Marcus is the only boy so it's, it was tough for me to accept, you know I always hid. I always had to wonder if I could go see Dad or not . . . do you talk to Dad today or don't you. . . . [I'd] go be by myself somewhere in the house . . . or I'd go to one of my smaller sisters, you know, I'd take care of them. . . . I was alone as a child and I'm thirty now and still alone.

When Marcus reflects on his childhood spirituality, he says:

> I was forced to go to church, you know, every Sunday get dressed up you go to church, probably 'til I was fourteen or fifteen, so, and I was the altar boy . . . probably only because I thought they wanted me to be, okay, so when I got the chance to stop going to church, I did.

## MARCUS'S ART THERAPY EXPERIENCE

When Marcus heard art therapy was part of treatment, he thought:

> That was a joke, okay? Bottom line I'm like, come on, you know, I'm not here for art class, I'm here to get better. . . . I had the bag on, the mask over my face, you know . . . well its been my mask my whole life. Its just to goof around—to be the clown—attention, I need attention, you know. I still need attention, you know, even though I feel I've progressed.

When asked to draw a picture of either his higher power or where he was in his recovery transformation process, Marcus drew Picture 1 (Figure 4-1), a pastel drawing. It has a little figure drawn in black on the lower left corner. There are black clouds above the figure raining down black rain. Two tall black, snow-capped mountains are in the middle, and the right side has a yellow sun in the upper corner over green grass and a green-leaved tree. Marcus describes his picture as

> a picture of myself . . . when I first came in. I, um, I felt like, uh, you know, it's a bad day out. I felt nothing was good about it. I'm being rained on. I know there's gotta be something better and that's why I have the sun, you know.
>   Well, its, its got the green grass—it's life, you know, it's life, but in between me and this picture that I had of life are these two big black mountains, you know, and it's a tough climb and it has been, you know, I had to look at myself

Figure 4-1

and I didn't like that guy . . . to me it was a picture, fine, okay. Here's how I feel, I'll draw a couple of mountains 'cause those are the mountains to go over to get to here. . . . It was the path I thought I'd have to take to get to a better place.

On the day when Marcus came in to do the Picture 2 (Figure 4-2), he was very sarcastic and appeared angry, trying to mask the unmet expectations he had for his sisters. He expected them to invite him for the Thanksgiving holiday, and they promised to pay a portion of his treatment costs. One of his sisters said she needed to take care of her own family and she could not afford to spend time or money on him. The task for the picture was to draw feelings about something Marcus had to let go of. He labeled the picture, "The anger I feel when I feel hurt." Of this black charcoal picture he said:

> [I] had myself on the right in a cage—it's a little stick man with a sad face and on the left-hand side of the picture is a picture of my family having Thanksgiving dinner—you've got Mom and Dad and five girls and I guess one of them would be my Aunt.

Two days after drawing Picture 2 (Figure 4-2) and one day before Thanksgiving, the situation with Marcus's family changed.

Figure 4-2

They finally called me the night before Thanksgiving and invited me over, you know, I thought they'd given up. But, um, Thanksgiving was a bad day for [me].... The beginning of Thanksgiving day, I had been offered a pass to go to be with my family, so I was ecstatic. The night before I didn't sleep, I was like I can't wait ... they're going to come pick me up. I had gotten a phone call and then I was ecstatic, but that morning my pass was taken away by my counselor. ... I had a previous engagement to go with the other clients to a breakfast at a place called EDI.

EDI stands for Easy Does It. It is the name of a local AA group that puts on holiday dinners for chemically dependent clients in treatment as a means of outreach.

This is a place where I thought I was gonna go sit with a bunch of other idiots like myself and, uh, we were just gonna sit there and have, you know, turkey and a little AA meeting afterward and it would be very boring, you know. I refused to go twice, and had words, big words between my counselor. ... I was surprised that they still let me stay here. ... I was asked to leave, either go to EDI or leave, you know, and I went upstairs to pack and, you know, used all the bad words to my counselor.

But then I decided I wasn't here for him, I was here for me and I went to EDI with the intention of not having a good time . . . there was no way I was going to have a good time. I wasn't gonna. Oh, I gave up totally. You know, Thanksgiving was not going to be a good day.

Armed with a desire to stay in treatment for himself and a bad attitude about the day at EDI, Marcus describes what happened that day:

Well, EDI, I guess you could say, was my spiritual experience. I went there with a bad attitude, and I was sitting there, and then I started talkin' to a few people, you know, I had the people from our, from Share around me also. And, uh, started enjoying myself a little bit. The dinner was good, you know, and [I] listened to the speaker afterwards.

And while the speaker was talking, I was just sitting there. And I had these really weird feelings going through my body, things I'd never felt before, you know, I didn't know what to explain it as, you know, I'm just leaning back and I'm like, what's going on?

Oh God, there were. I was warm and I was afraid that something was wrong with me, but I wasn't, you know—I was scared, but not afraid, let's put it that way. I was, I didn't know what was happening, but I wasn't worried about it. Yeah! It was, it's the strangest thing I've ever felt.

When asked to put a color on the feeling, Marcus said:

It would have to be yellow. It would have to be like I felt the warmth coming from somewhere . . . and it was, it was great . . . it was like I saw things happening before they did . . . they had a drawing, okay. AA has a drawing every now and then, for like the big book, and books, you know, literature and there was a drawing. They had three books and the first person got their choice, and I saw myself getting up and going up there, 'cause the ticket they had given me was going to win this thing, you know, and then they started to draw the ticket and I got up, like, you know, I knew, I just knew that they were going to pick my ticket and they did. Well, there was only one book I didn't have and the book was called *Came to Believe.*

*Came to Believe* is about AA's second step, i.e., "Came to believe that a power greater than ourselves could restore us to sanity." Marcus was connecting the strange feelings he was having and the circumstances of the day with his higher power whom he called God. He connected the energy he felt

with the presence of my higher presence. . . . That I finally came to believe not only in my higher power but in myself. . . . I feel I felt His presence . . . 'cause I felt calm, like an inner peace that I mean, come on, I was running around this place slamming doors, yelling, calling people names, I mean I was acting like a child, you know, and I wasn't going to stop that when I came back from this place. I was going to start off right where I left off.

And all of a sudden, "all the anger was gone . . . it was really strange." When Marcus received the book telling about coming to believe in a higher power, he perceived this as further evidence of God.

> Obviously, you know, it was like not only [that] I experienced it emotionally and in my feelings, but He wanted to let me know . . . my higher power . . . that this is what's happening to you [Marcus]. . . . Maybe I'm so skeptical . . . I could've wrote it off as a hot flash. . . . Obviously, I needed something more.

Marcus felt that he had received what he needed from his higher power and drew two pictures the next day in art therapy. Picture 3 (Figure 4-3) is a pastel picture which shows how Marcus's space in his life felt while he was using drugs. It is mostly black with a small faceless stick figure in the lower left and a small yellow sun in the upper right. Picture 4 (not shown) is a pastel picture indicating how his space felt on this day in treatment, the day after his "spiritual experience." It is a picture of a yellow sun which almost fills the paper. Marcus describes Picture 3 (Figure 4-3) and Picture 4.

> Space using, I've got, uh, my little stick figure of myself in the lower left corner and, uh, just a sea of black, but in the upper right corner there's a picture of my higher power. Now I associate the sun 'cause of its warmth, you know, and its greatness as my higher power. It's very small [the sun], you know, and I know that when I was using I didn't have any space. I always knew there was something else, but . . . I didn't care at that time. It didn't mean anything to me. . . . I didn't think I could ever get that far. . . .
>
> Space that day (Picture 4, not shown) is, it's just a picture, one page completely covered with the sun 'cause I felt warm and good and happy and loving and understanding and I could have saved the world that day . . . after the initial shock I realize I have to save myself first.

With the knowledge that he used the sun as his symbol of God, his higher power, Marcus looked back at Picture 1 (Figure 4-1) and saw that the sun was there on the other side of the mountains before he had consciously used that symbol for God.

> After realizing now . . . I know that this is where I have to be—On the good side of these mountains (Figure 4-1)—'cause He's there—my higher power the sun—He's there. Yeah, and there's life there. There's nothing on the other side of those mountains.

In the next session, Marcus drew picture 5 (not shown), a drawing of himself standing naked in waist-deep water. He felt like he would drown

Figure 4-3

with the knowledge that he was known and thus vulnerable to others. He tells about this picture and his feelings.

> Well, it's a picture of vulnerability . . . how we feel when other people really know who we are. . . . I, myself, hide behind being a clown, you know, and had myself half out of water, and after I realize how vulnerable I am and people see through that, I feel like I'm drowning. . . . [In art therapy especially] it's hard to hide who you really are. Very hard!

During the next art therapy session, Marcus wept most of the time after sharing Picture 6 (Figure 4-4) with the group. He had shared his drug history earlier in the day and was feeling very exposed. In the session, he took part in a mediation experience where he imagined himself reaching out to his baby self and he drew Picture 6 (Figure 4-4), a pastel drawing showing how he felt about this experience and how he felt about being valuable himself. There is a strong, somewhat monstrous-looking man, weeping and standing waist deep in water, holding a pink baby in the picture. A large sun, which Marcus now associates with God, is in the upper right-hand corner. Marcus describes the meditation experience and the picture.

> Well, we, uh, calmed ourselves. We were to look, picture ourselves as a child. I only, I have only one picture of myself as a child that I can remember and that's myself sitting with my little sister and I'm about eight, ninth months old and, you know, I got this little guy with a smile on his face, but he's just sitting there with his sister. Now, for me, all I could picture was picking him up and holding him. I didn't get enough of that when I was little. Okay, I probably still don't, but, um, I just wanted to hold him. I needed to hold him, you know, I mean.
>
> I really wanted, after I thought about it some more, I wanted to draw it—the picture—different than I did. I really should have drawn it a baby holding a baby....I drew myself holding this baby which is myself and I remember crying....

Figure 4-4

Marcus harshly judged his adult self and yet wanted to reach out to the baby while feeling a confusing mixture of "pain, sorrow, happiness and joy." Marcus describes the feelings he had toward both parts of himself that day.

> Well, I don't look like a nice guy, I guess, myself. I called myself [adult self] an asshole...'cause he is....The baby is innocence, you know, he

has a chance, you know I just, I needed to hold myself to get a grip on myself. . . .

The processing of this picture was, for Marcus:

> Very emotional, um, very emotional. I didn't expect to spend that much time on this picture that we spent that day . . . I was just sad. I mean I was . . . I pictured myself crying before we went over the picture, but when I thought we were going to go over it I thought I could just, you know, this is myself holding myself, and I'm not, you know. I felt sad and hurt.

Marcus describes the response of the group to his picture.

> They generally accepted it in a genuine manner. . . . They said I looked like Frankenstein, but . . . I drew myself like a monster, yes, but . . . [they were] very supportive. They came in and gave me the hugs that I was trying to give myself.

He goes on to talk about his experience of God's presence during the session

> near the end when I more or less lost control of my emotions. I know, He's always there. I know that now, you know, I just can't ask Him to be here when I want Him to be there 'cause He just, you know. When I let go, He was there. . . .
>
> Ever since Thanksgiving, He's [God, via the sun] been in every one of my pictures. He's always there now. Um, it's really strange. He's getting bigger and bigger, too. It feels great! I'm happier than most people can even imagine. I really am. I really am.

Marcus noted happily that the size of the sun, his symbol for God, had grown in size from Picture 4 to Picture 7 (Figure 4-5), saying, "He's almost doubled in size." Picture 4 had been done the day after his spiritual experience on Thanksgiving at EDI.

Picture 7 (Figure 4-5) is a pastel picture of how Marcus feels about his higher power which he drew in his last art therapy experience. The sun is yellow and larger than any other sun Marcus drew. It is in the center of the picture with hands reaching down out of it holding a red heart. The land is green with a blue border running along the top of it. Marcus tells about this picture.

> Uh, we were supposed to have a picture of our higher power and how we feel about Him. This was easy for me. I mean, I was done in like, what, three minutes? I had this quickly! This was there. Uh, you have a picture of my higher power which is the sun as I draw Him, okay, I draw Him as a sun. He's in the center of this page. He has two hands coming out from the bottom, holding a large heart and this was so simple for me, you know, because my

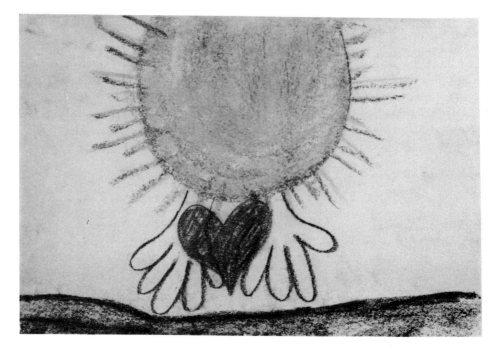

Figure 4-5

higher power—God, as I call him—you know, He's caring, He's loving, He's understanding. He holds all these things out to us, you know, and all we have to do is accept 'em. And, it was so simple for me to do this.... I feel He is here with me, holding me, and loving me.

Reflecting on art therapy's contribution to his spirituality and spiritual growth, Marcus says:

It's made me understand where I'm going and . . . how I'm getting there. . . . I look over these pictures I didn't even think of it then, but you know I look over these pictures, and, you know, I'm going from nowhere to everywhere. I see myself. I never thought I'd get over these mountains in the first picture, you know. Even coming here I knew—no way, it'd never happen. Letting go of my emotions and today's picture, you know, I have that warmth and I can see it when I look at the pictures. I can see how I've graduated. . . . I see me. I really do. I see myself growing and learning and loving.

Marcus jokes that he has decided to become an art therapist and talks about how he has been using art during his off hours at the treatment center.

I'll be an art therapist! . . . After homework, of course! You see, a lot of clients when they come into Share, they're scared. They have every right to be, you know. It's a scary step forward that most people aren't sure they want to take . . . we play "Win, Lose or Draw" at night. It's my own group therapy. . . . We just play it. Okay . . . the first night there were six people, three girls, three guys. . . . Last night we had fifteen people playing the game. It's good group therapy. It's a good release for people. It really is. I love it!

## SUMMATION AND REFLECTION

### Addiction History

Marcus was the only boy of six children and received both positive and negative attention for being a boy. His father was a "workaholic" who was rarely home. When his father was home, he physically abused Marcus but did not touch the sisters, because he did not believe in hitting girls. Marcus felt a lack of approval from his father that was administered with the beatings. Marcus consequently spent a good deal of time alone, hiding from his father. He also turned to caring for his younger sisters as a way to get attention for himself.

Growing up in this way, Marcus became desperate for attention and, to boost self-esteem, used grandiose comic routines. Cocaine, Marcus's drug of choice, gives a false sense of power and self-esteem. The caring he needed so desperately he gave to others, establishing his co-dependent traits early.

### Spiritual History

As a child, going to church and being an altar boy were a part of his co-dependence because he did it only to please others. He stopped going to church as soon as he was given the choice. He had no conscious faith in a higher power until his spiritual experience during treatment. After that experience, Marcus says that God became very real to him. He reports experiencing God as warm and loving and growing into a bigger part of his life every day.

### Art and Spirituality Experience

During art therapy, Marcus had many experiences of his growing spirituality through art. His feelings of personal powerlessness without a higher power are shown by the figure and the mountains in Picture 1

(Figure 4-1), as well as his unconscious inclusion of the sun which he later identified as his symbol for God. The colorless painful emptiness and co-dependence expressed through the impoverished drawing of Picture 2 (Figure 4-2) was important for Marcus. The tiny sun, which was there even in his darkest faceless time as shown in Picture 3 (Figure 4-3), was an important record as Marcus looked back. The growing, glowing yellow sun (higher power) in Picture 4 helped affirm Marcus's growing spirituality. Picture 5 connected Marcus with his fear of vulnerability as the reason for his clowning. The growing acceptance of his adult and needy self, as well as his child self, was apparent through his work in Picture 6 (Figure 4-4). His increased vulnerability and safety is shown through his now "very large" symbol for God shown in Picture 7 (Figure 4-5).

Art provided a place for Marcus to "see" again and again his experience of God and watch it grow on the paper through his drawings. He left treatment willing to be much more vulnerable and hopeful for recovery. He continued in long-term care at a halfway house.

# Chapter 5

## DANA'S STORY

### INTRODUCTION AND HISTORY

Dana is a friendly, extroverted young caucasian woman who is plump, although athletic, and who slicks her blond hair back into a slightly "tomboy" style. She seems to like attention, but is slow to trust. She is the mother of a 13-month-old son and has never been married. Dana was the second of four daughters in her family of origin. Her father was alcoholic and a sexual and physical abuser. He sexually abused Dana and her sisters. Her mother was the recipient of the physical abuse. Her parents divorced when she was eight years old.

Dana is now 27 years old and identifies herself as a co-dependent as well as an alcoholic and cocaine addict. Her first use of alcohol was at age 14 with a progression to cocaine use at age 21. Her drug of choice was alcohol before entering treatment at The Share Program.

Dana saw her father only once during her childhood after the divorce and once in the past year. In speaking about the effect of her father's abuse, Dana says,

> Um, it's kind of hard because it, it sort of buried a lot of anger inside of me. . . . I would have to say it more or less ruined my first 27 years.

Dana received treatment once previously at a private treatment center:

> Um, well I went through the detox, and about halfway through the first detox, they told me that my insurance wasn't gonna kick in, so they kicked me out and I was able to go back the next day, but only to start detox over again, so I was in detox for approximately 14 days. . . .
>
> I found out I had, there was something wrong with my knee, and I was five days under the rehab program, and since I found out I was having surgery, I didn't really concentrate on [the] program at all. And, uh, after, when I went in for knee surgery, they pumped me full of valium and that's all she wrote for 4 years. . . .

The effects of valium are similar to alcohol. After the valium was prescribed, Dana was immediately back into using alcohol. Before coming into treatment at Share, Dana had experienced an 18-month period of being "straight" followed by a relapse.

> I went out and I started using, uh, cocaine again. Slowly but surely I was increasing my, um, amounts and I was drinking very heavy—a lot, I'd say probably two cases in a day. . . . I just came here because I was scared of what happened to me the last time I used. I ended up stealing and, you know, my self-esteem was very low and I was very, uh, angry at myself, disgusted.

Dana describes co-dependent relationships with her family. She has:

> Um, a drug relationship with my sisters and, uh, . . . [I'm] very dependent on my mom. We used to, we lived together with my son. . . . I lived with my mom and she paid for everything that my son and I needed, not to mention she did give me money. She was an enabler. She also gave me money for liquor and, um, I just depended on her to be there when I wasn't for my son and, um, I don't know. We really depend on each other.

She talks about her co-dependency with her drug-addicted boyfriend.

> Yeah, my last relationship—my son's father—I was, uh, I was looking for a relationship and sort of just fell into this one and it went so fast that I think we met each other, two weeks—went out for two weeks and then we ended up moving in with each other a month later. We talked about marriage and everything and it was really—boom, boom, boom, boom, real fast. It happened real fast. So, um, I don't know. I just felt like I needed something and somebody, so I just turned my affections over and just went that way with it and, uh, I thought it was everything I wanted, but it wasn't.

Dana remembers no experience of her spirituality as a child. As an adult, her first experience with spirituality happened shortly before entering treatment this time. She describes this new awareness of her spirituality which came to her in a dream. She said I was the only person who she had told this story to, because she thought people might think she was "nuts."

> Mainly I became aware of it when . . . I think the first time that I had spirituality was when I decided to come here. . . . It was in a dream, I don't know what it was, but it was just a real weird experience, you know, bright . . . in my dream.
> It was just like, it was a fluorescent light, a real white fluorescent light in my dream and I just, you know, and it was right after a coke binge. . . . It was, uh, like warmth and like, uh, purity and, um, I don't know, just made me feel real comfortable and at ease with myself that, you know, finally I was able to realize that maybe, maybe this is it, maybe I better. . . . It felt like I was brushing up with death, you know and then all of sudden this dream came along and kind of livened me up a little bit and said, you take this chance now or you're gonna

blow it. [There was not a voice.] It was just a feeling, you know, I just felt totally warm and just full of, you know, like pure for that one moment and that was like real peace.

Dana stayed with an aunt for two weeks to think before entering treatment.

> I woke up and I said, "God, I, you know, this is it. I have to disappear." And I did. I disappeared for two weeks and then I decided to come in here. . . . I woke up the next morning and I told my mom that I need to come have treatment. . . . I went to . . . my aunt's house. . . . I was hiding from people, places and things.

## DANA'S ART THERAPY EXPERIENCE

Dana tells about her attitude toward art therapy in her last treatment.

> I hated it. . . . Because, well, from what I learned the first time in art therapy is that you can't change your feelings when you're putting 'em down on paper and drawing something. You can't hide what you feel. It comes out in the colors that you use. So, I hated it 'cause I didn't, I wasn't willing to be honest with myself.

In coming to art therapy at this time, Dana describes her attitude as having

> some reservations about it, but I was willing to give it a try, since I had come in here with an open mind. . . . "Oh, God," that's what I thought. "Here we go again."

The first day Dana was in art therapy, she drew two pictures. Picture 1 (Figure 5-1), an oil crayon drawing, shows how the space in her life felt when she was using chemicals. There is a peach-colored naked figure in the center of the paper with blue eyes and a unsmiling red mouth. Inside and filling the upper body of this figure is a small brown figure. The larger figure is surrounded by a grey scribble. A black scribble surrounds the grey on the sides and top. A yellow scribble line goes around the paper's edges on the sides and bottom.

Picture 2 (Figure 5-2) shows how the space in Dana's life felt the first day she was in art therapy. This picture shows a similar peach-colored figure in the center, but with a smile and moving to the left into a white scribble area. There is a band of orange scribble running around the back and the front bottom of the figure. A yellow scribble band comes next and goes over the head, behind the back and under the feet of the figure. A mixed black and grey scribble band is outside the yellow framing the top right and bottom sides of the paper. Dana describes her feelings and thoughts about these two pictures. She says, Picture 1 (Figure 5-1)

is my self inside of myself . . . surrounded by anger, shame and pain, with light surrounding that I can't get to. . . . I felt really like I was living in the dark side of my life, but as I was living the dark side of my life, I felt there was some sort of, of hope and . . . it's like I said, spirituality. It's, you know, it's all there, but it's like untouchable. . . . You know, it's [spirituality is] yellow.

Figure 5-1

For Dana the yellow in the picture connects with the light in the dream because it's a bright color. . . . The black is, is like, uh, it is like the evil part of me, you know, it's like part of me that I really can't stand. It's just real dark there.

Dana's attitude toward what she "can't stand" about herself is changing.

Yeah, I'm taking it in and processing it and turning it into something good. . . . Today, I feel like, pretty much that, uh, I'm sort of processing it bit by bit and, uh, whatever I feel that I'm getting upset about it, or you know, I sort of try to turn it over or whatever – just give it, "Take my insanity away, God," you know.

She describes the little person inside the larger person in Figure 5-1.

Well, I just felt really like, uh, you know, my outer body was there for everybody to see, you know, but the inside of me – my real feelings of how I really felt about myself – I was always putting up a front and, uh, when I was inside of myself, at least I could feel a little bit about what was really me and that's how I felt when I was using. I really felt like I really knew myself, but all I was doing was bullshitting myself.

Dana's tells about her feelings doing the Picture 2 (Figure 5-2) in the first art session.

I felt a little freedom, I felt a little, like a little bit of the air clearing and, uh, was leaving like the dark side of me behind and letting the pureness of my higher power closer to me. . . . I learned that I can have peace with my higher power.

The white space in Picture 2 (Figure 5-2) represents:

It's sort of the, um, space in front of me that I'm able to eventually walk into . . . the white is the open space. . . . The pure, open space so it's in front of me for me to have forward motion, you know. . . . The orange is just that, it's just a slight barrier between me and my higher power [the yellow space]. It's getting closer . . . [the dark black space]; it's there, but it's behind me.

I feel it's [Dana's spirituality] there. It's real light in those two pictures if you notice. It's not real dark, it's not real bright, but, ah, it's there.

In Dana's second art therapy session, she drew Picture 3 (Figure 5-3) showing her unhealthy repeating patterns, and a lifeline (not shown) indicating the ups and downs in her life. Dana used yellow to color in the alcohol bottles, and yellow rays are radiating from the cocaine. A yellow flame is coming from her broken co-dependent heart. Yellow is the color Dana now identifies with her higher power who she now calls God. The peach figure goes along the bottom of the page from falling on her head to landing on her back to praying to standing unsteadily.

She identifies the unhealthy repeating patterns in Picture 3 (Figure

Figure 5-2

5-3) as her former higher powers. She believes God would not give her anything that is bad for her, but that He allowed her drug use to continue. She even remembers praying to God for drugs.

> There was definitely spiritual life there, but it was all in the wrong. I think it was in [the] wrong, uh, sense. I was praying to the higher power for my drugs. . . . I always prayed to Him for it and I never went out looking for it without saying, "God, please let me score tonight," you know. . . . I think He allowed it. . . . Well, when I was, uh, drinking I always felt that I could, uh, do just about anything, any trick I'd be willing to do for it. . . . The third guy there [in Figure 5-3] is my burning love and my broken heart . . . for my son's father and, uh, I just felt like I was always begging for it and the more I begged the

more I hurt, the more I burned. . . . The last one there is, uh, myself when I'm really high and screwing things up like my 1985 Nissan truck which I was very proud of. I just felt really disgusted and like I was real angry, you know, that I did stuff like that [lost her truck].

Figure 5-3

She notices a similarity in the form of the ups and downs between the person moving along the bottom of Picture 3 (Figure 5-3) and her lifeline.

Oddly enough, it sort of takes the same shape as my drawing in, ah, its high and low points. . . . [The first dip in the lifeline represents] the child abuse years, sexual and physical. . . . I'm processing a little bit about, um, anger I feel towards my father, and feeling like that, I can actually reach inside of myself and just spark the little, the little tiny me, you know. And it feels real good.

I didn't know kids were supposed to be like that. I never understood it. . . . So sweet . . . it's like, ah, like I missed something. I know I did and it's hard to put it into words because I missed so much. . . . I didn't know that kids were supposed to be so vulnerable, so, so, ah, they're smart, too. They really are. . . . They know things. I think they know pretty much of everything. I don't think there are certain things. I think they know a lot . . . they know it in their head. They know it in their heart. They feel it. And I don't ever remember feeling anything in my heart when I was growing up. Only pain.

Dana drew two pictures about her Christmas holiday in the next session. She arrived in the session appearing very angry and defensive. She was focused on the unhappy day she had on Christmas day. Her first drawing, Picture 4 (Figure 5-4), was of Christmas day and the separation she felt from her family. The picture shows the peach figure of Dana on the left with a red broken heart and crying dark blue tears. The familiar yellow scribble band is behind her and turns to an orange band on top of her. A grey diagonal line cuts the picture into two parts. On the right side is a green decorated tree with presents underneath and a silver star on top. Next to the tree are three large figures smiling with one holding a package. There is one small figure in their midst who is faceless and holding a package. Yellow rays are pointing upward from the whole group of figures.

Figure 5-4

Dana became increasingly agitated as she drew and talked about her picture. She describes her feelings about Christmas day.

> Well, Christmas day was a real sad event for me 'cause I'm real family oriented. Uh, I was taken to the EDI club through the Share program and, um, there I just kept praying to God. "Please, please, somehow let me get home. I miss my son. I miss my family." Here in the drawing I'm separated from my family. Uh, they're celebrating Christmas without me, and my son is there, and I didn't draw his face in because I wasn't sure what he'd look like on that day.... I just knew that my higher power in there was darker, and I know [now] that through me and through them that my higher power was providing both sides of this picture.... Because it's right here with me—it's yellow, bright yellow, and it's bright yellow over here, too... above my family's heads....
>
> The orange is like, like I said, it's the part where it's there [spirituality], but it's not quite. It's, I noticed this is darker, too, and I, I, uh, that this is above me... the color orange is above me and it's like floating away and my higher power is coming closer to me. God [is coming along]... the yellow, the yellow.

Dana feels better about that day now as she sees the yellow on both sides of the picture. She now sees that God was present to both herself and her family in her picture as the yellow.

> Because I was able to process it through my higher power why things are the way they are and the way they were... I'm saying that through God we [Dana and her family] weren't really separated.

After processing the Christmas picture, she did Picture 5 (not shown) which is a drawing of a large yellow heart connected to two small hearts with a chain which has a small padlock at the end. Dana tells about Picture 5, saying,

> Because I wanted to get in touch with the feelings that I felt on Christmas Eve.... It sort of made me feel that, well I guess one day from the other really didn't matter, I guess I really had it all along... it was probably the best Christmas Eve I've ever had in my life. My drawing is of a yellow—bright yellow heart with pastel colors surrounding it, uh, yellow, light blue and light green with pink hearts, and I, um, I feel I was locked into love that day through my higher power—being able to spend that day with my son.... It was beautiful, just a day full of warmth and love and lots of hope for the future.

Dana connects the feelings of Christmas Eve and her dream before detox:

> I just felt really warm. It was like that bright light in my dream, you know, and it, uh, just felt really pure that day. I felt real good that day.... It was like a coming back experience and it was just.... I know through, through all that

love and hope that I have through my higher power, my son and I have a better future together.

During the group process, Dana's feelings about the holiday shifted.

> I was feeling real sad and depressed. . . . Well, after we got to talkin' about it, I realized that like what I was sayin' before with the yellow and the orange being above me and behind me and the yellow spirit's above my family so that we were all connected one way or another anyway.

In the next session, Dana drew her feelings about being vulnerable shown in Picture 6 (Figure 5-5). The oil crayon drawing shows a peach-colored figure tumbling down a river on a hill on the left side of the paper. The river is made of a blue line under a black line on the left, but becomes completely black on the bottom before it reaches a large brown boulder. After the boulder, the river progresses on to the right first black with a red line on top and then orange on the far right with three orange rays going up. The figure is popping out at the right end where the orange rays are, and she is smiling. The clouds at the top are, from left to right, grey, dark blue, and light blue. Dana talks about her feelings about vulnerability and Picture 6 (Figure 5-5).

> I'm real vulnerable (Figure 5-5) when I'm, uh, when I'm approached by anybody, anything. . . . It means, um, your feelings are being shown and, uh, you don't what 'em to be. That's the way it is for me. I get really depressed and angry, so in this picture I'm, uh, first of all I'm submerged in a waterfall of anger and, uh, disgust and it's flowing into a river and crashing against rocks. . . .
>
> The black is my anger. . . . The red is my depression and, uh, the orange is there again and I'm really not too sure why I put the orange there other than it was a brighter color than the rest of the ones and I needed to have some, where I'm jumpin' out of the lake, it's like I'm coming down into a, uh, more relaxed period.

Dana judges her anger and sadness, so these feelings are hard to express.

> I feel, I guess I feel better. I mean, I, you know, I, it's gotta be processed one way or another. You know, once I, well, you know, this is hard to do because when I get angry and depressed, it is mad or sad.

Dana believes her relationship with God gives her the strength to be vulnerable and show feelings which are hard for her to express. She also notes that in the lower right edge of the picture, the last color of the waterfall which helps release her is orange. Orange is the color Dana says she consistently uses as the color closest to yellow, her higher power

Figure 5-5

color. When she reaches the orange, she is close enough to her higher power to be freed or

> to pull myself out of the depression. . . . My sanity, my thinking, you know, it's . . . not a process of thinking, it's just like a momentarily flash, you know, it's like a, for me to, I mean, and like here I'm jumpin' out of the water and it's like, uh, the anger pit or whatever it is. . . . I feel He [God] gives me the strength to pull myself out of it.

Dana wrote this on her vulnerability picture the day she drew it:

> I learned today through pain and anger that recovery is definitely in my life, but also difficult. Picture means that when I'm vulnerable, it gets me caught up in a waterfall of anger and as I work through it — it gets to a point of depression which in turn I work through and it frees me to be me.

In Dana's next session the group did a meditation where they imagined reaching out to their baby selves. They were also confronted with the idea that they were of great value. They were asked to draw either the feelings they had about reaching out to their little self or how they felt about being valuable. Picture 7 (Figure 5-6) shows a picture of a peach-colored baby in a little pink cradle nestled in tall grass. There is a grey boulder separating and "protecting" the baby from a blue stream filled with brown fish. A green-leafed tropical tree is to the right with a colorful parrot in the branches. The sun is shining down from the upper right with rays of yellow coming to the baby. Rays of yellow are also rising up out from the baby. The picture looks safe, cozy, bright, and tropical.

Dana combined the feelings about reaching out to her child self and her attitudes about her own value in Picture 7 (Figure 5-6). She tells about her meditation experience and drawing.

> Well, when the meditation was going on, I felt it was really, really neat that I was able to, ah, as you were speaking the words of what we were supposed to be meditating on, I really felt like I was reaching out, picking my little self up and holding it, and as I was cuddling it, it became me that I'm holding. . . . She was just a cute little blue-eyed little thing with blond furry hair. . . . She was a babe, a newborn. . . . She was very happy. She stared at me with that little sparkle in her eye and had a little grin on her face which I know babies don't grin, but this one did. This one had a smile. This one was havin' a chance to come, come back and live it all again. . . . I picked her up and I held her close to me and as I was holding her close in my meditation, it became me. . . . I don't know my blood was running so warm that day I just felt really good. You know, it felt, it felt as close to love as I've ever been in my life, you know.

Dana said she has never felt connected with her child self and she felt

> very full, very alive. . . . [When she is using drugs, she feels] empty, nothing's left. There's no, it's, uh, it's like I said, I'm inside myself, there's nothing. Yeah, exact opposite. I mean, way opposite.

Dana says that the feelings brought out that day have stayed with her.

> This feeling? Definitely . . . it stuck with me. I keep, every night I think about it, when I write in my journal, I, I write about this, that I was in touch with my little self. Yeah, my little self is with me all the time . . . the picture is of a, of a, like a tropical setting and I'm in the midst of the grass and watching the water and the fish and all the nature and there's real bright colors and my higher power's there with [light] streaming down. . . . It's my little self in the picture. And, uh, I'm real cute. I'm in a bassinet.

Dana wrote these words on the back of this picture:

> This picture is me as a child [newborn] finally getting in touch with my inner self. I learned warmth and just what I missed as a child. I learned peace and serenity can be mine.

Dana says that when she held the baby, she felt like she was "hugging" herself. Her last drawing, Picture 8 (Figure 5-7) was of her transforma-

Figure 5-6

tion process. The group was led in a guided meditation about the transformation process from dependence to recovery. The group was asked to draw either a picture of their higher power who was helping them recover or a picture of their transformation process. Dana's picture shows her little tumbling peach figure crawling to Share on the left side of the paper and standing just before she reaches the door. The standing figure has yellow rays going up with a small yellow cross above. Grey and black rays and grey clouds are in the sky on the left side. The Share building is brown and green on the bottom with a grey outline and a yellow outline on the outside. A large and a small peach figure are coming out on the right side and are connected by a yellow line going over the place where they are holding hands. They are both smiling. A large yellow cross with yellow rays dominates the sky, and blue clouds fly overhead. The edge of Grateful House, a woman's half-way house, is on the right edge of the paper. Dana called Picture 8 (Figure 5-7):

"Transformation Higher Power Combo...." I connected with myself when you said the word transformation. It didn't take me too long to figure out what transformation was and how it affected me in my life and the program.... It means going from my shitty self ... and not being in contact with the inner me for so long—27 years—and, uh, going through the Share program and coming out with my little self right behind me, beside me, in front of me, wherever—it's gonna be there.

I had little spirituality when I came in; like when we were discussing in Pictures 1 and 2 (Figures 5-1 and 5-2), um, my spirituality hit me like I said in the middle of the night in a dream, and it was able to get me away from my "scene" which I needed desperately to do and, uh, it brought me to my aunt's house where I had a chance to think and realize that it just wasn't a dream and I brought myself to the "Hotel Share" and, uh....

Figure 5-7

Dana describes the yellow line around the Share buildling.

That's my higher power calling me in and it looks like a real warm place to be like secure like in the dream and, um, and a safe place for me.... [It's safe] because I'm here with my higher power and figuring out who "me" really is.

After treatment, Dana comes out on the right side with her little self.

As I'm leaving, it's [her higher power] much stronger and brighter. I got the yellow cross there and, uh, lots of streaking comin' down from it and below it is me and me, a little self and a big self, and we're getting to know each other through my higher power which is interlocking us together.... I'm not really sure how it's doin' it, but it's doin' it; it's, really, it's just a feeling.

Dana describes the halfway house she wants to go to for herself.

Grateful House is a, a place where you can, it's a halfway house and you can go there and, uh, further your recovery. Like, for me, it's a place where I need to be to process more of the garbage that I still have inside me.

Dana talks about how art therapy has been useful for her.

I feel that art therapy is, has, ah, brought me a lot closer to what I knew I had, but wasn't sure. I needed to, ah, grasp it and, ah, the way I grasped it is through my drawings.... It became more ... evident to me that it was there. All I had to do was look, look a little deeper in myself.

Like I said in my dream, it was the bright color and there's bright colors in my drawing and I know from my drawings that my bright colors stand for my higher power.... It's been a, a "way back" experience, let me tell ya.

## SUMMATION AND REFLECTION

### Addiction History

Dana has a possible genetic predisposition of the disease of chemical dependency via her alcoholic father. Her history of childhood sexual abuse with her father as perpetrator, her witness of the physical abuse of her mother, and the abandonment issues involved with her father's absence set her up for deep co-dependency issues. She experienced shame, abandonment, fear, guilt, and the resulting emptiness. Her mother had co-dependency issues with her father and she has co-dependency issues with her daughters. Dana has looked for men who would abandon her, women who would take care of her, and chemicals that would help her forget her pain and emptiness. Her alcohol use started at 14 years and progressed to cocaine addiction by age 21.

### Spiritual History

Dana had no conscious spiritual beliefs until approximately two weeks before coming to the detox program at Share. At that time, she had a dream with a bright light in which she felt momentarily pure and comfortable with herself. She felt that God used the dream as a way to tell her to take a chance and get into recovery before she died. She went to her aunt's house for two weeks to think about it and then she came to detox at The Share Program. As a result of this experience, she was open to her growing spirituality while in treatment.

### Art and Spirituality Experience

Dana expressed various aspects of her spirituality and spiritual journey in each of her pieces of artwork she made in art therapy. In Picture 1 (Figure 5-1), the color yellow, which she later identified as her higher power color, appears as the border showing her faith and hope even while she was aware of her powerlessness. In discussing Picture 2 (Figure 5-2), she describes the opening to the light areas as "searching for my serenity and my higher power" and said that art therapy is showing her that she can have peace with her higher power. Picture 3 (Figure 5-3) uses the color yellow to identify her past "higher powers" of alcohol, cocaine, and co-dependence. Through Picture 4 (Figure 5-4), Dana learned that she was connected to her family through her higher power even when they were not physically present to one another. Picture 5 allowed Dana to realize that her higher power did provide her with what she needed for the Christmas holiday even though it was not on Christmas day. Picture 6 (Figure 5-5) made Dana aware that in even the most difficult feelings of vulnerability, the color orange, which she identifies as close to yellow and spirituality, was at the end to get her back up. Picture 7 (Figure 5-6) was a way for Dana to affirm her spiritual experience of consciously reconnecting with her inner child through the physical world of art making. The yellow sun in the sky sent down rays which almost touch the yellow rays coming up from the baby. Her last drawing, Picture 8 (Figure 5-7), used a yellow outline and yellow rays and crosses to show that her treatment program experience was surrounded with her higher power and her spirituality. Dana went on to further treatment at a halfway house with an increased groundedness in her faith in her higher power and hope for recovery. She felt that art therapy was very much a part of this transition.

# Chapter 6

## MEL'S STORY

### INTRODUCTION AND HISTORY

Mel is a 23-year-old caucasian man who appeared to be controlled, quiet, smiling, and friendly at the beginning of his treatment at the Share program. During treatment he found anger lurking under his careful control.

After his birth, he was adopted by an older couple who were strict fundamentalist Christians with two grown biological children. When he was young, his brother and sister treated him as though he were unacceptable. They always knew that he had been adopted, but he did not find out until later.

He is a drug addict and co-dependent. He first drank beer at age 11. His drug of choice upon entering treatment at Share was crack, but he mostly drank whiskey. He accidentally found out about his adoption at age 12, and after that time he started using marijuana and "speeders," then cocaine the last year of high school.

> Uh, I was adopted at nine days and, uh, I lived a life—for about 12 years before I found it out. I was going through the drawers looking for drug money and I found these adoption papers, you know, and I went, so I confronted my parents with it. . . . They said, "Yeah, you're adopted" and all this stuff and you know, "we love you still" and I'm like why didn't you tell me in the first place. . . . I considered them liars and cheats and all that stuff. . . . I was already into the drugs. . . . So, I don't know what, how my reaction would have been had I not been doing drugs, but my reaction was to, um, hurt 'em as much as I could and I did that.

Mel's adoption and his biological parents are often on his mind.

> I got a lot of theories . . . that, um, I was a family baby. . . . I'm somehow . . . some way my family's involved in this because it was an under-the-table adoption at a hospital. Gone through my Aunt who now has Alzheimer's disease, oversaw the whole thing and it was through her, you know.
>
> Not usually do parents of 50-plus get a child . . . when they already had two kids of their own. . . . And there is, I do look like, um, my cousin's, uh, husband.

I spent my high school years smoking pot every day and, um, just going out . . . staying away. Seemed like soon as I found out I was adopted, I just rebelled against church totally. I never liked it in the first place, but I went because I was supposed to, you know, but after that it was all, I never went again after I found my adoption papers. I never went until recently, I went.

I was overweight 'cause my parents, you know, they were heavy eaters and they'd reward you with food. You know, so I took food as a, you know, as a reward and that was the big thing. . . . I was extremely overweight. It seemed like as soon as I found that [adoption paper], I didn't want to be alike 'em, I didn't want to be anything like 'em 'cause mom and dad are both overweight. And after that I didn't want to be anything like 'em at all.

A number of months before coming to Share, Mel had been detoxed in another treatment center for crack addiction. He did not think alcohol was a problem at that time. He describes the time after treatment.

I moved out of my house and got a job as a bartender, and I didn't do crack or cocaine the whole seven months between May and now, but I ended up being an alcoholic, getting shot twice, getting a beer bottle [broken] over my head, almost losing my right eye and, uh, but I didn't do coke. You know, I was like, you know, "I'm not doing cocaine, I'm fine." That's what I, you know, that's what I went there for and I succeeded, you know! But, uh, I was drinking a 12-pack a day. . . . I didn't listen to a damn thing. I didn't have a sponsor. I didn't have a higher power. I didn't have nothing.

## Mel describes his spiritual background.

I went to church . . . I went to a [fundamentalist church] and, um, I was the only kid there, you know, that went to a public school. Every kid in the whole church went to . . . Christian school—Christian High School or Christian grade school, you know, Christian everything. And I never fit in there. I never felt like I fit in.

Well, you gotta go to Sunday School, you gotta read the Bible, you gotta, you gotta sit at the table and tell, well you read the Bible every night, you know. I'm like, "Good Lord, I just got done eatin', I wanna go lay [down]. . . . " And it just got worse and worse. . . . And the Lord's prayer, I used to despise it. I swear, I used to hate that thing, you know, and the songs at the end of church, always had the same song every time.

## Mel thought God was about rules.

I didn't really have . . . anything about God. I went through my atheist stage, my agnostic stage, my totally rebellious satanic stage, you know, and all that shit. And I never really, you know, believed in God really. I thought all the people that went to church were a bunch of people that gossiped all the . . . all they lived for was to gossip. And if you weren't going out with somebody in church, you were a failure, you know. And it was just like they had to keep within their own. You know, the boy would go out with the girl and it would be all in church and girl, boy, church, you know.

Mel talks about his current spirituality and this treatment. He remembers nothing about being detoxed because he was in a blackout. His memory finally returned after detox as he was being dropped off at a shelter that is run by the local churches. Homeless people can spend the night, but they have to walk or find transportation to the next place to sleep. Mel describes this time and his ten-mile walk between shelters after the first night.

> This time I came in I, I still had stitches in my head from the beer bottle and I still wasn't sure [if he had a higher power] until when I got out of detox. I got my higher power out of Share. I didn't get it in Share. I got a temporary sponsor this year. That was the one thing that saved me, because he gave me a ride to the shelter and I didn't, I don't remember a day of detox at all. I remember getting out of his car—that's the one thing I remember after detox was closing the door and realizing that I'm out in Wheaton and I have to walk to Villa Park tomorrow to go to this ANONA Center. . . . So, I went in there.
>
> And I talked to the minister there. . . . So I'm talking to him for awhile [and] . . . he said . . . to turn it over to a higher power. . . . And I decided to do it, so I walked to, on the way to Villa Park that day, I'm like, you know, praying the whole time and, you know, I'm like, "God, get me through these 10 days. . . . " I didn't think, you know, anybody would help me. I'm homeless. I picture myself sleeping on a bench the rest of these 10 days. . . . I didn't know what the hell was going to happen. So, I just turned it over to God like I, I guess like I was supposed to do, but I did it without anybody telling me to do it which was, I think, what helped. No one told me to do it. I did it myself.

During the time between detox and rehab, Mel kept a journal with daily entries and several sketches. The primary theme of the journal is that each day he got what he needed to face the next day. The journal attributes this provision to God, Mel's new higher power. Mel describes his experience of prayer and developing spirituality during his ten-day "homeless" period.

> It was just like me talking to Him [God] at first. It wasn't as big as it is now. Slowly, it grew to that. It was a long procedure. It wasn't as fast as I think. . . .
>
> So, I, I went to, I went to ANONA for a couple of days. I got a ride from them every day. . . . And I'd do like 3 or 4 meetings there, and it seemed like every day the higher power thing would just keep [being] brought up in the meeting. . . . One day after 3 or 4 days, I ran into this guy who offered me a job. Just walked in and said, "Do ya need a job?"
>
> I said, "Yeah."
>
> I wasn't even sure I was going into rehab 'cause I didn't have the hundred

dollars, let alone the three hundred to get in, so I ended up workin' for him every day. He picked me up at the P.A.D.S. shelters. . . . He dropped me off at the ANONA Center 'cause we'd get off at 4 and I can't get into the P.A.D.S. shelter 'til 7, so I'd go to the ANONA Center after work, catch a meeting. I'd have a meeting every day and then I'd get a ride to wherever I needed to go that night from somebody. And, actually, I came up with $330 in five days.

I needed $300. I walked in there [Share for rehab] with $300, paid them and had the 30 bucks [left over]. . . . I walked in there and started my rehab and, um, oh, I also met my [new] sponsor outside, too, who's got 16 years sobriety and [is] an alcohol counselor and he just, he walks up to me and just talked to me and . . . I feel that God sent him now, you know.

It was just like, I was sittin' there, sittin', you know, sittin' there, I was sleepin' at the time on a hard bench, you know my head on the table and my cold cup of coffee sittin' next to me, you know, and he came up and he's like, you know, what's your story, you know. I must have talked to him for about an hour and I asked him . . . "I need a sponsor? . . . " After I met him . . . I felt more strongly . . . convinced that God was working, but not as strong as when you said that one verse in art therapy, that was it.

Another client in art therapy, on the day Mel mentioned above, said he wanted the God in the Bible to be his higher power, but he didn't know what he needed to get to God. I had told him that I remembered a verse from the Bible which said that the sacrifice acceptable to God was a broken and contrite spirit. Offering oneself as powerless is all that is necessary. Mel had heard me say this to someone else, and it had been important to him.

Uh, the one, God accepts the broken and contrite heart. After that, poof! No foolin' . . . I felt like I wasn't worth nothing. God wouldn't accept me unless I was, you know, living right and had a house and all this stuff and I was being a productive citizen 'cause I didn't feel like I was being productive. I thought, you know, I thought I was a bum and all this stuff. And then when you said that, I'm like, that really does make sense . . . I've got what it takes!

Mel feels he has seen God working in his life a number of times since.

Soon as I did that I called the one P.A.D.S. shelter where I was, Mary Magdalene Episcopal in Villa Park, and he [the priest] sent me a Bible and came out and visited me and I talked to the priest for a long time, and uh, after that I've had, just several spiritual experiences . . . so many. . . .

Like one night I was sittin' in bed praying, the cafeteria had been closed earlier and I was hungry as all hell and I'm like, you know, "God, I'm hungry. . . . " I was there and it was like 1 or 2 o'clock, so I walk down, I'm lightin' a cigarette and smokin' it and I look down next to me and there's a full can of pop, unopened, still pretty cold and about 6 saltine crackers. You know, it wasn't no . . . hors d'oeuvres, it wasn't no crab legs or nothing, it was saltines, but it was something to put in my stomach until the morning.

Oh, oh, like the cocaine crashes and stuff like I said I went through several of them. . . . I didn't think that I'd make it through it [he did].

Mel is grateful to be in a halfway house after his treatment and thinks God helped with that arrangement also. Even on his bad days now, Mel says he knows God is there.

## MEL'S ART AND ART THERAPY EXPERIENCE

Mel has drawn for as long as he can remember. Between detox and rehab, while in shelter, he drew Picture 1, a pen sketch shown in Figure 6-1. He says he felt

like my world was falling apart. . . . I didn't feel like I had my higher power yet. I had just gotten done eatin' and I had just gone into the smoking room. . . . I just felt like my world was just crumbling around me and it was all over with. I figured I was on my way to death, you know. I didn't think I would even make it. I'm like, I was thinking about suicide and everything, even then. I mean, I was. I didn't care. I was like, I don't know, walk in front of a train, nobody cares about me no more. Exactly.

Picture 2 (Figure 6-2) is Mel's pen sketch of "old demon alcohol" which he drew during his homeless period in response to a talk given by a pastor who thought alcoholism was not a disease but rather a matter of willpower. Mel drew the picture to say the "demon" of alcoholism is inside him and requires more than willpower.

When Mel returned for the rehab treatment at Share, he came to art therapy and drew Picture 3 (Figure 6-3) in wax crayon in the first session. The picture shows a rolling green landscape on the left side of the paper with a red sun peeking over the horizon and a blue sky with birds flying above. On the right side there are grey clouds, rain, and lightning, with a huge arm and hand coming into the picture and holding a pink umbrella over a little man near the middle. The man is using a pick ax to break apart a brick wall which is separating him from the landscape on the other side.

His first session was about transformation in recovery. On the day he did the picture, Mel wrote the following note on the back of it in response to the imagery he saw in the meditation. "[I] sort of saw inside myself and saw that it wasn't evil and dark, but bright and full of dreams and hopes." He says of Picture 3 (Figure 6-3):

Figure 6-1

[T]hat was my first art therapy, and I was, um, very, um, into the higher power thing. I felt that it had worked. . . . It had worked for me on the outside. . . . I got there and that was the impression I had, that somebody was like sheltering me from the storm, and now I feel like I'm still in the storm, but I'm also here. I am working still [on recovery] and I figure if I wasn't gonna, I might as well finish now, you know. I'm like I wanna put my mind to it . . . there I am workin' away. . . . Uh, the red sun. I don't know where that came from.

I am cared for, but it's not all. It felt like I was cared for, but now I had the

Figure 6-2

feeling that God was gonna protect me, but I had to do the work, too, some work, too. That was the first time I felt like that. And I think that was when you said that, that picture was right after I drew that picture you said the broken and contrite heart.

In Mel's next art therapy session, he drew Picture 4 (Figure 6-4) of his feelings about letting go. The picture shows Mel in a red shirt with a black empty hole in the middle which is dripping red blood. He is screaming with his mouth wide open, reaching and looking toward the

Figure 6-3

left edge of the paper. On the right side of the paper, there is a green
doglike monster with long, pointed eye teeth and dark red eyes. He has
Mel's red heart in his right hand and a bottle of alcohol in his left hand.

> [Picture 4 was about letting go of] a relationship I had with a using girlfriend
> for the last five years. . . . She was still using at the time . . . and I had to listen to
> my sponsor. As much as I hated to do it, I broke up with her, and uh, I'd
> become I guess addicted to her.
>
> I find it [co-dependence] a real big problem because, um, I find myself
> being attracted to women, but not just being attracted to 'em but also wanting
> to live for them. You know, I do as much as I can. The hole was like the empty
> space I felt. And when it was gone, even though I knew God was there, I still
> felt like there [points to the picture of the hole]. I had something ripped right
> out of me, an emptiness.
>
> That, that [the creature] was Mr. Addiction again in a different form, you
> know he's the one. I had to blame it on him at the time. I feel maybe a little
> different now. It was sort of his, my fault, but his fault. . . . I felt that he, if it
> wasn't for that stuff, you know, we might have still been together. . . . Um, green
> usually means sinister, ah, light green [the creature is light green]. . . . I usually
> associate red [the creature has red eyes] with evil, you know, I don't know why.
> You know, he's always evil. I don't know why, but red is evil.
>
> My hand felt stretched [in Figure 6-4]. I don't know what that means. It's like

I'm still . . . the tension is there. . . . I learned that strength is letting go and not holding on and changing your perspective on self-value.

Figure 6-4

Picture 5 (Figure 6-5) shows how Mel's space in life felt while he was using chemicals, while Picture 6 (Figure 6-6) shows how the space in his life felt sober. There is a small figure dressed in black and chained to a brown floor in a large grey stone block cell in Picture 5 shown in Figure 6-5. Through the bar window above, a very lightly drawn yellow light is coming through the window.

In Picture 6 (Figure 6-6), Mel has drawn a picture showing the same cell from the outside after he has broken out. The solitary cell sits alone on the green grass hill, and Mel's footprints have gone off the bottom of the paper. The ominous-looking red sun has risen high in the sky. Mel talks about these two pictures and the world of using and being straight.

Okay, the first one (Figure 6-5) was me in my using world, knowing what was out there 'cause there's a little yellow, hint of life that's on the out there. . . . I'm chained there, and I can't get to the light because of my addiction . . . the walls are high and the little tiny window. I knew what was out there, but here I am stuck all alone in my addiction, you know. . . . The yellow light. Oh, that means like the better life, God, or just living sober, the better life. I know it was there. I knew it all along, you know. I knew it for years what a sober life could do for me, but I didn't do it. You know, here I could see, I could see it, but I couldn't get to it.

Figure 6-5

Picture 6 (Figure 6-6) is described by Mel.

So, here I am. I broke out and I'm walkin' away from my, um, using world: my old friends, my old, uh, hangouts. That's basically what it was, just my old friends and hangouts and old life-style and everything that goes along with it. And uh, there's the red sun . . . isn't that a red, red sun? . . .

Mel saw the red sun as ominous, but said:

I'm going away from it sort of. . . . I feel like He's [God has] broken the chains and opened the walls 'cause I couldn't have done that by myself. . . . He broke it open for me. . . . With the help of my higher power I've gotten on the road to recovery. . . . That's about it, simple.

Picture 7 (Figure 6-7) shows Mel's feeling about being vulnerable. It shows a man crawling out of a turtle shell with the light green grassy hills barely seen in the background and the now even more darkly drawn

Figure 6-6

red sun beating its red rays down on the tired, sad-looking man. Mel tells about this picture.

> I feel like I come out [of the shell], but then there's this intense burn of standing up in the pressures and the, um, just being vulnerable, just getting fried in the process . . . by everybody, everything, just letting my guard down and just probably gonna get killed, you know, hurt emotionally or something.
>
> That's the old evil [red] sun. The old, all the bad people seeing me as I am, laughing at me. . . . Yeah, that's the old people, you know, laughing at me and, you know, there's me living the way I want to live, but there's these people, you know, ridiculing me.
>
> Um, just I'm crawling like I'm, He's [God's] giving me the strength to get out of there . . . [to at] least be there . . . even though it's hard to be there.

Picture 8 (Figure 6-8) shows Mel's feelings about having the Christmas holiday during treatment. He drew this the day after Christmas. He had dinner at the Easy Does It (EDI) club, a local AA group which reaches out to the clients in treatment on holidays.

The picture shows a black tree on a black landscape with a black sun in the sky. Behind the tree a fire is blazing, outlined in controlled black lines. Mel says of his feelings and this picture.

Figure 6-7

Oh, the holidays were terrible. I didn't like it, um, even though I knew God was around I didn't feel like, it's like these people [at EDI] wanted me to have, like a, a real good time, and I didn't want to have one. I wanted to wallow in self-pity and . . . I just felt like the whole world was burning. . . . I felt so angry. . . . I was, that's, the red is the anger and the evil inside of me. . . .

Yeah, that felt like it was just empty [the black sun] that day. I felt God was with me, but not as much as He could've been. I felt let down emotionally.

Mel said in group, after drawing the controlled, outlined Picture 8 (Figure 6-8), that he felt like screaming. I asked Mel if he would like to allow his anger to explode or "scream" on paper. He got up from the processing group and proceeded to vigorously draw seven pictures in several minutes. This series, Pictures 9–15, is not shown but is described in the following text. "I decided to draw it like screams, like my anger, so I drew the first one" (Picture 9), a black and red scribble with his trademark scrawled into it, was intense "utter anger . . . turmoil."

The second picture in the series is (Picture 10) a red flame with a

Figure 6-8

yellow center surrounded by black and turning blue on the right. Mel says his feeling "was semi-intense which was the fire burning . . . hoping to deal with the anger."

Picture 11, the third in the series, showing a black landscape with a barren tree and a light blue sky and river, has the hint of a red hump coming up in the lower left corner. For Mel drawing the picture felt "like settling down . . . desolation."

The series fourth, Picture 12, shows a large yellow-green colored volcano with red coming out of the top and a black sky. Mel says of the drawing, "I got more angry again for some reason . . . got a volcano erupting . . . and I felt like it blew up . . . anger erupting after dormant years."

Picture 13, fifth in the series, shows a picture of an outer-space view of the eruption from a blackened earth. Red fire is at the bottom of the eruption with the black figure of Mel, engulfed in the outburst, entwined in the explosion at the top. Mel says "it was over with and I [had] just been relieved."

Picture 14, sixth in the series, shows the bottom of a large bland-looking tree trunk surrounded by blue sky and planted in the light sickening green....It felt like still evil in the base of me, but I felt still like I could grow....I associate green with...I associate green with it. Its been grown over, but it's still there, you know there...something underneath it.

Picture 15, last in the series, is a picture of a white heart surrounded by pale blue. Mel says of it:

And then the final one in that series is just me feeling at peace...spent, exhausted, cool, calm....

Mel associates all of the pictures in the series with his spirituality.

Um, just the, after the anger came the mellowing and, uh, the realization that, uh, God was helping me go to, to develop these things. It was like, well, for God and me to do this, I guess. He wants me to experience myself....Yeah, He wants me to feel myself. That's what I have the feeling of like you got to get to know yourself.

The group did a meditation in the next session about reaching out to their child or baby self. It is designed to help the participants gain a deeper understanding of their great value as unique human beings. The clients are asked to draw feelings about being valuable or feelings about reaching out to their child self. Mel chose the second idea.

The Picture 16 (Figure 6-9) shows the adult side of Mel walking toward a house and the sea while holding the hand of the child side of Mel. Looking through the window of the house, one sees the sea and the first yellow sun Mel has drawn in art therapy coming up, rather than the inside wall of the house. Between the beach Mel is walking on and the house is still a small patch of the light green Mel refers to as "sickening." Mel talks about his experience of his picture.

Uh, that was getting in touch with my inner self....We did a meditation before this to get in touch with my inner self, and I had a wonderful experience of me picking up myself as a young child of about a year and a half, two years old, you know, and just walkin' with him and, you know, it was just, you said you could plug it in anytime you want and I do that all the time....I have been doin' it [visualizing reaching out to little Mel] a lot....I plug it in whenever I feel bad, you know, like I have a bad AA meeting or something. I'll just plug that in and it works! And so, it's just like I feel at peace with myself.

Um, I just feel that's how I am to God, just a little helpless baby, you know, just in need of help.

We talked about Mel's experiences with art almost a week after he left the Share program and was already in a halfway house. As Mel looked at all of his work in one place he was delighted to notice that his first work

Figure 6-9

done in art therapy, Picture 3 (Figure 6-3), where God was caring for him while he was also working at his recovery, had the same theme as his last work, Picture 16 (Figure 6-9). God was still caring for him as he was continuing to care for himself. Mel wrote the following on the back of his last picture:

> I rediscovered my inner child and felt a new kind of peace and love which I guess is self-love which I have been searching for with all the wrong methods, and now that I've rediscovered it, I'll be damned if I'll let it go.

## SUMMATION AND REFLECTION

### Addiction History

The strange unrevealed details of Mel's adoption and biological roots have resulted in a basic uneasiness in Mel. Even things which appear good have an unspoken underlying "evil" or sinister feel to them. He was raised by an older couple who were both compulsive overeaters, and he was told that there was something wrong with him by his adult siblings who were natural children to his adopted parents. He felt as though he didn't fit in, but was told he was loved.

He was brought up in a strict rule-oriented fundamentalist church where he was not accepted, and consequently, he felt that he did not fit in there either. He heard that God was loving, while at the same time he experienced people talking about him behind his back and a lack of acceptance.

Mel began using marijuana and beer at age 11. When he found out about the truth of his adoption at age 12, it seems as if he used it as an opportunity to rage about his underlying uncertainties and shame. He denied everything and everybody in both his family and church and headed into open rebellion and drug use.

### Spiritual History

As has already been stated, Mel was raised in a strict church with many rules. This rigid structure combined with the lack of acceptance and care he felt caused him to experience himself as evil. He came to hate the church and deny God's existence by becoming atheist, then agnostic, and even a believer in Satan.

The awareness of his total powerlessness over his addiction and his belief that death was his only alternative perhaps allowed him to be open to the pastor at the shelter for the homeless after his detoxification. Although the pastor used big words and Mel thought what he said sounded like "religious" talk, he decided on his own to turn his life over to God on his ten-mile walk to the next shelter.

The circumstances of the rest of his shelter stays, the time he spent in rehab, and his acceptance into a halfway house were all day-by-day signs to Mel that his higher power was with him step by step. He realized that what God wanted from him was just himself. After his expression of belief in a higher power, it became important to Mel to do his part each day to make his life work. He seemed to become increasingly conscious of the fact that even in little ways, he was getting what he needed each day.

## Art and Spirituality Experience

Mel told me he was doing art therapy before he even knew there was such a thing. His journal of survival from his time in the shelters is interspersed with sketches about his feelings. Picture 1 (Figure 6-1) is an expression of Mel's powerlessness and inability to hold his world together any longer. Picture 2 (Figure 6-2) expresses Mel's feeling that "evil" is a part of him and that willpower will not be enough to help him.

Mel's first work in rehab, Picture 3 (Figure 6-3), shows his belief that God is strong and there to help him, but that he must also cooperate with the work to be done. In Picture 3, the red sun which Mel later describes as "evil" and "ominous" also appears on the horizon of recovery.

Picture 4 (Figure 6-4) is filled with the "evil, ominous" red and the "sickening" green of Mel's co-dependence and chemical dependence. He is screaming and powerless again. In Picture 5 (Figure 6-5) he is small and powerless again, but now there is the hint of yellow "life" coming into the picture. In Picture 6 (Figure 6-6) after his release from the cell of addiction, there is a new enemy to face as the ominous red sun is getting higher in the sky. At this time, the veneer of Mel's strained, quiet smile from the beginning of rehab was wearing thin, and his anger was becoming more visible in his body language, talk, and art.

In Picture 7 (Figure 6-7), the red sun with its red rays were at full heat. Mel was still aware of God's faithfulness, but he was also aware of the ridicule, laughter, and lack of acceptance he had felt in his life that showed up in the red of the sun.

His experience of anger and "bad memories" of Christmas's past finally caused the red to flare into the controlled flame of Picture 8 (Figure 6-8). Mel allowed the "scream" of this flame to burst into fullness in the black and red scribble of Picture 9, to recede in Picture 10, and to reappear pushing into the silence of Picture 11 as a red lump growing in the lower left corner. The "sickening" green, the angry red, and the black all come together in the active volcano of Picture 12. The final explosion for the moment comes as Mel's anger is carrying him into outer space in the explosion of Picture 13.

Peace and a certain groundedness is established in Picture 14, but the "sickening" green at the base indicates that the working through of this anger will be a process that will need to continue. The airy quality of Picture 15 shows a lightness that Mel has not shown in his previous artwork. Mel felt that God helped him to do this series of pictures and wanted him to know himself and experience these feelings he had kept under such control. Mel said that in this series it was the first time he had ever allowed himself to draw without being careful about how he drew.

Picture 16 (Figure 6-9) shows a yellow sun coming up through the window in Mel's house. The figure of adult Mel is strong and holding his child side firmly. There is a sense of peace and a lack of denial about the "sickening green" which remains in the corner of the picture.

Mel is in a halfway house, and he says he is experiencing each day as it comes. He knows he has a tremendous struggle, but today he is sober.

# Chapter 7

## SAM'S STORY

### INTRODUCTION AND HISTORY

At first glance, it is easiest to notice Sam's long, though styled, hair and "with it" clothes. After being with him for a short while, one realizes he is earnest, quiet, and open. In a group, he is happy to share when asked, but is soft-spoken and gets easily forgotten when he is not asked to speak. Sam is a twenty-year-old caucasian man who started using marijuana at twelve years of age. Cocaine was his drug of choice upon entering treatment at The Share Program. His maternal grandmother was alcoholic and died of alcoholism, but neither of his parents are alcoholic.

Both of his parents worked when he was small, and he has few complaints about his childhood memories except when his parents were not home. His father was a policeman, and two of his police co-workers, who worked a different shift, took care of Sam and his younger brother during the night shift when their parents were working. When asked about how these baby-sitters treated Sam, he says:

> Um, it's not so much that how they treated me wasn't good, it was like a big mind game against the children—me and my brother—and, uh, they used to do strange things like with our cat. They'd say, you know, "We're having cat soup for dinner tonight" and they would literally have my cat in the oven with it on and me and my brother would have to run and rescue my cat.

Sam brings up episodes with these caretakers frequently, and they are often in his conversation. Sam describes another abusive game his caretakers played.

> Oh, that was "hide-and-seek" for us. It was supposed to be fun. They used to, uh, if my brother was it, I would have to go and hide and they would take me and handcuff my hands behind my back and muzzle me and stick me at the top of the closet and lock the door with the lights off and leave me there overnight.

Sam reports that while growing up he had no interest in spirituality. Upon coming to treatment, his attitude has changed. Sam animatedly

93

describes a spiritual experience he had with his higher power in the detox program before he came to the rehabilitation program and art therapy. He had never had any kind of feeling or experience like this previously. Sam says:

> This client comes in and he's a new client here in detox and, uh, we have like a mutual attraction to each other and, uh, we just hit it off right away, talking all day long and at night. He started—it wasn't preaching to me—but he was talking a lot of religion and, uh, experiences he had had through God and through his spirituality and religion and, um, at the end when we were done talking right before I went to bed.
>
> I got down on my hands and knees to pray for the first time in my life, probably, and, uh, as soon as I opened up to God, I, um, my body—like from head to toe—just felt elevated and just tingled and I didn't want to open my eyes because I felt like I was being lifted off the ground—like lifted away from all the burdens I'd been through and, uh, it was probably the greatest sensation I ever felt, better than any high I ever had.

Sam has been aware of his growing spirituality in treatment and currently has two higher powers. He explains:

> I have two [laughs]. Um, I recognize the meeting tables at AA and NA as my higher powers and like I was saying before about . . . meditating during quiet time. . . . Today is Tuesday . . . it was last Thursday at the AA meeting during quiet time when I closed my eyes, someone was looking me right back in the eyes, and as I slowly focused in, it was a picture of Jesus Christ. And, uh, I figured he was my higher power. God came to me.

### SAM'S ART THERAPY EXPERIENCE

Sam says that he has experienced the spiritual part of his recovery "for the most part through art." In Picture 1 (Figure 7-1), Sam drew how it felt to him to reach out to his child self in a meditation he took part in. The pastel picture has a medium blue background with a large black "whirlpool" circle in the center and a very pure white smaller circle in the upper left-hand corner. There is a stream of white light which feels like energy which is either pulling toward the black or the white. Sam describes his meditation experience and the picture he drew.

> I think I remember it as, um, when we were supposed to see ourselves as a child, you know, we were supposed to imagine ourselves getting closer to hold the child. I could picture me as a child, a very small child, but the closer I tried to get, the more it would fade and it turned . . . it's like my mind turned into a whirlpool. . . . That was the first day.

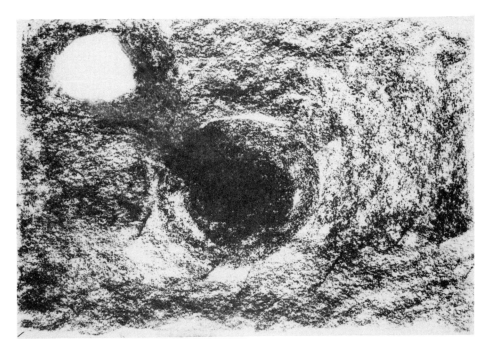

Figure 7-1

The day Sam drew this picture, he wrote on the back:

In this picture I'm the huge whirlpool spinning in fear and emptiness—reaching out for clarity and purity for myself.

Sam saw the white circle as his child side which was being "sucked" into the circular black whirlpool.

In Picture 2 (Figure 7-2) Sam drew where he saw himself in his recovery or transformation process when he came to the second art therapy session. The pastel picture shows brown cliffs on the left and the right with a blue waterfall in the middle. There are brown trees with green leaves, green grass, and red and yellow flowers on top of the left cliff. The similar trees and flowers are dwarfed by a very large tree with big visible roots on the right-hand cliff. There is a blue sky above, and the blue water is crashing on huge brown rocks at the bottom of the waterfall. Sam describes this picture:

[Picture] two is kind of a reach for my recovery after seeing two clients here relapse the day that they left and come back to a meeting. . . . This picture was a day after that meeting and, uh, it was a picture of a waterfall with a very rough bottom and rough surface to the top, but the top was very beautiful . . .

real clear . . . and the dominant tree on the right was the good side of light. . . . It has got very powerful deep roots that can get through and hold onto even rock . . . they were just busting out through the rocks and that nothing was stopping that tree from growing, and it was a very strong and dominating tree. . . . It was the happy, the bright, the clean.

Figure 7-2

Sam connects Picture 2 (Figure 7-2) with his "spirituality through strength and, uh, determination, and myself." Sam said that the bottom was symbolic of using. The top right is the place of sobriety. He described himself as being "halfway up the cliff" on this day, "wanting to be as close as I can be to that very powerful tree." Picture 2 (Figure 7-2) has further spiritual connections for Sam.

I think there's a few things in that picture that have to do with my higher power. I think the tree dominates all the other things, but, um, the flowers here on the right were, um, in my first vision were of people, you know, having fun, smiling, being clean and eventually it just turned into . . . just beautiful flowers. I mean endless, you know, until you couldn't see but woods in the background.

Picture 3 (Figure 7-3), drawn in oil pastels, shows Sam's feelings about a "co-dependent" girlfriend he needs to let go of. The background in the top half is grey and the background color around Sam is yellow. The girlfriend has on a red shirt and is blond. Sam has on a blue shirt and has brown hair. Sam explains:

> That's, um, a picture of me waving good-bye to my girlfriend because, um, I've known her for two years and I've been using for two years and now that I'm clean . . . she knows she's a co-dependent. We need time away from each other and it's me being honest with myself to work on myself. And uh, that just shows, I think it shows . . . how much I really care for her, but I don't know what's between us. She's very beautiful in that picture.

Sam says of the yellow background's symbolic meaning: "it's the good side of me. Kind of shows that I want a brighter future."

Figure 7-3

Picture 3 in Figure 7-3 showed Sam with another dimension of his spirituality. He says, "I think maybe towards honesty to myself and to others, not holding back and repressing things into me, like I always did."

In Pictures 4 and 5 shown in Figures 7-4 and 7-5, respectively, Sam shows how the space in his life felt while he was using chemicals and how it feels now in his sobriety. The pastel picture in Figure 7-4 has diagonal lines of boxes with alternating black rows and medium blue rows. At the upper left is a yellow box and in the lower right is a red box. The pastel picture in Figure 7-5 is of a large yellow sun which almost fills the paper. At the top is a row of small rectangles starting with a yellow rectangle on the left. The rest of the rectangles are orange, light green, and light blue. The row of rectangles on the bottom from left to right are black, blue, black, blue, and red. Sam tells about these pictures and how he experiences them.

> The picture while I was using (Figure 7-4) . . . I pictured it as the blues and the blacks . . . like stairways always having to run up and down and never really knowing which direction I'm going, and in each corner I had a picture. In the bottom corner of red, which I think symbolized death or hell . . . and at the top I have the bright yellow corner which I'm reaching for now which is the good side of life—that's the term I like to use now—the good side of life, the clean, the pure.
>
> I see it (Sam's space now, Figure 7-5) as being really open and my higher power having a lot to do with it. Really bright, really powerful, and at the top of the page I have bright, happy colors, you know, nice, happy colors, and at the bottom I know that if I ever fall again the blues and the blacks—that if I ever hit the end of the line—I'm going to die.

Sam wrote the following of Picture 5 (Figure 7-5) on the day he drew it.

> Being clean and sober, I'm as one with myself and my higher power. . . . If I reach for the sky there's lots of beauty, love and very bright.

Sam's use of blue and black in Pictures 1, 4, and 5 (Figures 7-1, 7-4 and 7-5, respectively) is interesting. This combination appears to represent situations he finds threatening. When I asked him what colors he associated with the abusive off-duty policemen who cared for him as a child, he said blue and black, like their uniforms. He also said that the apartment where they cared for him in had many "up and down steps."

Reflecting back on the consciousness of his spiritual connection on the first day of art therapy, Sam says:

> Not the first day, no, and I think that that white spot in my picture (Figure 7-1) was my higher power telling me that he was there, but I didn't really realize it until I drew it, and I still didn't know exactly what it meant, but I knew something was slowing down the whirlpool in my head, and it was that huge white beam coming through the sky. I mean, it was a very ugly picture,

Figure 7-4

but then you have this beautiful white pure clean beam just like slowing everything down, kind of pulling me back up.

In defining art therapy's contribution to furthering Sam's spiritual journey, he says:

I think the main thing that helps me through my journey is mediation and, uh, then putting your meditation out on paper with the art, and it just really makes things a lot clearer, 'cause when it's in your mind, or when it's in my mind I'm not exactly so sure of what it was until it comes out on the paper, and once it's on the paper it's really defined. . . . It's so clear to make out, you know. In your head it may be a clear picture, but you don't totally understand it and it helps a lot.

Figure 7-5

## SUMMATION AND REFLECTION

### Addiction History

Sam has some good feelings about his childhood, but the experience he had with the abusive off-duty policeman caretakers who watched him while his parents worked made a deep impression on him. During the times that Sam came to art therapy, he mentioned these two men several times. He still seemed to be deeply affected by the frightening experiences he had with them.

Sam has a possible genetic link with chemical dependency through his maternal grandmother. His drug use started at 12 years, quickly progressing to cocaine addiction. Sam is aware of the possibility of dying as a result of cocaine use because of what he has seen. He came to The Share Program with a serious attitude about recovery. His cocaine addiction had progressed rapidly, causing him to seek treatment at age 20. He went home to live with his parents after treatment and had plans for outpatient aftercare counseling.

### Spiritual History

Sam has no spiritual history that he is consciously aware of until coming into the detox program at Share. Through his interaction with another client, he became aware of his need for a higher power and prayed expressing his powerlessness. He had a physical sensation after the prayer and the spiritual aspect of recovery became very important to him after this.

### Art and Spirituality Experience

Art therapy was the part of treatment where Sam experienced the spiritual part of his recovery the most. In the session where he drew Picture 1 (Figure 7-1), he was able to both see his child self in the meditation and feel the pull of the whirlpool of addiction away from this "clarity and purity." He was able through his picture to feel the pull that both the purity and the "fear and emptiness" had for him. Through Picture 2 (Figure 7-2) he was able to see how relapse and addiction looked to him and encourage himself to take the hard climb to recovery rather than die on the rocks of relapse. This picture helped him to deal with the fear of relapse without ignoring it while still looking at other possibilities. In Picture 3 (Figure 7-3), Sam identified yellow as the color for his higher power, and he surrounded himself with yellow (he later also identified the white light in Picture 1 (Figure 7-1) as his higher power also). He made concrete on the paper his need to separate from his co-dependent relationship. Through Pictures 4 and 5 (Figures 7-4 and 7-5), Sam became even clearer about the use of blue and black for confusion, manipulation, and evil and his use of red for hell. Interestingly, his pretty blond "co-dependent girlfriend," who he needed to let go of, had on a red sweater in Picture 3 (Figure 7-3). He also became stronger in his use of yellow light as not only his way of expressing his higher power but also including himself as "one" with his higher power. Art was a way for Sam to express the pull within him to both good and evil. He was literally able to watch his spirituality grow and become more visibly real through his art experience.

# Chapter 8

## KATE'S STORY

### INTRODUCTION AND HISTORY

Kate is a very pretty blond-haired, blue-eyed 25-year-old caucasian woman who is both a recovering drug addict and co-dependent. She was a client in The Share Program and seemed tired and hopeless at the start. She referred to herself as "hard" in her first session of art therapy. Kate experienced many traumas as a child, but she says she was "mostly happy."

Neither of her parents were alcoholic during her growing up years, but her paternal grandparents were both alcoholic. Kate's mother has become alcoholic during recent years. Kate had her first drink at age 11.

Kate was the first born of three children, being followed quickly by two brothers. After the birth of the second boy, her parents got divorced. A year later when Kate was four years old and her brothers Ken and Nick were three and two, respectively, Nick drowned in an accident at her gramma's house. Soon after, her mother almost died in an accident and a close uncle died. Kate remembers vividly the day of her brother's death and its impact on her life.

Um, my gramma told me to go, go find Nick, go find the boys because we were at my gramma's house, but she said go find the boys because it's time to go out to eat. We need to wash up before we go out to eat. I went to look for my brothers. I looked all around. I was calling for Nickie. I said, "Nickie, Nickie, Nickie, where are you?" And I couldn't find Nick anywhere.

I found Ken. He was in, playing in my Dad's sailboat which was on a trailer, and I asked if he's seen Nick, and Ken said, "No." So, I continued looking for Nick and couldn't find him, you know. My gramma and grandpa had a three-car garage, and all of a sudden I stopped in the third, in front of the third garage.

It was like something stopped me . . . then, uh, it was and then I heard this, I felt this feeling. It was a feeling with no fear, but I was wondering what it was. I remember there was no fear, no fear at all, but it was different and I felt really alert and all of a sudden this voice said to me, this man's voice and it was a deep, deep voice and He said it slowly, He repeated himself twice so I could

103

understand. He said, "Kate, Kate, Nickie is in the swimming pool, Kate. Nickie is in the swimming pool." And He said it slow and loud and in a really deep voice. . . . When He talked it wasn't anything I could hear with my ears, it came into me, and it, it was just, I knew it was God. It was just no doubt about it because it's the way. I don't know how I knew, I just knew.

I, as soon as the voice left me and the feeling, of, of—it was kinda warm. There was no fear whatsoever and normally you would feel a fear when you hear a voice from nowhere, but it was like all fear was taken away, and as soon as that voice left me I was terrified, I was terrified. . . . I didn't know why that voice had told me where he was, and I felt that it did and something was wrong. After it left me.

I started running and then in my head I think I was saying to myself, "Run! Faster, faster, faster, faster, faster, faster, faster." You know, and I ran, and I ran right to the pool. And I ran to my gramma's house and told, told them that he was in the swimming pool. Course I didn't know to say drowned because I, you know, I just knew that he was in the pool and I knew that it was something wrong.

And I told them and they, the way that I guess I told them they both ran out and then they called the ambulance which back then it was, it was fire, fire trucks came out. And I remember that night he was laying on the sidewalk and they tried to, um, the paramedics were trying to save him and they were doing all kinds of stuff and I thought—he was my baby brother, he was my closest one. . . . Yeah, he had fuzzy white hair, he was my baby. He was my little baby. . . .

## Kate did not go to Nickie's funeral.

I think that my, that people, somebody baby-sat us because of what my mom was going through. For us not to see our mother like that. And my mom also remembers me saying that day about the voice. I was so, trying to tell her about the man's voice that talked to me and nobody really knew what I was talking about, you know. There was too much going on, so they didn't know. I'm just a little kid, and you know, I wasn't the main thing that was happening, but she remembers me, and I talked about it for years. She didn't know what I was talking about and I didn't know what it was at first.

## Kate reflects on her ideas about God at that time and now.

I don't know if I did or didn't [believe in God before the accident] because I was that age. My gramma, my gramma was very, very religious very religious. . . . Ah, I know that He's been here. . . .

## Kate experienced sexual abuse and nightmares starting at age seven or eight.

There was a little bit of sexual abuse. Um, once my gramma's cousin's husband or something like that . . . when we were staying at my gramma's, and my mom was in between divorce. [When this happened, Kate was] . . . 7, 7 or 8. And 11, 12, and I've been raped a lot of times.

I used to have nightmares when I got baby-sat, and I, I started having dreams about the Devil and I could swear I seen the Devil on my wall. It lit up my whole room on my wall and I had dreams about the Devil. . . . I used to have dreams that were so real that I can still remember every detail of the dreams.

## When Kate was 14 years old, she says:

I got a boyfriend and I fell in love. He moved and three weeks after he moved, I found out I was pregnant and I called him and I told him. He laughed like it was funny and he said, "So, what're you gonna do?"

I said, "I'm gonna keep it. I don't believe in abortions."

He said, "No, don't do that, you know, you're too young and I'm too young." And he was the same age as me and I just was so hurt, you know. I don't remember what else we talked about. I just remember him laughing.

I remember them telling me at the abortion place they said, "You don't really want to have this done, don't do it, you'll regret it for the rest of your life." And I did it and said I wanted it and I did it, and I really didn't want it and I regret it to this day. And I hate myself for that.

## Kate talks about her drinking and behavior after the abortion.

It [drinking] started going full force after the abortion. . . . I, I dropped out of school. I wasn't going even when I went. Around people—just hanging around with people that were a lot older than me . . . I was experimenting with whatever [drugs] I could get my hands on. I didn't care. I didn't care, anything to make me feel good.

## She felt:

Suicidal. . . . I tried it, I get my years mixed up still right now, but I tried it after September, after I had the abortion, and uh, I think I did it to see if my mom really cared. And then, I got stuck in a mental hospital which was, ah, really bad.

There was abuse going on. Just staff with the clients . . . they wouldn't let you cry, get out any feelings. If they caught you with a tear coming out of your eye, they'd make you drink this stuff—they called it mellow yellow. It was yellow shot glass and I said I wanted to cry. Leave me alone. I didn't want to drink that stuff because it made you like a zombie, and they said if I didn't take it the next step would be to have male security guards come in and pull down your pants and they give you a shot, a shot in your butt. And um, I didn't want that to happen.

If they caught you not swallowing it and spitting it out somewhere, they'd do that, too, and if you still were fighting it they'd put you in straights till whenever they felt like taking you out—strap you in a belt. And I totally felt that that was wrong . . . I really didn't want to kill myself. I think I just wanted to see who really cared. 'Cause if I really wanted to kill myself, I would've. But I, I just wanted help, and that was the wrong kind of help. I didn't need that.

## At age 16, Kate says:

I went down into the desert in Southern California. I, we and a girlfriend and four guys, just decided to screw everything and let's go see what's out there. I had a beat up old Rambler which we didn't know if it would make it, but we were going to try it, so I didn't tell my mom, but my girlfriend told her mom and she said it was okay. She was only 15 and I was 16, so I had a friend to go with me. I wasn't the only girl, so and we all were about the same age, so we went and we made it. I don't know how we made it. We had to stop with the car and let it cool off, but we made it out there. One guy knew somebody out there in this little desert town. The only way to get in and out is to drive because there is no other transportation.

## Kate describes her life since as:

Up and down, up and down... life in the fast lane. I was, I had such an overwhelming life and every day—one day I could be in LA and the next day I could be in New York... drinking and partying. Looking for something that wasn't out there. Yeah, looking for me... I searched the world.

So, I had tickets that some guy bought me to go out of this country. I got scared and I started thinking how well do I know this person, and I started thinking they could just sell me in a different country and I could never get back again.

Kate subsequently had many relationships with men, and finally she says,

"I sold my body, done everything I could to survive." She says that recently:

I started noticing people around my age, and they had the happiness and love... and things I wanted. They had a boring simple life which I always thought that's not what I wanted. I wanted more than that. I tried to look for more because I felt that I didn't have a normal life, and I deserved better. But I don't want that now. All I want is a family, happiness.

### KATE'S ART AND ART THERAPY EXPERIENCE

## As a child:

I remember I always liked art.... Of course, anything to do with nature and life and I loved art, anything to do with art. Drawing, pottery, you know, when I went to my dad's house—I had a stepmom, too—and she was a very creative person, and she'd get all kinds of art books out and have us do projects and stuff like that.

The first time Kate came to art therapy, the topic was vulnerability. The clients were asked to draw how they felt when they were vulnerable. Kate drew a scribbled, abstract design with a red center, surrounded by scribbled medium blue. The red center has six wavy lines going out into the blue area. There is a black border around the whole picture. Kate describes her first session and Picture 1 (Figure 8-1):

> I was looking forward to it, but I didn't know what to expect. And, uh, I didn't remember, I didn't know what to draw. I was kind of frustrated that day, and I don't remember what for. I was frustrated. I was looking for something that wasn't there—that I could not see, and that's where my . . . picture [Figure 8-1] came in; it answered a question I had in my mind. . . . What am I looking for; what am I missing in my life? . . . [The answer] was God.
>
> I drew me and the world around me. Me, well, this picture I done in less than a minute and I had no idea what it meant at the time. I just drew me, which was red, and I wanted me warm and then I drew the blue for cold around me in my red. I have my little squiggly line reaching out and I'm trying, I'm trying to reach out into the coldness and black which was the world because it was dark, cold, too, it was colder than the blue. The blue was more or less the people, the places.
>
> Okay, you had a poem that you just happened to have found, and it went with this picture. And with that poem it totally explained my picture totally to me. It goes perfect with that picture.

Kate was referring to the following poem, written by Ulrich Schaffer (1980):

> *He meets you in gentleness.*
> *He comes close.*
> *He takes your coldness*
> *and warms you from inside.*
>
> *You can melt,*
> *and if you do,*
> *streams will flow from you*
> *to give life and renew the land.*

"He meets you in gentleness"—I was thinkin' that was God, and "He comes close"—I feel that He is by, through this picture, He takes my coldness which is the blue and the black and He warms me from inside, me, the warmth, the red in the middle. I can melt which are my little squiggly lines coming out into the blue, and if I do, streams will flow from me, "will flow from you," you know, that's what it says. And that's still my little squiggly lines. They're kind of, they're soft and wavy like they're melting so I'm trying and that would give me a new life and renew the land. But I'll be breaking it, I'm gonna break this ice here . . . this poem just, I don't know.

Figure 8-1

It was just fantastic that you, and you just happened to have had it and it just happened to have fit it perfectly and it was just, seems like it fit it so perfectly that it's almost unreal. So, I really felt that it was meant to be this way. I felt that God was giving me a message—I'm so hard-headed He was giving me a message that He's here to, ah, be faithful, and open up.

I felt that He came through my artwork that day and that was a feeling that I can't really describe. It was a feeling of good . . . I just, I was stunned. I was really stunned. And that's my first picture and it had lots and lots of meaning—it just had lots of meaning for me. And it took me less than a minute to draw and I had no idea what I was doing when I was drawing it. I was just kind of drawing it, three different colors and then it, it had so much meaning to it. That's my favorite one. And nobody else would understand it by lookin' at it. So, it was a message, I felt it was a message to me. And I'm doing what I'm supposed to be doing. I'm on the right track.

At the next art session, Kate drew a lifeline and an unhealthy repeating pattern. Her repeating pattern drawing, Picture 2 (Figure 8-2), shows repeated rapes and unstable relationships ending in abandonment, alternating with the use of drugs and alcohol. Kate describes her work that day:

This is my pattern that was for a long time and I was always left alone. Even when I was alone, even when I was with people, I was alone. And I didn't see much day, I seen only night. I tried to, ah, hide in the day and come out at night. I was alone. Even when you see me here with people, I wasn't really with people, I was alone, and that made me think I didn't like people.

I can't do what I'm doing in recovery and stop drinking or using drugs if I'm alone 'cause I can't be alone. My number one priority is God. I just, I just feel so strong, strong about God. I feel that He's been here. I feel I wouldn't be living today if it wasn't for Him.

My gramma, when I ran away, my gramma used to have a, I didn't know about this, but, ah, she used to get everybody together at the church and they would pray for me, just four people would pray for me because I was out there, alone out there not knowing what I was doing. . . . She was my favorite person. Ah, I just feel like He's always been here for me, but I've pushed Him away.

He still watched over me because He knew that I really did believe, but my head was so messed up, I, I didn't understand anything at the time. I was so screwed up mentally for a long time.

Figure 8-2

The third time Kate was in art therapy, there was a guided meditation where the clients were asked to imagine their baby selves and reach out to that baby. The baby Kate saw in the meditation as her baby self reminded her of how her brother Nickie looked as a baby. Kate drew Picture 3 (Figure 8-3) to express her feelings about reaching out to her baby self.

The picture is of a landscape with hills on either side which come down to wavy blue water. A large yellow and rose colored sun is rising into the blue sky. Kate called the picture "Brand-New Beginning." Kate describes the meditation experience as

> peaceful, amazing, different.... I got as close as [an] arm length to the baby with the baby reaching out, but I was scared to pick the baby up because the baby was so brand new.... The baby looked, ah, it looked like it could be a couple months old.... I think it was [cute], yes, it was me.
>
> Yeah, she had white fuzzy hair like a little angel with blue eyes, but I was scared, I was scared to touch her 'cause she was so little and innocent and sweet and I felt, I felt that I didn't want to hurt her, because she looked too sweet, too innocent, too new. I didn't want to damage that new.... I felt that she was helpless that I was scared to touch her.... Yeah, [she was] very beautiful, I loved her. I loved her so much I was afraid to touch her. She was a beauty.... She [the baby] wanted me and she didn't care about what was predicted about me.

Kate says of Picture 3 (Figure 8-3):

> This is, uh, before man stepped on earth. And everything's new and untouched, brand new, like a brand-new baby. And it was scary to wanna go there 'cause it was so new, scary, just like the baby!

The next session was about transformation in recovery. Kate appeared agitated when she came into the art therapy room that day. She was hesitating to do the third step in the AA program because she was afraid she couldn't do it "perfectly." The third step is "Made a decision to turn our will and our lives over to the care of God as we understood Him."

The assignment was to show where the person was in the transformation process of recovery and how they felt about it. Kate drew Picture 4 (not shown) of a large tree in the center of the paper with a trunk which is black on the left side and brown on the right. On the top of the tree there are green leaves throughout, but there is red fruit only on the left side. Sunlight is shining through the leaves on both sides. There is green grass on either side of the tree at the base. Kate tells about her picture.

> This one had my second most spiritual feeling. My spiritual awakening. Yes, this tree... this picture was about transformation, and I learned from this picture that, that I am on the third step of... recovery.

Figure 8-3

And what I actually learned from this picture is that God is telling me, "It's time, it's time to turn it over. It's time to turn your will and your life over to me." That's what He told me in this picture and where I got that was from my tree here. . . . I got little fruits on it, but it's only half full 'cause I was just starting, and I got some sunshine coming through the branches and colors — colors have a lot to do with my pictures and feelings. Uh, the tree trunk is brown, and I have a very full tree, and of course I have some black. Black to me means empty. It means nothing, like an empty black room. No fear, no nothing just empty, emptiness.

Well, this tree is me, and I didn't realize there was black in it until after we talked about it, but this black in the tree to me was my body and I, and I have this empty spot in it and at the time in my life when I drew this picture I had that empty spot inside me, and I was trying to figure out the right way to do a third step the perfect way.

I came to realize that there is no perfect program, and I was procrastinating in taking my third step — turning my will and life over. But what I didn't realize was that I could do that every day. So, that space was empty 'til after I drew this picture and got the message that it's time to make your third step.

So I did my third step and I turned my will and my life over and I feel good. And I can do that everyday and I can know that, so this made me take my third step which I was procrastinating it for a long time.

Picture 5 (Figure 8-4) shows the picture that Kate did in her last art therapy session. The clients were asked to draw a picture of something they needed to let go of and/or their feelings about letting go. Kate was struggling with letting go that day as her treatment was coming to a finish.

In her picture, she is the figure on the left, dressed in a black dress with black tears running down her face. The figure is stretching both to the left where it is superimposed over light black reaching into yellow and to the right toward the things Kate feels she needs to let go of as she prepares to leave treatment. Kate tells about the picture:

> My picture . . . was about letting go. Uh, I had to let go of friends and family. It shows all different kinds. . . . If you notice none of them are smiling because they're not very happy people. So, I didn't put no lips or anything on 'em.
>
> Ah, I'm, I'm trying to let go of my boyfriend if I have to, but he's hanging on to me harder than I'm hangin' on him 'cause I'm, I'm further in my program than him. He's also in the program. Mail and bills—I can read a bill and let it wreck my whole day. And I need to let go of little stupid little everyday things and turn it over. School—I had to put off school because it's too much for me, and I need to work on myself and my recovery and school takes up a lot of time, and I, I have to put that off for a while.
>
> I'm on the verge here. I'm halfway into darkness, which is empty and pain inside me. As in my tree, I did not realize this 'til I looked at my pictures together. I've got my black in my tree trunk. I'm also wearing black. I don't know why. I have black tears. So, this is, this is my empty pain. I think I'm lettin' my empty pain out and I'm going, going through it to get to my sunshine and my new life right next to it, but it's gonna hurt, it's gonna hurt.
>
> And the way getting there and letting go of all these other things, but in order to get happy, I have to feel my pain. And that's what I'm learning to do right now, and I know that I won't have to go through this ever again. Once I make it there and I know that I have to keep looking back on some of these things that I had to give up and the people I had to leave and I have to remember all these bad things and things that bothered me so that it won't come back. I can stay over there. . . . Yellow means happiness, serenity, peace . . . in God, and in myself, my regular self.
>
> It [turn it over] means to let God totally come into my life and help me figure out what to do when I don't know what to do. And I may not know consciously that He's working through me. . . . I just know He's here. I know He's in me. I know He's with me. I don't know how I know, I just know. I feel it.

### Kate talks about her immediate plans after treatment.

> I'm gonna go home, but not home where my parent, my mother is. My mother is drinking now. She didn't drink 'til after I left. I'm going home with my boyfriend who's also recovering. I know that if something happens, he

Figure 8-4

could end up relapsing, but I really have strong faith in God and myself and in
him that I think that this might be the one out of a hundred that might make it.
I have that hope. I understand that and all I can do is pray that it does and
worry about what I would do if he does relapse. . . . If I feel that's jeopardizing
my sobriety and I'm unhappy, I can go stay at my sponsor's and wait to get into
a halfway house. So, I do have something to do if it does not work out. And I
have that feeling in me to where I realize that I would have to let go, if it comes
down to that, for myself because I want to get to this happiness over here
(Figure 8-4), so I'm going to have to do what I gotta do to get there. And I can't
do it alone and I, I can do it with meetings, but it'd be a lot harder without
God. With God by my side and behind me it makes it a lot easier.

## Kate ended by talking about finding herself and who she is.

I looked all over the country for me . . . I'm finding me. I don't know totally
yet [who I am]. I just feel happy. I feel more at peace . . . childlike. . . . I figured
it out, it's the simple things out of life I want, like just out, playing out in the
garden, you know, havin' a yard to play in, you know. I don't know. I don't
know. I'd like to decorate and do little things that really I get a thrill out of,
just little things.

## SUMMATION AND REFLECTION

### Addiction History

The divorce of Kate's parents, the death of her brother, her uncle's death, and the near death of her mother were traumatic events early in her life, all happening before the age of six years. She had experiences of sexual abuse starting at age seven or eight. She started using alcohol at age 11. Her pregnancy, boyfriend's rejection and subsequent abortion and suicide attempt at age 14 preceeded her dropping out of school at 16 years of age. At this time, she ran away from home a number of times. Coming out of all of these chaotic circumstances, she still describes her childhood as "happy." Neither of her parents was chemically dependent during her growing-up time, but her paternal grandparents were alcoholic and her mother has since become alcoholic.

Kate kept the chaotic events, confusion, and emptiness in her life going in her adult life through many relationships with men, drug use, and going around the country pursuing this life. She came to her co-dependence looking for men to take care of her and, instead, finding men who would abuse her sexually and leave her. This had been her history. She came to her chemical dependency with the disease already in her family.

### Spiritual History

The dramatic spiritual event where God spoke to Kate on the day of her brother's drowning made a deep and lasting impression on her. Being caught in the midst of the tragedy, Kate's mother was not able to hear her story about God. Kate has little else to say about her spirituality previous to her treatment at Share, except that she has always believed in God. It seemed almost as though she had not missed a beat spiritually from the day of her brother's death until that first day in art therapy. She remembered and expressed her feelings about the early spiritual experience on that first day.

### Art and Spirituality Experience

Kate had had a positive experience with art as a child, but had not been consciously aware of her spirituality through the art. Art therapy provided a place for Kate to express and have her spirituality validated. During her first art therapy session, she felt that Picture 1 (Figure 8-1) related powerfully with a poem I happened to have. The poem and the picture affirmed the strong spiritual experience she had had as a child and gave her a current way to relate to God's presence in her life. After this session, her attitude visibly changed to one of being more open and willing throughout the treatment program. When she did Picture 2 (Figure 8-2), she was very aware of her powerlessness over her co-dependence with men and her chemical dependency. In the session with the mediation about reaching out to her child self, she had the feeling of being "brand new." Picture 3 (Figure 8-3) from that session is one of the earth when it was brand new with nothing on it. She expressed hope for herself and her future. Picture 4, of her brown and black trunked tree, deeply affected her and helped her to see how she was holding back from turning her life over to her higher power and thus keeping herself empty. The last drawing, Picture 5 (Figure 8-4), showed her the confusion and difficulties she was still having in letting go and making healthy decisions for her life.

When she left treatment, she was going to live with her newly recovering boyfriend. She had planned outpatient counseling, 12-step meetings, and an alternative plan of action if her living situation did not work out for her.

# Chapter 9

## DAVE'S STORY

### INTRODUCTION AND HISTORY

Dave is soft spoken, thoughtful, sensitive, and intelligent. He appears to listen and consider before he enters into a conversation to share his ideas. For most of his adult life, he has been a part of the corporate structure, successful and fitting in with his three-piece suits, intellectual-looking glasses, and charming smile. He is a 47-year-old caucasian man who identifies himself as both a recovering alcoholic and recovering co-dependent.

He started drinking after his first semester of college, but his co-dependency developed far sooner in his dysfunctional family. He describes himself as being "dry" for 18 years and only sober in the last couple of years. When he says dry, he means that he was not using alcohol, but he was not really content or at peace. With this growing sobriety, Dave has been reviewing his values and changing his way of life. Underneath his corporate image, he has reconnected with the spiritually alive and creative, graphic artist and poetry writer he remembers being as a young boy. Dave tells about his early history.

> I was born in [a large city]. . . . I had one sister who's . . . younger. . . . We were fairly poor when we started. . . . I can't remember hardly ever seeing my father when I was very young. . . . He was working. He was a depression person and he never got over it.

Dave describes his non-working mother of his early years as:

> I guess, possessive and [a] vain woman in hindsight, and uh, kind of, I spent most of my time with her and, looking back, had the feeling that, uh, I was her possession. . . . I know looking back also that she, uh, drank a lot and even now is addicted to painkilling drugs, prescription drugs, although I didn't realize it until very recently.

The family moved to the country where Dave's dad went into business:

> We all moved . . . in the country and, uh, started a new life up there and it turned into quite a . . . reasonably successful life compared to what it was. Uh,

and I think after about ten years we then became solidly middle class, economically.

## Dave looks back at his family of origin from his current perspective.

I use the terminology now, but we were definitely a dysfunctional family. . . . I can never remember any real feelings or honesty ever being expressed in our family. . . . I guess I was a pretty sensitive kid and I always, I always liked to read and draw, but somehow gradually I started to fit the mold of the achiever. . . .

Okay, it's only recently that I've been able to think back and remember some of the things that happened when I was young 'cause I really blotted a lot of them out and, uh, I did pretty well in school. I always felt that I was the hero of the family. I'd somehow salvage respectability for the family and everybody was counting on me. I was going to be, somehow I got it in my mind I think my parents kept drilling it in to me that I had to be a doctor, first of all because the Jewish son who becomes the doctor is the true champion and also I know my father figured that during the depression only doctors survived in a reasonably comfortable life.

## When Dave uses the word "Jewish," he speaks of it in terms of:

Only nationality. My parents were, uh, very hypocritical. They never prayed. I'm sure that even now they don't believe in, that there is a God. Um, but they love . . . they liked to associate with the trappings of Judaism, although maybe once a year they went to synagogue. Uh, most of the trappings consisted of cooking!

## In summing up the change he went through as a child, Dave says:

Yeah, even when we moved . . . although my father was doing very well, he still continued to work whatever hours he could work. . . . I had no contact with him whatsoever. . . . I guess to sum this up, uh, although I loved literature, I loved art. I had a sense of spirituality when I was a kid, and I was very sensitive. I gradually learned how to encase all of that and I became an athlete, a pretty good athlete. Um, I moved more into the areas that were expected of me, I think. I loved to work with my hands, I love to use tools, uh, but that was, my family kind of frowned on that. I was being pushed more toward the whatever it was they expected of me . . . it was something that would grant the family respectability, and the arts was not the area. . . .

## Dave began drinking heavily in his freshman year of college.

I started college [in my town]. I did pretty well my first term there . . . then something happened at the end of that first term. It was like somebody pulled the plug on everything that I'd ever been. . . . The way it felt was like I suddenly became nonfunctional. . . . Unfortunately just at the same time, although I'd never had anything to drink in my life, I went down to [a] college . . . bar with some friends to celebrate the end of the semester, uh, and had one drink and that was it for me. It was like instant addiction. Uh, and after that I would pretty much be drunk every day for the next ten years, almost from the very start.

But, nevertheless, uh, there I was starting the second semester [and] suddenly hooked on alcohol and, uh, I ended up moving back home. Looking back ... I think one of the problems I was experiencing was just the problem of separation and ... somehow I just wasn't separating very well. In fact, I think now in hindsight, too, uh, I'd never learned for many more years after that how to properly separate from any relationship, and that's gonna be [the] theme in my life I think ... the proper way to separate.

## Dave now defines himself as co-dependent at that time.

It was, co-dependence, was unconscious blending of life with someone else, uh, and uh, in this case with my family ... probably with my mother, but being unable to break away—that's what I meant by separation. I think dependency has to do with separating these invisible strings that I wasn't aware of and not knowing how to become my own person, and being sucked back into this dependent relationship with my family.

I think the alcoholism had a lot to do with the pain, the depressive reaction, this tremendous pain I was feeling and I suddenly had found a painkiller.... The pain came from the co-dependency within the family, without a doubt. And, uh, and although I had an interest in spirituality, um, I didn't know how to pray, I didn't know how to relate to God or a higher power truly, and so I couldn't—it was a gravity that was tugging me back in.... I didn't understand what was ... causing me tremendous pain ... and then when I could anesthetize the pain, then there was no reason to feel it, so, uh, that's the way I stayed throughout another whole year.... Finally [the college] suspended me....

## Dave changed colleges, went to night school, and continued drinking.

I was still passing, but grades were lousy, and then that was during ... the Vietnam crisis, ... so I joined the air force and, uh, all during that time somehow I still knew that art, writing, and spiritual things was at the core of my life. I just couldn't do anything with it because I was just drinking and feeling bad all the time....

## Dave requested an overseas assignment and got it seeing much of it through an "alcoholic haze." He describes this time.

I would always try not to drink during the day, ... but I always went to bed drunk ... but there was something in me still trying to come out.... I would also spend time in my barracks room trying to write and there was something in me that just wouldn't come out.... I always had to write drunk and then splint it when I was sober, uh, which meant I would get these half-formed thoughts on paper and then try to patch 'em up when I sobered up which wasn't very often.

## Near the end of his tour of duty, Dave met a girl and she got pregnant.

I decided I would stay ... and see my child born. ... I had some drinking friends, but I hadn't really had a girlfriend until I started going out with this girl. ... It was the beginning of the classic wounded bird/hero helper relationship ... I was the rescuer. Without doubt.

I was drinking, continuing to drink, um, and uh, I got a flat in this town where I was working. ... I didn't do very much writing, I was working and drinking. ... Within a few years, I'd gone from being a $60 a week programmer to being—having responsibility for all operations in the company, 1,000 people, all the manufacturing, materials and everything.

Dave married the girl: "Later, a year and a half after my son was born ... it was a stormy relationship from the start." Now, nineteen years later, Dave is in the process of being divorced from this woman. He says regretfully that the divorce is needed, "because it's the first time our personal boundaries have been established."

Dave goes back to describe his drinking pattern at the time of his son's birth and his decision to quit.

I was really drinking heavily and anything I could get my hands on, but only after work. ... [One day] I put down my beer and I walked out of the pub and I didn't have another drink for a year and a half. ...

I just sweated and went through this acute withdrawal for about two weeks— not sleeping, just sweating. I went to work every day, and I went through the withdrawal stage. I didn't know why I did this ... but I didn't have another drink, even after work. I would go and I would sit in the bar while everybody else drank. And, uh, then my career took a jump, that's when it really started to take a jump.

Dave's career jumped with his "dry" controlling behavior.

I wanted to be the rescuer for the whole company. So, I became a dry drunk par excellence ... very goal directed, and uh, so I started to become extremely successful at work. ... Now that I couldn't squash my feelings with booze, I somehow managed to bury them completely, stuff them completely.

Dave says he began drinking again on his wedding day.

On the day we were married, um, we had a small party ... everybody was pressing champagne on me and, of course, I had no idea I was an alcoholic. ... I finally had one glass of champagne and it took me another year to stop drinking from that moment. ... I stopped drinking, uh, just through sheer willpower. Not knowing I was alcoholic ... I became a dry drunk from that point, 1971. ... The dry drunk lasted until 1986.

Dave describes his spiritual reawakening.

I was transferred back [to the U.S.A. and] ... it turned out in the States the company was falling apart and I wasn't accepted there. ... I had another ...

bout with depressive illness. . . . A friend in . . . Canada gave me a job . . . [and I was] driving back and forth to . . . Illinois on the weekends. . . . Emotionally, I was really totally drained, and I just couldn't relate. . . . While I was working in Canada, I was making these long drives [and] I would listen to the radio a lot.

And coming through southern Indiana there's kind of like a little Bible belt, and the only radio station I could pick up through part of that area was a Bible station. And Christianity at that time was totally alien to me. I mean, I did have a belief in God. I didn't know, ah, but that's basically it. . . . This was 1982. Um, and there was a guy who had a Bible study program on called "Jay Vernon McGee." He had this southern accent; he was a "down home" boy, and the first time I heard it, I almost broke the radio knob I turned it off so fast.

I made these trips for a long time, but then after a while there wasn't anything else on, so I listened a little longer, and then a little longer, and finally I started to get interested in what he was saying. And so, I listened regularly then, and then when I got this job back in Illinois, he was on at seven o'clock in the morning . . . then I started reading the Bible naturally, and finally I wrote him a letter. . . . I said that I had started in my Church of the Oldsmobile, which was what I was driving at the time; at that point I said I experienced a conversion. . . . It was strong, but I still had inward skepticism.

I knew I was on the right track, but I'm a very rational, analytical person, and it was starting on the gut level. The thing that started to really end my marriage as it had been was the fact that I was reading the Bible, and this would drive my wife crazy. . . . She claims to have, certainly at that time, to have no belief in any religion whatsoever.

## Dave first went to AA in 1986 at a friend's invitation.

She said, "Why don't you come to an AA meeting with me? . . . " I said, well I used to drink a lot. . . . Finally, I went. I went to one meeting and I said, so that's what's wrong with me! And I suddenly realized what I had to do. And this is after how many years? Fifteen or sixteen years of being dry . . . everything started to come clear.

I just kept going [to AA] 'cause I knew I had to keep going and then. That spelled the total end of my marriage 'cause my wife, she was having a hard enough time accepting me reading the Bible, but to go to AA meetings when she didn't think in a million years that I was an alcoholic was absolutely unacceptable. And so, we ended up separating then.

### DAVE'S ART EXPERIENCE

## With AA and growing spiritually Dave's creative self has re-emerged.

In 1981, when I had this tremendous crash, I did some writing and some drawing then, uh, but I couldn't, it didn't catch. I couldn't get validated with it. I mean, I needed it, it was therapeutic, uh, but it just kind of withered.

Dave took a class I taught a year ago where he says his creative work

was validated. And that, in fact, has formed the basis of a theory I have, at least not only in my own life but in other people, too, about, uh, the importance of validation in a very strong way . . . in another deeper sense — in a spiritual sense of validation as a continual lifelong process and, uh, so that was the turning point for me, that class.

Dave ties his spiritual growth to several things.

Through AA, through a lot of Christian studies, um, and interestingly through my understanding of natural sciences from a spiritual point of view. Uh, the isomorphism, I think, of how spirituality just ties everything together.

Um, the more I turn my life and will over to God, the more kind of a sense of everlasting, continual life and brotherhood comes back to me. . . . I have a divergent analytical sense. If I'm confronted with an experience I'll go all over the place looking for alternatives until I converge, ah, but my converging now has to be on Christ. I've already explored all the alternatives and, uh, so I no longer search.

Dave believes he lost his creative expression via the addictive process:

I think I was blessed with some artistic ability from the time I was small . . . but I never had enough confidence, or to put it the other way, too much fear to pursue it — not enough courage or whatever it was. So, I got diverted with other things — addictive stuff, and um, various obsessive/compulsive behaviors for years and years . . . the last couple years I've suddenly rediscovered my blessings and, uh, decided to pursue them with a little more courage.

Dave says his spirituality and creativity are growing.

I'll get struck with this really vivid image that I'll kind of nurse for a while and sometimes it'll come even in words or phrases or which I'll write down. And other times I'll write down some words or phrases which then develop into an image.

I think because I've had a lot less training in art that I had in writing that my preference is for writing, but I think inside me they kind of are granted equal force.

Spirituality for me is an internal expression of meaning . . . a truth that can only be expressed through sometimes poetic or graphic images, but often escapes words or other reductionist communications.

Dave tells of his first powerful art experience in recent years.

I think the very first, well, a few years ago . . . 1982 . . . I had done a linoleum block cut Picture 1 (Figure 9-1). This was at a time when I was going through a particularly traumatic period of life. . . . I was at home. . . . I just wanted to do one . . . the cut is of a bicycle rider embedded in an image, really.

I was doing a lot of bicycle riding. I was reading a lot of Carl Jung and this image just came to me of the, uh, kind of the Jung's concept of the shadow, the oriental ying and yang image. . . . I think of some integration that was starting to take place in me.

I had dissociated so many things that, uh, this image just formed in my mind of this bicycle rider where the wheels formed kind of . . . an elliptical eclipse where the light and the dark mutually eclipse each other, um, and yet form the total light of what we are. Kind of a good and evil, ying/yang, uh, bipolar totality and that I was somehow riding that totality and starting to integrate it into me as a whole. . . . I just was aware that I had this image that I wanted to put down. . . .

## For Dave, the block cut, Picture 1 (Figure 9-1), relates to his spirituality.

Okay, the image (Figure 9-1) I think was an expression of the intertwining of good and evil in me, and that the evil was this inescapable—consequences of this fall which the more I try to suppress, the more it came out in my fears and, uh, doing things that I told myself I would never do, and uh, the more I try to squash it, the more it popped out, and I guess basically the fact that I couldn't control it—there was no way I could control myself, how I acted, or how other people acted and yet I also knew that there was the possibility of good in me.

## Dave relates the darkness and light in Picture 1 (Figure 9-1) to parts of himself.

I would have been riding into complete darkness and that's much more how I felt at the time. That I wasn't yet heading into light. I was coming together, but I was moving into darkness, but the thing that was significant was that the front wheel—the circle—was actually radiating light and the back one was radiating darkness, so light was out in front. . . . But I know I was going into darkness . . . and full blast as you can see. . . . I mean I'm, that rider is riding hard. . . . It's a real thing and the light is being radiated from a dark body and so it's the total blending of the light and the dark in me. . . . Everything I'd dissociated was somehow starting to pull together.

Now it's—at that time I had to project out of me—I couldn't feel anything inside myself at the time. I didn't know who I was. I had no relationship really with God on any kind of meaningful basis. Um, it was as if I had to see something with my eyes to even start, so, to me this is a projection out of this muddle inside myself. That was the first step.

I was just, it was like, uh, doing, uh, shadow puppets on a screen. I had to see on some screen the fact that I was starting to change. I couldn't feel anything inside myself except I was still in a lot of pain. Inside I was still undifferentiated as far as feelings or understandings went. But it was like, really like doing shadow puppets. This was the first one and starting to see that even though it was a two-dimensional image, it did come out of me and there was something stirring in there that was trying to express itself.

## Dave is aware of God in his life then when he looks at the block now.

Figure 9-1

Oh, yeah in that, that was God trying to get me to change...[giving me] some insight into me, starting to come together enough to a whole, enough so I could start to develop my spirituality. And it was a sign, I guess.

Yeah, it was very powerful [at the time he made it]...but I knew that it had said something. In a way, it gave me some hope. [I'm] still in the darkness, but confidently. I mean, that looks pretty confident in there, too, which amazes me considering when it was done. But certainly into the darkness because I can't know what's ahead.

Experimenting and enjoying drawing about a year later, Dave remembers:

I had this wonderful sense of peace afterwards, um, and all it was was a salt and pepper shaker and a jar of mustard, but I had this really good feeling, relaxed feeling that I hadn't had for a long time...it was my non-logical part of me, my non-controlling part trying to tip the balance back again.

A year ago, seven years after the making of the linoleum block, Dave had an opportunity to draw a number of pictures in a class which I taught. Pictures 2 and 3 (Figures 9-2 and 9-3) were drawn on the same day. Picture 2 (Figure 9-2) shows the time-oriented mechanical man part of himself that Dave believes people see.

Picture 3 (Figure 9-3) shows who the real interior Dave. The head in Figure 9-3 is brown and the scribble around the head is black. The book is black, connected with a small red lightning bolt to a spiral or "vortex"

Figure 9-2

that is black with red and then blue coming out of it. The blue turns into a brook. The tree has green leaves and a brown trunk, and the sun is yellow and orange. There is green grass around the tree. Dave describes these two pictures and their meaning to him. He says that Picture 2 (Figure 9-2):

is pretty cartoony, and I think it was a very surface image. I didn't have to dig very deep for that. That was the very first drawing, so it was more of a cartoon really. And then, uh, but the other one just popped out of me. I didn't expect to see that on paper at all. So, uh, I'm glad I did it. I think it told me something about myself very quickly.

I was really evolving here (Figure 9-3) . . . there was a big change going on there at the time. . . . This just came out of me. . . . I love the simplicity of nature. . . . I somehow reach a full depth of understanding of nature through books. And this is a very biblical-looking text here. . . . I don't always directly experience nature. I have to come at it from a slant which is maybe a spiritual understanding first, and then that's converted into a direct experience of natural things.

I think the black certainly, I'm surrounded by black and white while I'm staring at this book, and the colors don't come out until I get transformed through the brook into the natural setting. I think it's, uh, the book itself is very sterile, but it does lead me to—the written word leads me to fuller experience and living and life. . . . I think in some respects I'm going from this sterile into the rich here and that I've found my way there through books.

Exactly what it says that I was coming back to life in a way and that I have to think that that book is the Bible . . . when I looked at it a few minutes afterwards, I thought that [it was the Bible]. . . . Oh, yeah, He [God] was leading me to life.

Looking at it a year later, Dave now feels this picture was prophetic.

It says to me that I've gone from one universe to the other through this little vortex in a way. . . . It's literally coming through some hole in one universe and emerging on the other side. Because a year ago I was reading about it and now I'm living it, so I know I've gone from one to the other.

Um, no, not easy, no, not easy [his transition], but wonderful. . . . I've observed my life and really enjoyed making this transition. . . . I like looking at 'em [the pictures], because I mean they just, ah, are tremendous milestones.

Through Picture 4 (Figure 9-4) Dave sees his co-dependent tendencies which have kept him isolated. Dave describes this picture.

I've always been a rescuer. This picture is of a lifeguard, a very grey lifeguard sitting on a black high chair—very high chair—casting a dark shadow, but looking over a bright beach and water where everybody's having a lot of fun and throwing beach balls and sailing, um, and, uh, I've always felt like the distant isolated rescuer.

I wrote under here [the picture] . . . "participating only in the way of

Figure 9-3

responsibility, outside the joy, living with the threat of catastrophic intervention and being at fault of having to be ready to rescue, up high, out of touch,
but with a good view and vigilant, reluctantly trading the closeness and contact
and ecstasy available for a very secure and powerful, even admirable position,
a certain feeling of self-repugnance, untouchable and really yearning for
acceptance." And that's exactly how I felt.

Comparing Pictures 3 and 4 (Figures 9-3 and 9-4, respectively), Dave
says:

Figure 9-4

Well, certainly the grey and the black colors...[meaning] cold and, uh, separate, out-of-touch, isolated...and then in both cases the world of warmth and other people are separate, but close, nearby...as long as I feel I'm responsible for what everybody else does, I can never participate, and I'm more permanently out of touch there. I'm in a position of authority and responsibility, and that removes me from participating.

Picture 5 (not shown) is a drawing of Dave's childhood recollection. A large grey-haired teacher in a blue shirt points her finger at the shamed

Dave, who hangs his head between two other children. Dave has brown hair and a red shirt. The child on the left has black hair and the child on the right had blond hair. Both are wearing green shirts. Dave describes the episode and the picture.

> Okay, this was a poignant episode in my life . . . this picture was at a time when we were singing. It was a chorus of some sort. It was in the third grade. . . . I was doing so badly that I was messing up the people around me and finally the teacher just said, "Dave, would you please just move your mouth," and so, number two crushing defeat was music! And, uh, so this picture is of Mrs. G. pointing at me over the top of her piano while I'm in total humiliation.
>
> But, um, it shows how, uh, lack of encouragement at the right time can literally destroy a kid's, a whole area of kid's growth. Um, and also, if you don't grow up with, uh, a belief in a higher power in the home, or have access to a higher power when you're young, that an incident like that can even more destroy a growth area because you get to be so totally dependent on adults and parents for validation that when they are, you know, less sensitive than you'd like them to be, then that's your sole authority.

Dave compares the boy in the picture to the person he is again becoming.

> The picture is simple because I'm not worried or afraid to make a simple statement, afraid that somebody would be critical of it. I just say simply what I mean and at one time I would want to qualify or look for approval, you know, modify things for approval, but now I just say them simply.
>
> I just feel totally grounded in God most of the time, anyway, and that the more I feel like that the more I know that what I say is coming from me. . . . I really understand how God is always there—it's just me that moves away from Him. And, uh, but, uh, I may go through difficult experiences, painful experiences, but I, God is a loving God for me and He makes it okay to say simple things that I believe in. . . . Yeah, acceptance of whatever I am, I am.

Picture 6 (not shown) is of another early childhood recollection of Dave's which has meaning to him now. Picture 6 shows a picture of a small boy in a red wagon waving to another boy who is rowing a row boat out in some water. The colors are bright and the sun is yellow. The scene is natural and peaceful looking. He tells about the picture and its meaning for him.

> I was, uh, probably only five years old in this picture. It's a picture of a little boy in a green rowboat who was me. . . . On the land sitting in a little red wagon is another little boy waving to me. . . . That little boy is my friend, Matt, who was . . . I guess you'd say at that time the word was retarded. . . . He couldn't get around by himself, but I used to tow him around in this red wagon. . . . He

couldn't communicate, he couldn't speak really, but, uh, we were friends and I remember in this picture I'd towed him down to the lake, left him there and then got in this little green rowboat.... This was on vacation ... at a lake.

I just have an affinity for just basic natural things of water and bark and woods.... I was away from that for a long time, but I know in some of the poems I've written recently I try to take the most mundane parts of nature and have written poems about them, I mean cornfields.... Somehow I'm tied up with nature, I mean, that's where I feel better.

Dave remembers this time as an enjoyment and acceptance of nature and even the parts of it that our society calls handicapped, i.e., Matt. Dave contrasts the natural life-giving setting of this picture to his desire for control.

I have such a clear picture of that choice that we have between what we do and what we make, um, and that the choice is only in one of two directions— life or control. And the way I distinguish internally as to which way I'm going 'cause sometimes I'm not sure is that if I do something and I feel like somehow I've gained an advantage from it over others, then I know I'm in the wrong mode and I'm in control.

Dave describes Picture 7 (not shown) of another childhood recollection.

Ah, this is a pretty vivid picture of ... someone's fist slamming into my right eye, throwing blood out of my nose.... This was, uh, from an incident in my childhood when I stood up to the playground bully who was bothering us by stealing our basketball and, um, I got beat up pretty bad in that fight.... I had to walk downtown to my father's little shop ... walking through the streets of downtown and into his little shop all bloody.

Dave compares Picture 7 to Pictures 1 (Figure 9-1), 3 (Figure 9-3), 4 (Figure 9-4), and 5.

Well, one thing is, I think, that comes out in all these pictures is, uh, being solitary in a certain way.... Again, it was just me in the fight and everybody around me watching.

My parents are, and were and are, fearful people. And they don't have any belief in a higher power, really, and so the consequence of not believing in God is fear. So, they live in fear, and I can remember I was—they passed their fear onto me in a way that most parents do, always worried that I would do something to get hurt.

Dave describes Picture 8 (Figure 9-5), a picture of what he yearned for as a boy.

This is a rear view of a middle-aged man and a little boy. The man kind of has his hand on the boy's shoulder, on the back of his neck and this was supposed to be my father.

There's a kind of a slightly exaggerated distance between the two of us and . . . I think this is what I would . . . have liked to have happened after the previous picture when I got beat up 'cause I can remember, I don't remember my father ever touching me. Even then, he didn't comfort me when I came in all bloody and beat up.

## When Dave drew the picture, he says:

I felt a sadness. . . . I still do because, you know, getting beat up was no big deal really especially since I got my licks in, but uh, it's funny that I even think that that's what, uh, I never, until I drew that picture, I never thought that that's what I would have wanted. I didn't even remember that part, but now it seems to be the most important part of the incident.

Well, now I'm grateful for every experience that I can recall. I mean, there's nothing I wish hadn't happened . . . that's the biological father that I never really had a closeness to and now I have a spiritual father who I can't ever pull away from.

I think, I think I've gained strength from every experience. Although I would have, I wanted that closeness at the time, um, in that picture I am self-reliant, I'm standing on my own . . . that I ended up being self-reliant and in maybe finally a good way and not bitter and destructive.

First, I had to get a relationship with God before I could have any kind of decent relationship with anyone else. That's the way I feel. . . . I think by being isolated, suffering the pain of isolation, then finding God, then being able to come back and establish relationships with people . . . I know that the only way I can avoid isolation is having a relationship with God continually and then that is the enabling power that lets me relate to other people in an empathic way, too, especially.

No, I know I lived that way for a long time. I mean, I had relationships. I wasn't totally isolated, but I was in a spiritual sense. I was around people a lot, and I did things with people, but um, I didn't embrace them. That's what I'm saying in the same way that my father isn't embracing me in this picture. I related to other people with a certain distance which was a result of my feeling of isolation or depression.

Dave drew Picture 9 (Figure 9-6) and Picture 10 (Figure 9-7) at the end of the "Inner Child" class. Figure 9-6 shows a partially opened door surrounded by black on the inside. Outside is a colorful day which is very similar to the landscape and colors in Figure 9-3, which was one of Dave's first pictures in class. Dave describes Picture 9 (Figure 9-6):

Just the door opening from a dark room onto a lush garden and, uh, but that's really the way I felt, I think. This was right at the end of the class. . . . Actually it's interesting because uh, it's a, it's a recapitulation of the very first drawing (Figure 9-3). . . . Just looking at the two, uh, it's basically the same scene of nature . . . but the thing that really strikes me here is, uh, in the earlier

Figure 9-5

picture in order to get to that peaceful natural setting . . . I had to do it through this convoluted way through a book and through some mystical vortex to get there, whereas in the later one, all I do is walk through a door and there I was. . . . Yeah, why make it hard? . . . "knock and it shall be opened."

Well, I liked it even then when I did it. I realized that, at that time, it just seemed like a cliche, and I wasn't real proud of it, but then maybe the basic, the fact that it is a cliche, it's like the twelve-step cliches which seem so simple but are so profound. It goes along with the "Let go, let God" type of simplicity. . . . I liked it when I did it and I still do . . . where I am today? Oh, well, I would, uh, the door would be behind me by now. . . . Oh, I'd know it was there, yeah.

Dave goes on to describe the last drawing, Picture 10 (Figure 9-7):

This was the last one, yeah . . . another abstract, um, picture with vivid colors—green, orange, red, black, yellow, blue . . . it's got a lot of energy in it,

Figure 9-6

to say the least! [laughs]. Um, it's certainly different than Mr. Corporate Man at the beginning . . . there's this, uh, kind of caldron of energy in the middle and then at the very top, like balloon captions in a cartoon, there are little bubble kind of faint drawings in each one. Uh, one has a car, the other has a cat, and the third has a house and a woman.

Um, and, uh, this was at a time when, uh, my marriage was definitely gone. I guess these are like conventional sort of like icons that are in these bubbles, um, but they're kind of faint . . . floating off there like on little umbilical cords and about to break off and float away . . . but the real activity is going on in the kind of the gut area of the picture.

Yeah, so, I think these little bubbles with these kinds of icons of conventional life look like they're about to pop off and float away, but what's left is a very, uh, vibrant commotion going on, not too organized either. . . . I think it's like, ah, raw energy going on in there and uh, again, I could tie that back to that linoleum block and that's the driving energy that's in me . . . an unformed . . . alive chaos.

I haven't talked about it, but chaos . . . again, going back to the relationship between natural science and spirituality, one of the hot topics of science now is chaos, and uh, it turns out that chaos is self-organizing. Now this is an incredible discovery that um, through a process nobody really understands now . . . it turns out that chaos has an intrinsic organization to it where everybody has spent their lives trying to control chaos. It turns out if you leave it alone, it organizes itself.

I'm letting go of . . . these comforting symbols and letting my chaos organize itself, or letting somebody organize it for me [laughs]. The only one who's ever organized anything for me before! . . . God sorts myself out for me. "Let go and let God" is the cliche I used before. . . . I'm somebody who has to validate something, some way that natural science even, I have to draw an analogy with something that I can be analytical. . . . I think that, uh, the universe is holistic, if I can't find and analogue to something, then I doubt it because I think that God transforms Himself in many different ways. If I only see one instance of something, then I have to question it.

Dave says the theme is the same in Pictures 1 and 10 (Figures 9-1 and 9-7):

Basically, I'm going on pure energy into the unknown.

I did all these pictures in a very short time, apart from my linoleum block, and although I've been writing for years, probably these pictures are as expressive as anything else I've—any of the writing I've done. It's nice to see them all together to go through this . . . puts them into a sense of meaning altogether.

I think the themes, they illustrate something . . . they really drive it home and that is that I spent my life learning how to be where I am now. I guess in the same way I couldn't have got to where I am now unless I went through these pictures.

Figure 9-7

I'm grateful for all these experiences. I don't think I would've ever got to the relationship I have with God now if I had somehow bypassed the experiences, although I didn't think so at the time. . . . I'm grateful to be alive; I'm grateful to be alive through it all.

The difference is with my relationship with God now. It makes all of this different is that all of these incidents where I, um, was apparently alive, where there was a fight or something else, I didn't live through those with a sense of composure that I can have now. In other words, there was always a strong element of fear at the time and that I went through them on adrenalin but afraid, whereas now, I can go through an incident with an inner sense of peace. . . .

## SUMMATION AND REFLECTION

### Addiction History

Dave was born into a poor family with an emotionally isolated "workaholic" father and a possessive mother who wanted to "mold" Dave. The family was dysfunctional with "no" expression of feelings. Dave's mother drank quite a bit and has gradually developed into a prescription addict.

Dave liked to read and draw, but art was not what would bring the family desired "respectability," so Dave gave up creativity for a more analytical approach. He took over the roles of the "achiever" and "hero" that the family wanted.

Dave describes himself as being instantly addicted to alcohol at the end of his first semester in college. He also had great difficulty separating from the enmeshment in his family at that time. He flunked out of college after doing poorly due to depression and drinking.

Dave enlisted in the air force and went overseas, drinking heavily the whole time. Overseas, he dated a girl who got pregnant, and so he stayed there. He describes himself as the "hero" to her "wounded bird" role. He married her 1½ years after their child was born. He stopped drinking a couple of times, went through "dry drunk" periods, and finally went to AA fifteen or sixteen years later and got really "sober." He went through terrible withdrawal times with each dry period, but did not realize he was alcoholic until he went to AA.

### Spiritual History

Dave grew up in a nominally Jewish family, although he remembers having a sense of his spiritually as a child. As he took on his hero role and got more deeply imbedded in his addictions, spirituality moved into the background.

During a difficult period in his life, when he was suffering from depression and job troubles he gradually started listening to a Christian program on the radio during long cross-country commutes. He

He says he went from being initially turned off to being gradually converted.

The fact of his increased ability and desire to share feelings, combined with his growing spirituality and entrance into AA, threatened and eventually ended his marriage. He has felt as if he is going into the dark on his journey of faith, but he has become less afraid over time and more risk taking and faithful. His trust in God is opening doors, and he feels as if he is coming back to his true self that he left in childhood.

## Art and Spirituality Experience

After giving up art as a child, Dave did some artwork during his depression and job troubles in 1982. The work was not validated by anyone and even though it had meaning for Dave, the seed did not take. He did not start working again with art until the last year. The linoleum block that he carved in 1982, Picture 1 (Figure 9-1), has even more meaning to him now and actually shows one of the great themes of his recovery and spirituality. In a difficult time, he was able through this piece of art to project out his own fear and show that he was willing to ride into the darkness. He sees that as a real movement of his yet unnamed faith in that dark time. When he did other drawings at this time, he remembers feeling "peace" in "turmoil."

Picture 2 (Figure 9-2) was one of the first drawings he did in the class a year ago. He sees it as "cartoony" and superficial, but it is portraying a role he plays rather than that of his true self. In Picture 3 (Figure 9-3) he was able to identify a process through his spirituality which would release him into his natural self, but he was still intellectualizing that possibility.

Through Picture 4 (Figure 9-4) he was able once more to look graphically at his isolation from life that his role caused. Looking back for childhood roots of this behavior, Picture 5 revealed an experience of shame when an authority figure in his life put him down. He feels that had his life been grounded in faith or a functional family, it would not have been as devastating. Through Picture 6 Dave looks at a different sort of childhood experience, the experience of being one with nature and accepting the whole and the handicapped or the light and the darkness. In Picture 7, shame is once again admitted with the attack of the "bully." In the light of the faith and wholeness that Dave has come to through his higher power, he can once again become vulnerable about these fears and shameful events.

Through Picture 8 (Figure 9-5), Dave identified his childhood longing to be comforted by his dad to whom he could not get close. He says that now he has a "spiritual father I can't get away from [God]."

He relates Picture 9 (Figure 9-6) back to Picture 3 (Figure 9-3) because both have the themes of going from death and darkness to life and light. The picture in Figure 9-6 is a much less analytical, more natural transition. This time he goes right through the door of faith.

Picture 10 (Figure 9-7) is a mostly abstract picture through which Dave continues his spiritual journey by letting go of the old clearly-defined controlling ways and finding the real "activity" in the "gut." He says that science is finding that chaos is self-organizing, and he thinks God is involved in this order. He has decided to increasingly move into being himself and to allowing God to sort his life out.

# Chapter 10

# ANN'S STORY

## INTRODUCTION AND HISTORY

Ann is a soft-spoken, shy-appearing person, with lovely fine features and a quiet gentle laugh. She was the middle child of three, with an older and a younger brother. Neither of her parents were drug or alcohol dependent. She is a 24-year-old caucasian woman who identifies herself as a recovering co-dependent. She has been in recovery for three years. She works in a helping profession. I met Ann when she came to some workshops and a course I taught. Ann describes what co-dependency means for her.

> I get into relationships with people who I kind of, I sort of feed into whatever they're doing. Um, I also take care of people. I'm a big caretaker, and that's how I try and get people to, that's how I try to feel safe and loved. And I'm always in control and I'm always the martyr. . . .
>
> I get a real high when I can take care of people and I can fix the situation. . . . I feel real good about myself and I'm energized and I've just . . . taken care of the world and the situation that this person just couldn't figure out or fix or was so upset and I just slipped in and was so in control and fixed it.

When Ann was two years old, her parents became missionaries and moved the family abroad. The family spent four years in a warm sunny country where Ann remembers being very happy and content. The family returned to the United States when Ann was six years old. After their return, her mother worked full time, went back to school, and was in bed most of the rest of the time. Her mother experienced chronic depression and anxiety for the rest of Ann's growing up years. Ann's father started a home improvement business and was caught up working and doing estimates for most of his waking hours, leaving Ann with the care of her younger siblings, the cooking, and the other household chores. She became a practiced caretaker and pleaser and forgot who she was in the process.

> I think that's why I was so lonely. I think I grew up real fast and I still feel a lot of times like I have, like I'm faking everybody out . . . that inside I'm really just

this scared little seven-year-old girl and I mean, it's been like that forever 'cause I always, I faked it for so long. I don't know when it's real or not.

Ann tells about her feelings during her college years after leaving home and the beginning of her three-year recovery from co-dependence.

I wasn't alive, like I was dead and I had nothing inside . . . I lived my life for other people, and I lived my life through being with other people, and so I felt like I had nothing inside. I remember talking for hours and hours, my friends telling me about their lives and their relationships and there it is, and I would be so into that and feeling all their feelings and you know, and that felt like being alive. . . . I needed to get that lost in people to feel alive. . . .

I was that connected in with people and I was that connected with my mom. I mean, it was real hard to get out of my family that's just, that's what closeness meant. Um, and in the last, three years ago it started like a few seconds a day, I would feel alive and then a few minutes and then a few, you know, one day at a time. . . . I hit my "bottom" 'cause that's when I reached out for help and decided that I really couldn't live my life the way I was living it.

Ann describes the difficulty she had breaking with her family pattern.

Yeah, 'cause it was one thing to break my pattern with my friends, it was another thing to break the pattern with the family. And it felt like I was gonna die or they were gonna die.

Ann still sometimes feels "dead" when she goes home to her family.

It's still empty, um, or numb . . . 'cause when I go home I feel dead and that's just like depressed, but then I also slip into all this, like I get real. . . . just start getting really down on myself and say, it's just all these horrible things I tell myself about how bad I am. . . .

I just, um, at my lowest, at my lowest low there was a time when I cut my arm because I had so much pain inside and I didn't know how else to, I mean I just wanted to get it outside of me, I guess. . . . When I did it, it worked. I stopped feeling, I stopped feeling all this pain and like, all I can feel is my arm, so it worked. . . .

Ann talks about where she is now in recovery and says she feels alive

. . . most of the time. I get, when I get real busy I get, I lose that, um, it's still, it's a constant struggle, but I still have to always pull away and do retreats or do my art and that always centers me, or music, music centers me. Um, but most of the time I feel alive. And it's like I have this, I have the steps or the skills to get out of it when I feel dead or numb. I know how to get out of it.

Remembering her recent spiritual history, Ann says she left her conservative background

and went to the Episcopal Church. So I did a complete turnaround. Um, the school that I went to from third grade through eleventh grade was very, very,

very fundamentalist. I mean they had like a don't swear, don't listen to rock music, don't drink, don't smoke, don't dance kind of ideal. It was all works, it was all external, and that's what it meant to be a Christian.

Earlier, from age three to six, Ann remembers different feelings about God.

I couldn't see God, but I could feel him. . . . I mean [at] that time there was so much playfulness and joy and freedom and that's what I think of when I think of God.

If she drew her early feelings about God, Ann says:

I would use every color! All I thought at first was orange and yellow, and blue and then purple and then pinks. . . . I always saw God with nature. Um, being at the ocean and, um, in the woods. . . .

Ann's very early experience of God changed in later childhood.

And then the other experience that I had of God—but I don't think it's really God now—was, um, became pretty predominant throughout a good part of my life until just recently and that was God as, you know, um, God as this judgmental person who I had to be and do certain things in order for him to approve of me. . . . I just kept hearing that I'm not good enough, you have to be like this, you have to do this, you can't [see] things—all the way up 'til when I got into therapy.

Ann says, "organized religion and education" changed her beliefs because

that was also at the same time that my life changed because we came back to America and there wasn't enough time for me and I would always struggle to fix my parents or fix the situation or change it because it was different, and nobody was happy and I couldn't change it.

Through therapy, Ann came back to her belief in a loving, accepting God:

I just started realizing about halfway through that no matter what I said to him [her therapist], or no matter what I showed him, he still reacted the same way to me and he was always benevolent and interested and caring, and it didn't matter what I did or said . . . he always wanted to know why and was always concerned about the deeper reasons, not what I did but who I was. . . . I started being able to look at myself that way and then somewhere in there I realized that, I realized God was like that, too. And it kind of just stretched Him out, and I realized He's not so freaked out about what I do or say. It's who I am that he cares about. I just realized it, and it just totally changed my view of God.

I went to the Episcopal Church . . . nobody was demanding anything of me. Nobody expected me to do anything. They just respected me as a person and there was all this mystery and all this art like in the mystery and I just loved that. I felt at home and I've stayed ever since. And God's just gotten more benevolent.... My family thinks that I, um, have lost the faith and headed for hell or something worse.... I have been able to move, I feel like to a faith that's more true to me. That was one of my separations from my family ... to be able to say, no, I don't. It doesn't fit me, and that's not who I am, um.

## Mostly, both making art and being with God feels the same to Ann.

When I'm really with Him, like when, you know, I'm, just like my little girl with Him and we're playing ... everything is full ... it's like I go beyond myself.... I think we know instinctively where to look.... I mean, looking for God is the right place to look. We know it's, there's something outside of us, but it's not people or things....

I'm still, I feel like I'm pretty near the door. I can walk in and then I'll walk out and I'm always moving, but it is like coming home.... It was when, it was during my therapy when I started dying to, um, all my adaptions and all this outside stuff. I think that's dying to myself.

I think that's, I think that's what it means and we have to die continually to yourself every day 'cause your real self—who you are—I don't think God wants to kill that, I mean, that's perfectly in tune with Him.... I think that part of me got, I see it as it got, it got hidden behind all this stuff ... every now and then I can touch the Center ... through art or through God or through being with nature, or with a group of friends....

### ANN'S ART EXPERIENCE

## Growing up, Ann says:

I knew I had talent.... I took some classes in high school and really liked it, um, I don't know there was always something, it was the same feeling as when I was in nature and so it was like I would keep going back to it, just, um, it was just one of those things that helped center me.... It's just an un-self-consciousness and like an otherness, um, it's like, it's just like play and freedom and love.

## At other times Ann says her co-dependency is acted out through her art.

No, my co-dependent art's when ... it's not out of joy. It's just out of, well, I have to do this and, um, people are expecting this, or people know that I paint, or I told them I would do it, and I'm gonna do it ... I don't just enjoy it.

## Ann talks about the connection between her spirituality and her art:

When I did it, there was something powerful about art; there was something transcendent—I would never have known what that word meant, you know, I could never put my finger on it—but there was something about art that always drew me . . . something that always seemed to promise more, or to promise a path. . . .

I mean I can't point to a time when I said, "Oh, my art is where I find God," but that's when [2 years ago] . . . I took that hold of art as a way to recovery or as just a way to express myself or as a way, you know, searching for that other or for that love and peace. . . . I had a conscious intention to do it for that purpose of reaching whatever that was that I couldn't name.

Some time after Ann began therapy, she did the drawing shown in Picture 1 (Figure 10-1). The faces are blue and purple on the outer edges, going into orange and red where they join. Pictures 1–3 (Figures 10-1, 10-2, and 10-3) use similar colors and trace the Ann's process of separating from her co-dependency with her mother. Ann describes Picture 1 (Figure 10-1) as

two faces, sort of, they look exactly alike. They're so generic and nondescript, um, except that they're like connected in the middle. It's like they were maybe connected next to each other and then they're being stretched apart and like gum, or like they're sealed together in the middle, the stretching is pulling them apart and they're being stretched and, um, the colors on the outside. It's just so cold.

I mean to me they look like metallic or like stones or something. They were just cold . . . just cold and dead. But the stretching's real. It's real painful and there's real, there's a lot of conflict and a lot of guilt and just real painful— that's all the fire associated with the red and yellow . . . like a tearing.

Ann describes Picture 2 (Figure 10-2), which uses the same colors.

I didn't like this one as much. . . . I was really, really feeling like I was tearing away from my mom and like I felt so horrible about it and so guilty and I mean all these pictures are about, about what that was like, but I think a lot of the impact was just visually to see how connected we are, and it's like Siamese twins. That picture is like a Siamese twin picture and it's like lobotical surgery- . . . [when I see it now] it makes me feel sick.

Um, when I was that connected it felt safe and that's what intimacy was or that's what closeness was, but we weren't close, we were just the same. . . .

The distorted face in the picture is hard for Ann to look at, but

it just makes me feel something, and it seems like something honest and it was something real. . . . For so long everything had been okay and I was okay and everything was fine and you know, everything was just fine. And, um, I didn't really need God . . . this was like admitting my pain or admitting something that wasn't nice, and it's not a pretty picture. Here's one of the first . . . NOT pretty pictures that I drew.

This one just disturbs me . . . 'cause it's not, it's not pretty. It's ugly. . . . That's what it felt like, that's what it felt like closer than the one [Figure 10-1] up there.

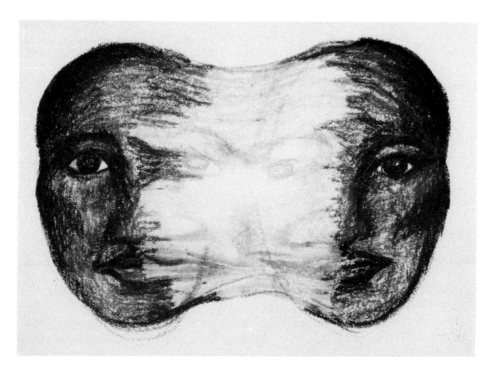

Figure 10-1

Considering the idea that new babies and old people look alike, Ann says:

> I look kind of pretty much reborn! I mean, it started then . . . I just think He's [God], He's on the other side of it. I went through this really — my bottom. When I hit my bottom. I hit it spiritually, too. And I said before that you can't be close to yourself and not be close to God, you know, it all goes in line and I hit a bottom in every dimension of my life. . . . I had felt like eternally far away from Him. . . .

Picture 3 (Figure 10-3) shows a drawing with the same blues, purples, and oranges as Pictures 1 and 2 (Figures 10-1 and 10-2), except a new color is added with the warm tan of the little figure in the center right. The eyes and the background are primarily blue, and the orange rim around the figure looks as though it has been blown open. Ann tells about the experience with her therapist which the picture depicts, and then she describes the picture.

> I mean for a year and a half . . . I could not look at this man in the eye. . . . He said . . . "I want you to look at me."

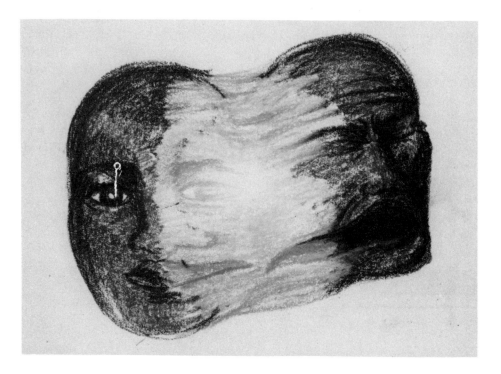

Figure 10-2

And when I looked at him, it's like, it was horrible and terror and what happened was like I got really small . . . and then the world just exploded, and there was like nothing and just terror. . . . I had so much fear . . . he could see me, you know, he could see me, I realized. . . . It was terrifying, and I felt like everything, like the red and the orange. You know, maybe at once it formed a nice little circle and it was out there . . . it was letting him see what was really there, and it was really, really scary . . . 'cause it just felt so little and so small. . . . It's like a little naked person curled up and hiding like from all this explosion. . . . These eyes [in the picture] are like monster eyes . . . and they're gonna get me. . . . And that's what I expected of God, too, for so long.

Ann wrote a story in which one of the characters is a described as "porcelain-faced mouse-child." After reading the story, I looked at the shy, fine-featured face of Ann and remarked about how fitting the words "porcelain" and "mouse" were. Ann seemed very surprised because she had had trouble with her skin as a teenager and had made two clay faces to show just how ugly her perception of herself has been. These faces are Pictures 4 and 5 (Figures 10-4 and 10-5, respectively). Ann describes her feelings about herself and the creating of these faces. It is interesting to

Figure 10-3

note that the face in Picture 4 (Figure 10-4) has the same cheek pulled out that is being pulled in the face of Ann in Pictures 1 and 2 (Figures 10-1 and 10-2, respectively). Ann was not aware of the distortions in the cheeks until it was brought up in our interview. The face in Picture 5 (Figure 10-5) shows that same side of the face caved in as though the separation has been made. In the Picture 5 (Figure 10-5) face, Ann wanted to show the deepest extent of what she perceives as her ugliness. She tells about her "porcelain mouse" and why the word "porcelain" surprised her even though it came from her story.

> I laughed when you said "porcelain-faced" 'cause I don't see myself as that at all.... Um, see, when I grew up, I always had the acne and felt like my, you know, I would counter my, my bangs were real long, and I would have all this hair, and I would hide and I wouldn't look at people in the face, and I just felt so ugly and so ashamed and just so bad and horrible, and I carried that around with me for so long and then I did this [the clay faces], so this is what it looks like....

Ann tells of the circumstances around creating the clay face of Picture 4 (Figure 10-4).

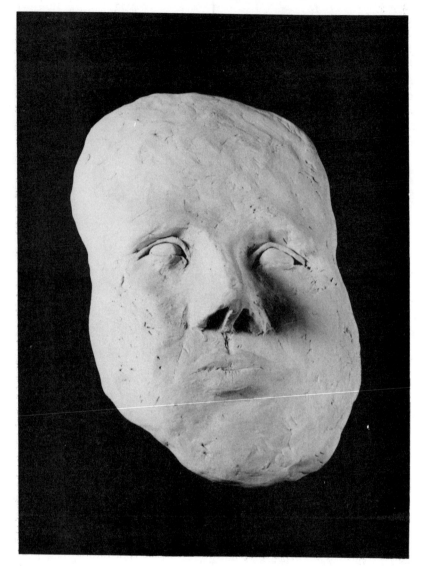

Figure 10-4

There was a time when I couldn't really look at myself in a mirror because when I would look at myself, my face would distort, and it was like a visual hallucination. . . . I thought I was so ugly. And when I looked in the mirror, it would misshapen so I thought one day, I thought one day, if I could shape this in clay, maybe . . . that would help me.

Who am I? . . . that was one of the things that I knew art would help me find. 'Cause when I put something out there and created something, I just, it was hard to deny that there's something inside me if I can create something.

I went out and bought clay and I sat at the kitchen table one night and I did this and I didn't think about what it was gonna look like, I just started doing it, and the more and more I got near to the end, like I moved away from the table and I started kneeling on my chair and I'd have to get up and leave it because it made me so anxious. . . . I knew I was done because I couldn't look at it anymore and I wrapped it in paper and put it away for a few days and then took it to therapy. And I haven't seen it since [in the mirror]. . . . I put it outside in clay.

I think all my portraits focused on the parts of me that I don't like or the parts of me that I'm ashamed of or parts of me that are painful and that's really true, and these are all the things that I never thought God could accept and so I couldn't, you know. I couldn't accept them and um, as I do them, it's almost like I can look at this now and I can accept it and I have this feeling like He, He knew it was there all along, and He could accept these before I even thought of it. I don't know. It's just, being able to look at all these that are spread out here and I just, I know that He's had His hand on me all along, and I've been going through a process, and I feel like maybe one by one He's been saying, "Okay, now you can look at this, it's okay, you can let it go." And He does that with maybe each one.

Actually I feel like, I feel like He says I'm okay and I say, "No, I'm not, no, I'm not. . . . See how terrible I am? This proves I'm so horrible. . . . This is why I'm not okay. I look like this."

And then, He's standing there saying, "Well" [ho hum], and then I can look at it and say, "Oh, that's not so bad." And then I can put it away, but He's put it away a long time ago. He doesn't see that in me. He sees me a different way. . . .

It makes me a little bit queasy [now], but I don't have to run away from it. Actually, I kind of like it now, I would maybe like to one day paint it and then hang it on the wall! . . . Quite a switch.

Ann talks about the face in Picture 5 (Figure 10-5) and showing it to her therapist:

There were two clay faces I did and I had the other one out, but this one I didn't bring out 'cause this one was disturbing to me, just this ugly face.

I had done this one (Figure 10-4). It's like it didn't scare him or shock him. Even my whole story about this hallucination, visually, it was like, you know, we talked about it and it didn't shock him, so I thought it was almost like, well I'm gonna show you how horrible it is . . . so I did that one (Figure 10-5) and it was the same response!

Ann tells about Picture 6 (Figure 10-6), a charcoal drawing. She is represented by

this little person curled up because I feel so small inside. . . . Pretty strange all the way [out west] in the rocking chair, but I she [mom], I still felt so much conflict, and there was so much control, and just like I'm in her hand . . . [and yet] I felt like the only safe place was home because the world was so cruel, and

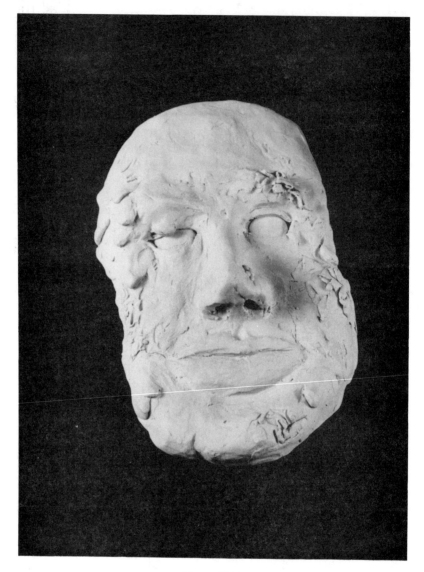

Figure 10-5

I was so young and vulnerable and unprotected . . . so this is the world and
outside and this is all the demands, the pressure and home with mom would be
safe. And I still want to run home to mom sometimes.

I get nurtured, but I don't feel safe to let her really see me . . . it seems
like there's been a lot of times when I've told her things or said I didn't like
things or gone against the view of who I'm supposed to be, and she hasn't liked
it, or . . . anything in any way is insinuating on . . . her ability as a mother.

It's not my mom's hand that's gonna be able to keep me safe in all this, but it's God's. The world still feels that way sometimes. It can even be that cruel and I feel real powerless in it, you know, and I want something other than myself to help me negotiate all that. . . . I feel like I have a nice, gentle parent now [God]. . . .

Figure 10-6

Ann explains the "important" charcoal drawing, Picture 7 (Figure 10-7). She had felt the paradox of such numbness containing so much pain that she actually made a cut on her arm. The cut enabled her to feel the pain, but she was agonized at what she had done. The next time she felt this desire for self-destruction, she drew this picture which shows the bundle of strangled feelings lying underneath her skin. Drawing the picture actually drew out the pain in a far less painful way than the act of physically hurting herself. Ann tells the story of doing this drawing:

> I told you about how after I graduated I'd been through a really low period, and there were two times that I cut my arm . . . and I knew I just didn't want to do that, but I felt so bad and I felt that would be the way out, and so instead of doing it, instead of cutting myself, I drew about it. And it was the same

thing—it was the same feeling that got me past that bad point, but this is what it was about for me.

Um, it's like this is me, this is me, my feelings in here . . . there's something that's wrapping, wrapped around me that's just like suffocating me, and um, it's this, whatever it is, it's like exploded at some point, so it's been ruptured by all the pressure, and um, on the surface I can look like everything is fine, you know, everything is just fine, and you couldn't see this picture under here unless like these are the cuts here. Do you see these sections here? They've been cut, they've just been cut open and you couldn't see what was underneath that it unless you, unless that had been cut open . . . after I cut myself I could cry, like I was so upset and so depressed and so bad and then I hurt myself and then I could just cry. Part of it was just I couldn't believe I had done that, but . . . that let me feel what I was feeling and got me past that stuck point and this picture did the same thing for me.

An acrylic painting, Picture 8 (not shown) is of a many-colored opening peeking through melting snow. This was a hopeful image for Ann. She describes this painting and its meaning for her:

It's like a snowbank or something over a lake, and . . . part of the snow has been blown away or else has melted, and the thaw is beginning . . . that's like all

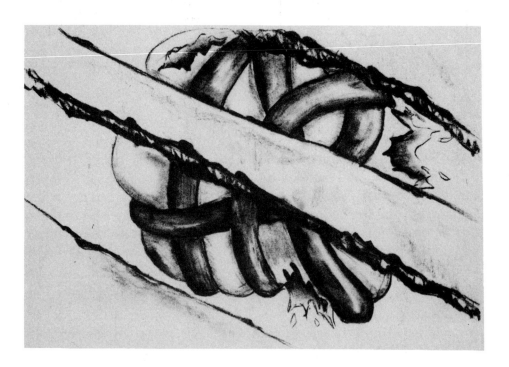

Figure 10-7

my feelings and a lot of need and it was like all coming up . . . it was all covered
up and buried and frozen . . . angry is red and excited, and yellow is happy;
green's not scared, though—green is such a wonderful color. Um, blue—sad,
oh, I think brown is sad . . . there's a full rainbow . . . it's real hopeful. . . .

I think I was feeling, that was when I was starting to trust him [her therapist]
. . . the winter was gonna end soon and you could tell, I mean like the first
signs of spring, I just wanted to paint my first sign of spring. . . . I knew it was
gonna change. I knew it was gonna thaw. . . . It took me a long time to trust
him. . . .

Picture 9 (Figure 10-8) was drawn in black magic marker during the
course I taught which she took. She says that at that point in her
recovery, there was only a little "closet" or box left that contained the
things about herself that she felt great shame and pain about. Her
picture shows that box. She describes this picture and its meaning to her.
The box is similar to the one in the story she wrote during the course, a
story that metaphorically used the image of a box for her co-dependence.
It also described her recovery process using this same imagery.

My big foot (Figure 10-8). . . . I have thought about this one so often . . . it's my
feet standing next to my box . . . it's still a mess there [in the box]. I could go
through times when . . . I was so ashamed and felt so bad. . . . I let go of a lot of
it and the rest I could contain and it didn't overwhelm me or consume me, but
it was now in this closet [box]. That's what this is, a closet. . . .

Um, when I left therapy and I had it in my closet—this thing in the
closet . . . I felt like I was supposed to just leave it be with that, that there were
gonna be some things that I just would always be there, you know.

But when I did this one it was because I was not gonna just leave it be like
there was something, some part of me that was just gonna be that way and I was
just gonna have to adjust to it. I just, I can't accept that.

Um, this is one more of those pictures where He's [God's] standing behind
me . . . just waiting until I'm ready to pull it out 'cause He already knows
what's in there. . . . He, He's just waiting. He's not afraid. I mean, He's been in
there more than I have probably. Um, He's, I mean, He's in there, too, I think.
And when I'm in there, He's in there. . . .

Picture 10 (Figure 10-9) has three separate pictures on it. The oil
crayon and marker picture was also done during the class. The design at
the top is a picture of Ann's disease and recovery. The rainbow colors of
her healthy childhood on the left are covered by the black scribble lines
of co-dependence in the center. On the right, the black begins to dissipate,
and the rainbow colors show again as Ann's recovery progresses.

In the lower right part of the paper, shown in Figure 10-9, is another
small drawing of a woman holding a small girl on her lap. The woman's

Figure 10-8

dress is pink, and the little girl's dress is dark blue. Ann says the picture of the mother freely holding the little girl shows

> what safety or security feels like and security to me isn't at all being trapped in or roped in. I mean freedom is, freedom is being held in security. . . . I mean we're both just like totally there . . . [that's] how God is with me . . . that same feeling of God holding me or being around me. . . .

A small girl in a dark blue dress in another separate sketch in the lower center of the same paper has no face and is alone in the center of a large oval shape surrounded by black scribbles. One squiggly purple line is coming into the oval shape. Ann describes the picture of the girl in the oval.

> That was me and my space. . . . I went through a time when I just hated God because I couldn't feel Him hold me, you know, I couldn't feel Him touch me. I thought He was, what good was He . . . I'd pushed him kind of away, but He was, He was still surrounding me and if I wanted Him, He'd give me a line back to Him.

Picture 11 (not shown) is an abstract wax crayon drawing with a large swirling purple circle containing a squiggly purple line going toward an

Figure 10-9

orange and red circle in the center of the larger purple circle. Ann describes this picture saying, "That's God, God and me." God is the larger purple circle, and Ann is the orange and red which is lightly contained and connected in the purple.

Near the end of the class, Ann brought in a piece of artwork, Picture 12 (Figure 10-10), that she constructed with a heavy mirror background painted to look like green marble. Fragmented pieces of a broken mirror had been attached to the background with copper wire, which is part of the design. Ann tells what it means to her.

> I did this at a point in my life where I'd gotten real far away from myself again, and um, it was because of all the demands of work and people expecting me this and that, and friends and church and just everything had gotten back outside of me and I was operating on how I was expected to.
>
> Um, and this is what came to my mind. . . . I tried to make it so that the glass would be different levels and different, a little bit different angles, but there's a lot of you and you're all cracked and broken and that's what I felt like, like each one of these might be a different expectation or a different rule or whatever . . . so when I look at it, that's how I feel like inside.

So . . . the real me is behind this, hiding behind this and this isn't me, I mean all these expectations and things. When you look at a mirror, you see a reflection of yourself so anybody looking in here would see themselves . . . and when I get into my thing [co-dependence], I become everybody else and I'm not myself anymore, so all the mirrors, I was just mirroring everybody else and I was just a bunch of little shattered, just a lot of little different mirrors in different places and trying to just be everything for everybody. . . . I wanted the glass and the sharpness because of that, 'cause it's just, it's painful and it's a dangerous kind of thing. . . .

I don't even know if I offered 'em to Him [God] like even with a "Please accept this, or is this good enough." It's just like, "Oh, well, here it is. . . ." I don't think this is what's really me, but I've always thought it was, and I mean, it's what I do and I just know He sees beyond that now and it's like, "There you go. You can have this one." And it's just fun to give it. It's just fun to have out.

Um, part of my being able to finally go in the closet and look at it and open it up is not having to hide so much, you know? I don't feel like I have to be so ashamed about all these things any more.

Ann reflects on her art, spirituality, and recovery.

Figure 10-10

I think where I'm in, where everybody told me I had to get to by reading my Bible and praying and repenting, which is sanctification, I'm getting to with my art. . . . God's art is getting me to there, of being a part of that and, um, it's just like rather than being this horrible painful process along the way it's just, even the process part of it's being, is just kind of fun, you know. . . . There's so much joy and just peace in it that I, I just get drawn, keep being drawn, just like back to my art I keep being drawn.

I lost my spirituality, you know, when I lost me and by letting me take things about me out and look at them, things that I'd shut off or cut off and look at them. I mean, I, I thought of recovery — to recover. I've been able to fully recover those things and take them back and also let them go, let go of all of them, a lot of the painful associations, the shame or the guilt; um, but I've been gaining me along the way and that includes, you know, my spiritual side, and it includes being open to my self and to God and to other people.

## SUMMATION AND REFLECTION

### Addiction History

Ann's first memories are of happy, sunny times. At age six, there were radical changes within her family. Her mother and father both worked very long hours, had problems redefining their spirituality, and had trouble readjusting to a radically different life-style.

Ann took over the caretaking role for the whole family. Ann was desperate to please her mother and became enmeshed in the process of trying to make things better.

When she went to college, Ann found herself continuing her pattern from home of becoming almost totally lost in other people and only experiencing their joys and sorrows, not her own. On her own she only felt dead or numb, and then she would beat herself up for being more of a person.

The depression and pain of working through this brought her to a self-destructive place where she cut her arm one day in an effort to feel something. During this phase, she saw a therapist for two years during which time she did much of the art included in this work. She has been in active recovery from her co-dependence for three years at this time.

## Spiritual History

Ann's first feelings about God were ones of freedom, love, joy and play. The warmth of these feelings changed as she was exposed to the growing trouble in her family and the rule-oriented, fundamentalist Christian school she attended. Her concept of God gradually became one of a God who rigidly judges and needed to be pleased. This remained static until she entered therapy, and the therapist's constant acceptance and care gradually brought her to the place where the concept of a loving, accepting God was possible for Ann. Over the period of her recovery, she has reconnected with the loving, joyful, playful God of her early childhood.

## Art and Spirituality Experience

Ann is a person who turns naturally to art. In Pictures 1 and 2 (Figures 10-1 and 10-2), Ann was able to communicate the pain of her enmeshment with her mother and the struggle she experienced in freeing herself of the deeply imbedded, co-dependent behavior in this relationship. The acceptance by her therapist of these images of pain helped her to come to believe in an accepting God again. The fear, pain, and shame of being seen as she really was by her therapist is communicated in Picture 3 (Figure 10-3). In that picture, the orange of the fire of the previous two pictures is a protection which was blown apart with the therapist's accepting gaze.

Pictures 4 and 5 (Figures 10-4 and 10-5) continue this process of Ann, offering what she judged about herself to her accepting therapist. Allowing the therapist to become her higher power (in a very real sense) allowed her to experience the love and acceptance that she needed to believe in a loving God once more.

Picture 6 (Figure 10-6) shows the terrible choices for Ann in her co-dependency. The large, smothering mother love reaches its stranglehold out from across the country, while facing life in the big world without it seems chaotic, stressful, and very frightening. Picture 7 (Figure 10-7) takes an interior look at the stanglehood of Ann's co-dependence as she "cuts" apart her flesh on the page to see the cords of her co-dependency binding her true feelings. Making these truths concrete through her art and having them continuously received by her therapist was bringing Ann closer and closer to the realization of a loving God.

In Picture 8 the snow is melting to reveal the colors of Ann's feelings and the new life of spring in her recovery of self. Picture 9 (Figure 10-8) shows this hope once again as Ann makes concrete for herself the idea that much of her pain and shame has been worked through and accepted, and the rest would fit into this little box. Even while toying with the idea that this box of shame was hers to keep, she now knew an accepting loving God who already knew what was in it and was not shocked in the least.

Picture 10 (Figure 10-9) traces several stories. The top makes concrete her hope, faith and belief in her recovery process. The little girl in the center shows the pain of that process. The girl and woman on the lower left show the gentle loving relationship that Ann has come to know with God. Picture 11, a freely drawn abstract, affirms the gentle, easy loving relationship Ann now has with God.

The fragmented mirror construction, Picture 12 (Figure 10-10), shows the terrible pain and brokenness of the disease of co-dependency, but Ann's soft smile and current knowledge that her real self has been hiding behind that picture all along takes the pain out of the artwork. She is grateful for recovery. She is continuing in her recovery, working a Co-Dependents Anonymous 12-Step Program and is feeling content with healthy friendships. The last time we talked, she said, "If I feel like I'm missing or if I need guidance or God, art is where I go."

# Chapter 11

## NELL'S STORY

### INTRODUCTION AND HISTORY

Nell looks well-scrubbed, clear, and open and has the serene, free qualities of a child. She is soft-spoken, gentle, and very alive in her responses. She is a 52-year-old caucasian woman who identifies herself as a recovering alcoholic and co-dependent. She is in a helping profession. I met Nell when she enrolled in a course for which I was the teacher.

Nell was the middle child of three in her family of origin, with an older sister and a younger brother. She was raised in a rural midwestern town. Her paternal grandmother lived with the family "off and on" during her growing up years, and Nell remembers her as more of a mother figure than Nell's own mother. Nell describes her pious Scandinavian father as the family "patriarch." She says that her mother also was of Scandinavian decent and in reality had more "power" in her family than her "strict" father, since she had "ways" of manipulating her husband to do what she wanted. Nell talks about her parents.

> I have, you know, kinder feelings really about my dad than I do about my mom ... as accepting me more as who I was. Whereas my mother, I felt as though my mother wanted me to be who she wanted me to be and sort of, you know, molded me. ... In our family, um, the only acceptable way of being was happy and well-adjusted, and um, if you had problems there was something the matter with you and you weren't handling things well, so we didn't have any problems in our family 'cause that would have meant something was wrong and NOTHING was wrong in our family ... feelings weren't allowed. ... I learned, somehow I learned to trust, um, maybe that came from my gramma or from just from the steadfastness of my mom and my dad. Both were always there, you know, and I learned how to trust, but "don't talk and don't feel" were, you know, definite rules and, uh, the only feelings you could have were happiness, joy, contentment. You couldn't be angry. You couldn't be sad.

Nell describes her relationship with her paternal grandmother.

> Well, she just was always there for me and she was, the way I perceived her, was totally accepting of me and she didn't have any, I didn't ever feel any expectations from her as to who I was supposed to be. I could just be me.

158

Whereas my mom I didn't feel that way about. And my dad, I didn't, I felt more that way with him, but with my mom, it was definitely the "be what it is that is the right thing to be."

## Nell discusses the development of her addictions.

Well, you know, I can look back on it and I can see it developing. At the time I wasn't aware that it was developing . . . it's the drinking that was my addiction — the alcohol and . . . co-dependence, yeah. . . .

I have two sort of memories as a younger child. One was mom and dad drinking a beer and just worrying sick that they were gonna get drunk. And the other one was that, that alcohol was for medicinal purposes.

Well, it was early on, but then my dad ended up having some problems with his eyes and went to the doctor. The doctor said, a drink before dinner . . . would help to relax him . . . when I came home from college, then I would get to have a martini with them . . . then I began to have this, this idea that, that it was sophisticated to drink, you know.

The, um, first time I ever drank I got drunk and blacked out. Now, that is a real indication right there that, that somehow I'm not going to be able to tolerate the, um, alcohol, but I didn't know that at the time. And that's when I was in high school.

I went to college, yeah, and had some, a few drinking sprees, but not, not a whole lot, but always very intent on learning to hold my liquor and being able to drink anybody under the table almost from the time, you know, sure I can hold my, I can hold it, you know. I'd go out with the guys or with a date and I'd be able to drink just about as much as anybody could. Um, and I just, and early on in our marriage, our friends were drinkers and that was, that was important. . . .

I probably over the years I just gradually developed more and more a feeling of guilt when I would, um, realize that I had drunk too much the next day and I had, I had blackouts over the years and that's usually what gave me the biggest feeling of guilt. . . . I would have these terrible guilt feelings and, "What did I do?" "What did I say?" "Did I embarrass myself?" "Did other people know?"

Yeah, and, and, you know, it got so before we went to parties, before we went out I'd have a drink or two because, because I wanted to get that buzz on before I got there and maintain that buzz, you know, the whole. And the increased tolerance was there and the, um, inability to stop once you've started . . . even if I would contract with myself to have only three drinks through the evening, I could not stick to that, you know.

I quit drinking seven years ago. . . . The first open meeting I went to, I felt this is where I belong, you know, I just knew it. . . . There was such a feeling of acceptance and, you know, of being okay who you are and, and that love, that spirit of the 12-step meetings was just overwhelming to me, overpowering.

I was having, um, and I was probably drinking, um, at least a quart of wine a day. I, um, at least and more often than not it would be the more alcoholic one—like the quart of sherry. . . . I would drink more and I would black out sometimes, or just have little gaps in my memory the next day . . . it never interfered with my work. I was, I think I, I'm a high-bottom drunk. . . .

### Nell talks about the roots of her addictions.

I think that co-dependence was there, I think that was there from the time I was little. I think that was so much a part of my family of origin. I think that I took care of my mother from the time I knew what her needs were, from very, very early.

I think the alcoholism was there also from the beginning because I believe biochemically I have that predisposition because there's alcoholism in my . . . my mother. . . . Well, I think she was, an alcoholic. . . . I believe she could be.

### Nell tells of her co-dependency with her chemically dependent son, Ray.

I could tell that there was a very definite co-dependence between Ray and me. . . . I would do things like make sure he got up and went to school, make sure, I did things for him and I should have, you know, that would have been better to allow him to. . . . I was taking responsibility for him, yeah. And, I mean, it was agonizing for me to see him doing this to himself. And, I mean, emotionally I was very, it, um, what's the right word . . . enmeshed.

And what's interesting to me is, is what I've gotten in touch with fairly recently is this same feeling, um, of needing to, and it's this co-dependence that I had for my mom, I have the same feeling with Ray. It's, it's like somehow I have a responsibility for her I had, for her, especially for her emotional stability and the same I have for Ray. . . . Caretaking, more, not physical needs as much as emotional needs.

### Nell traces her spiritual journey.

I have felt pursued by God. . . . Somehow I was able to get a feeling of a personal and loving God from the time I was little. . . . My [maternal] grandpa had a farm in Nebraska and we would spend some, week or two or whatever, there in the summertime and this was one summer when we were out there and for some reason I was sleeping alone in one of the bedrooms upstairs. . . .

I loved being on the farm and there was just always a, I think I've always also felt a feeling of oneness with nature and the universe somehow just going together, you know. And I woke up very early one morning and as far as I know nobody else was, there was nobody around. . . . I remember waking up and it was summer and the window was wide open and looking out and, and smelling the air and the dampness of the earth and, and you know, little bit of a breeze and hearing the doves making the, the mourning doves making their, their sound, their cooing, or the call that they make. And feeling that, just feeling somehow a oneness with the universe and a total, you know, peace within and outside of me and a presence of God and a presence, you know, just knowing God as a loving God, caring God and I, I don't know how old I would have been, you know, maybe six or seven or so.

We always went to church and to Sunday school every Sunday and, there was just a, I don't know, there's just a knowing for me that there was a . . . God was present.

## Nell also sensed her spirituality through her paternal grandmother.

And, um, she was a person who was content just to be, you know, she, um, like she, I have memories of her ironing and humming and being at peace or sitting and darning socks and humming, you know, she was a very peaceful presence for me and a very loving presence for me. . . . She never had to say, "I accept you as you are and you don't have to be anything else for me" because I felt that from her.

And so, so, for me God, God is not male or female, you know. I mean God is much more than, you know, all those feminine characteristics of God are there for me as well as the male.

I went through a period when I was 28, 29, 30 when . . . I asked all the questions, "Why, why, why?" "What's life all about?" "Who am I?" I questioned God. I questioned whether to believe in God or not.

When I was 28 I had an image come to me . . . in my mind like I'd never had before. . . . My parents had come to visit us. . . . My mother was telling about this guy, a one-time acquaintance that they knew that had bludgeoned his wife to death. And this image came into me of me, you know, do it like that with Mike [her husband] . . . like I'm bludgeoning or chasing him or trying to get him with a sledgehammer or something . . . my husband, yeah. And, I mean, I could not, I did not know what that meant. And it frightened me just, and I thought, "Does that mean I am capable of doing some harm to Mike or to my kids?" you know. What does that mean? What does that mean? . . . That just triggered all of this soul-searching. "Who am I?" "Am I who I thought I was or am I somebody different?" "What do I believe?"

## This was Nell's first realization that she might be capable of evil.

It was the beginning of my shadow coming to me. It was like, you know, God saying, Nell, you're ready for this now and I didn't believe it and I didn't even know what it was, you know. And it scared me to death. And I couldn't tell anybody else about it. And Mike was in graduate school and we had no money. I knew I needed counseling . . . I was trying to figure out what in the world was going on with me.

I mean, there was a real strength there that I can see, somehow God was with me in all of this, in all of this doubting and all of this searching and at the time I didn't know that. At the time I even thought about suicide. If I was capable of . . . being bad, right, then I wanted to kill myself.

Yeah, [I'm human] like all of us, but at the time, you know, it was I could only see the good in me, only those qualities that were acceptable was all and I couldn't accept . . . because it hadn't been accepted before by my parents, by my family, you know, you're only good, you're only helpful, you're only caring ... I wasn't acceptable. That, I mean, you know, it was like I couldn't be both at that point ... I didn't embrace the shadow in me in that time.

## Nell chose to believe in God and her creativity started to flourish.

I accepted where I made the choice for myself, "Yes, I will believe in a God." Until that time, I think that I had believed because that's what I had been taught and so at the age of 29 or 30, I made this conscious choice ... I came to a ... spirituality from within myself as I went through that. After I went through that, it was like I claimed sort of, I claimed more for myself ... that which I have known all along. ... I wrote a poem about that ... I just had a need ... the way I expressed myself was to, to write a little music and write a poem. ...

I mean, in my whole life, I have, you know, "Who am I"—it's sort of been ... it continues to be my journey. It's learning more and more who I am and going deeper and deeper inside myself to find this out ... that's my Journey.

## Nell is still answering the same questions.

God has been pursuing me all along. It's like there's nothing, I can do nothing but to do this. ... Well, now if I look back on it, I can see that I've always been on it [her spiritual journey]. ... God has pursued me. ... God has been pursuing me my whole life and asking me to find out who I am, you know. ... In 1968 when I was doing this ... I didn't know that that was part of my journey, I hadn't heard the words, "spiritual journey" at that time.

Um, to me, spirituality is that which is life-giving ... spirit has to do with that which enlivens, that which animates life ... and so, for me, spirituality is that which is life-giving. ... I was thinking about spirituality, you know, in Genesis where God moves, the Spirit moves over the water—the Spirit and then life is created out of that, and so that's life-giving. The Spirit is life-giving and then God breathed into Adam and Eve the breath of life, and it's the same word in Hebrew for Spirit and for Breath—Ruah, so ... from the time the Bible was at least put down in writing—the Old Testament—the Spirit has been what is life-giving.

## Nell sees her spirituality growing slowly over time. She also sees now as she looks back that God has been with her from the beginning.

I always called myself a Christian, but it's like it took a more personal, personal twist and ... that's when I really started journaling more ... sort of sporadically ... I started writing down a few things.

## NELL'S ART EXPERIENCE

In spite of Nell's other creative expression, she didn't do graphic art.

My mom was a great crafts person. She did a lot of crafts and always for a useful means to give, to sell. . . . For some reason I never did any of that stuff and I never did anything graphic, in graphic arts creatively at all and I think somehow, you know, intuitively, unconsciously . . . I knew that would be taken from me, too, if I did it, from my mom. . . .

It wouldn't be mine anymore. Somehow it wouldn't be mine. It's like with finishing any of this stuff [her clay artwork], I don't want to finish this 'cause then it's not . . . I don't want to glaze it because then it's gonna be a finished, it's gonna be, maybe a finished project is what I started to say, and then it's gonna be for somebody else to, to, maybe it's accept or reject, but it's more than that . . . to have. . . .

Nell tells about, "My Scabby God," the clay figure, Picture 1 (Figure 11-1).

Okay, in the program that I was in . . . which was 2½ years ago . . . a program in spirituality and spiritual direction. . . . Well, we did some . . . clay pieces. . . . And they're very primitive, but I have a scabby God, which is my shadow . . . after reading one of the myths about "Scabby God/Proud God" I can't remember exactly what it's called, but the Scabby God sort of represents the shadow and the Proud God represents the persona in this myth that was read. And after we had read the myth, our instructor sort of led us on a guided meditation where we meet our Scabby God and our Proud God.

At the time, I wasn't even aware so much that they were Persona and Shadow, you know. But anyway, and it just was very interesting to me because my Proud God was like a knight in shining armor . . . this Proud God, I said, looks perfect, but is hard and unloving and brittle and this Proud God sees the Scabby God as repugnant, repulsive and the Proud God doesn't want to talk to the Scabby God, uh, and it's interesting, as I looked at it afterwards—the Proud God also reminded me of my mother.

The Scabby God in this guided meditation, the Proud God and the Scabby God meet, I can't remember exactly, but the Scabby God then gives you a gift in this guided meditation and what the Scabby God gave me was himself. And he jumped inside my body, you know.

I didn't know quite how to feel about it! You know, I didn't know. It was like what's he doing . . . surprised, yeah! And I didn't quite understand what he was doing or why he was doing it. He enters my body. He's extremely totally malleable. He allows himself to flow into the form of my body. This form flows, follows the form of my body and lines the inside of my body all over from toes to head. His shape is my shape and that's how it was. I don't want to separate him from me again. I don't know how to do it, where to tuck him away for safe keeping, that's what we were supposed to do with this gift—tuck it away for safekeeping. Well I didn't know how to tuck this, him away 'cause he was inside of me, inside my body again, so he just stayed there inside my body. And at the time, you know, I really didn't know, I mean, I've come more and more to know my shadow, you know, since then.

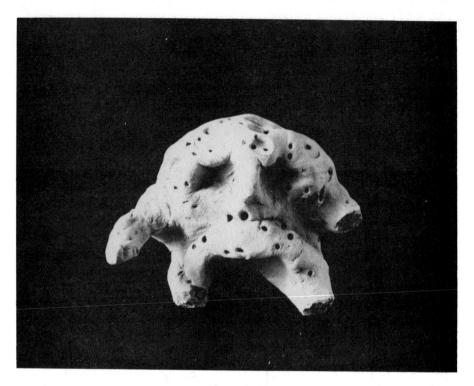

Figure 11-1

This was twenty years after Nell's scary image of hurting her husband.

It was like now I can just accept it.... So I made the [Scabby God of] clay.... We were supposed to make a clay piece of the gift, to represent the gift that was given to us, and so, my Scabby God was the gift and so, so I just made a primitive piece, you know, form of the Scabby God.... I loved him ... I still love me. And see, he says I have feelings underneath. I am real underneath, accept me, accept my feelings.... He gives me the gift of himself with open arms. Oh, at first I don't know if I want him. He jumps into me and it's like, well, okay, if that's the way it's gotta be ... this is it, yeah!

I think when I was making him it was sort of a love/hate thing now that I think about it ... making the clay. It was like 'cause he was ugly, you know, to me he was ugly, and he was sort of amorphous, just ... he was like a blob that was his head and his arms and his legs. He was very primitive, his arms and his legs sort of . . . came out of his head and, um, he was all pockmarked and anyway.

I really, I do love him . . . I'm sure the making had something to do with it, yeah. Oh, yeah, because I know then afterwards somehow we had to talk about it and I really cared about him then. I really, so it was in the making, that's probably really true, in the making of him.

Well, you know, because if my quest is to know more and more of who I am so that I can be more and more God's instrument in the world, um, the Scabby God is a part of me that, and you know, the shadow, my shadow is a part of me that, that has been unconscious that I repressed and suppressed and so, now I'm embracing my shadow.

Okay, the like the more I can accept who I am the way I am. The more I am okay with myself, the less need I have for anybody to, for a co-dependent relationship or anybody to meet any of my needs one way or the other. I mean, because in meeting other people's needs, I'm truly meeting my own needs, you know. I mean, like with my mom, in meeting her emotional needs, I was really . . . I was keeping her connected to me.

## As Nell accepts her "Scabby God" she feels she is:

More, for me it's more, um, you know, accepting the unacceptable, you know. . . . That which has not been acceptable before now becomes acceptable and that, there's a gift in the fault, in the shadow. We don't get rid of it. We learn to recognize the gift in it and so, and that's really what I believe.

## Nell talks about some clay pinch pots, Picture 2 (Figure 11-2).

Two summers ago, we went out to this retreat place . . . retreat center and I did a little bit of pinch potting. . . . There's something terribly significant and I can't tell you what.

I had all these pinch pots inside of myself that had to come out. And so, I went out and I searched and I searched until I found clay because I couldn't get clay. You know I couldn't get just this plain old clay. And I, it was like I was compelled to do this and I honestly don't know why, but there was something in the making of these pinch pots that, that was a statement of my wholeness somehow and I made all variations of an expression of my wholeness because, you know, you make them by starting with the blob and then keep going around and turning them around and around and around and around and around. . . . The shape, definitely, yeah.

## Nell unwraps the pots, exclaims over and caresses them, showing them to me.

Pretty. And here's another! And see, they come out so beautiful? Aren't they beautiful? . . . And then here's the little one. See, my family thinks I should do something, make them serviceable and I don't want to.

I like their roundness. I like their, and I like their unfinished. . . . I mean they're finished for me. I like the fact that they're not anything that anybody

Figure 11-2

can put value on, you know. That anybody can.... If I finish 'em then I'm gonna have to give 'em away or I'm gonna have to make somebody else appreciate 'em and I don't wanna do that 'cause then that's gonna distort. Now maybe that's not true see 'cause I've never really done anything artistically that I have had as a finished product.... But something in me doesn't want to.... They're finished as far as I'm concerned.

Last year Nell had a dream in which she abandoned her child self in order to be with some "important" people. Nell wrote a note some time after expressing her feelings to this child who she had treated as unacceptable.

"Dear little child, I want to tell you again I'm sorry for abandoning you all those many years ago. You needed me to take you home and I abandoned you in your time of need. Let me take you home now. I am here for you now. Come take my hand and together we can find our way home. We can lead each other. When you feel lost, I'll show you the way and when I feel lost, I'll trust you to lead me and I know that together we will find our way home."

She talks about a poem she wrote to her child self at that time.

It was very cathartic. . . . I don't know, put it out made it more concrete. . . . I didn't set out to write a poem at all, you know, but it just sort of poured out of me.

I had, you know, met her [Nell's inner child] in guided meditations other times . . . more and more in getting to know who I am, knowing that, um, there are wounds from early childhood that, um, you know, are ready to be sort of looked at and ready to be redeemed and healed.

Nell feels that all the events of her life have helped her continue to answer her question, "Who am I?" After the dream and poem about her inner child, she signed up for a local college class I was teaching called, "Discovering the Inner Child." During this class, Nell became very interested in doing more work with clay. Nell explains a clay dove she made, Picture 3 (Figure 11-3).

I was telling you earlier about the experience I had when I was a child on my grandfather's farm waking early in the morning and the experience of . . . unity with the cosmos and a feeling of God's presence and of the goodness of all of creation and of me and, you know, this peace, this peace that came. And so, and that memory came back to me for one of the exercises that you had us do in class. . . . Joyous childhood memories! Yeah, yeah. And, um, and that memory came back to me right away. And I don't think I'd thought of that in years, you know, but it came. It jumped out at me, so I, I, you know, in order to honor that or to represent that someway, I made this dove because it symbolizes waking up that morning and looking out of the window and hearing the doves and, and feeling, you know, smelling those country smells and, you know, feeling the presence of God.

Nell lovingly caresses the dove as she talks to me how this art differs from her poetry, writing, and music.

It is, it's different. I'm tactile. It's, um, you know, it's got something concrete that I can hold, that I can feel that I can. . . . I don't know, it's interesting. It's like I can do something for it at the same time. . . . It does something for me and I do something for it by touching it sort of . . . it is a part of me, absolutely.

[I'm] Peaceful and content and, um, just, I feel that it brings back almost that same feeling that I had, you know, that morning of that.

She joyously realizes a dove brought her first consciousness of God.

Oh, a dove! . . . I mean, talk about peace, right?! . . . I've never put that together before. You know, and for the last few Christmases I've wanted to have this dove on my Christmas cards every Christmas! I mean, a dove. Somehow I've wanted this peace, this embodied and I found 'em. More often than not I've found Christmas cards with the dove, you know. Isn't that something?

I hadn't put those two together. It feels, it fits! You know, truly, it does. It's like another piece. You know, it tells about, oh, it shows me the connectedness

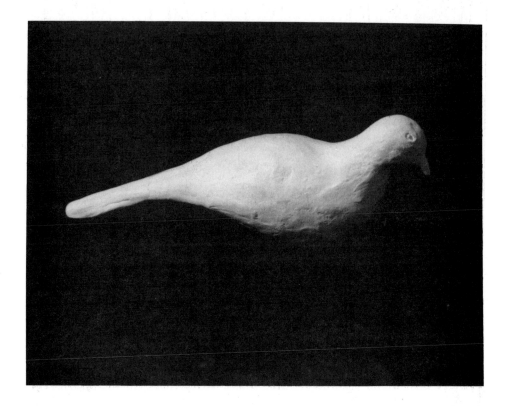

Figure 11-5

of all of me, you know, from way back. It does, just, in a new way, and you know, in a fuller way . . . it had to be a dove.

## Nell adds more answers to the question, "Who am I?"

I am peace. I am one with the universe, you know . . . God and I are one sort of, you know. Yeah, I mean I can say that sometimes. . . . It's all of the same piece here we're talking about. All the same . . . it's the same as the universe. The same bit of an atom is the same as the universe to me.

I never thought in terms of it being recovery of me, but in certain, in certain, yeah, I mean, it is . . . I've found recovery most in terms of my alcoholism, you know. In terms of what alcohol did to me and, I'll tell you I knew even in my drinking days, I knew that, um, I couldn't continue to grow spiritually if I continued to drink. . . . I was on the journey as my alcoholism was progressing and somehow, see God kept hold of me through all of that so that, one of the things that He kept telling me in my mind over and over was, "If you don't quit drinking you're gonna lose yourself. You're no longer going to be on the journey. You're gonna deaden yourself so much. . . . "

Recovery answers "Who am I?" by helping Nell find what she has lost.

Yeah, and reclaiming everything. It's like reclaiming all these pieces of me that I denied, you know. Um, like accepting them back into me. They were there all along, but accepting them as being a part of me. . . . Well, 'cause God, for me, God made me the way he made me! I mean, you know, so for me, the more I can know of Nell, the more I can be who God created me to be, you know, warts and all like they say. . . .

Nell looks back lovingly at her dove and states its importance to her.

Well, you know, 'cause it represents a part of me that, that, um, you know, part of me that, you know, connects me to the universe and to God. . . . This would be another exercise in quiet time. Just spending time with this piece, you know, just holding it, caressing it and looking.

When Nell was in the "Inner Child" class, she made a small baby out of clay. When she shared it with the class, the tenderness with which she held it was something indescribable. The class was silent. The moment felt sacred to me. Nell tells about imagining and creating her clay baby and trying to understand how that baby might feel. Picture 4 (Figure 11-4) is of the baby.

The image that came to me was this baby, this fairly new baby. I'd say less than two months old and, um, there was something about embracing this baby, this, you know, accepting this child within me, this tiny baby in me. And I'm, you know, this is the way she came out and this is the way she's supposed to be and, but I didn't really know exactly how she was supposed to be before she came out. I didn't have a real vision.

As I see her, she's lying on her back and she's totally open and totally vulnerable. She's not protecting herself against anything. Her arms are raised sort of just in openness, slightly above her head. Her legs are probably kicking a little bit. Um, she is, she's not afraid. She's not afraid of anything yet.

And what's interesting was somehow after I did this, I can't remember if I told you this or not, well, one thing her arm broke, all right? And that, but then I glued her arm back together again. Both of her arms have come off and I've glued them back. And like maybe that she's not supposed to be perfect or whatever.

I put myself in her position on my bed, did I tell you that? And I thought the, I really felt when I did that that the feeling I was gonna have was going to be one of reaching for somebody, but it wasn't that feeling at all. What it was was that feeling of total self-involvement in the healthiest of ways. Total self-appreciation, just delighting in being herself.

It was just astounding to me and to sort of kick a little bit and to raise my arms and, and there was no, and it was that feeling of total self-acceptance, of . . . being able to be vulnerable, being able to, to just be herself, like without, naked, naked, without any . . . no shame. I mean, to me, the more I can accept myself, the less I need to hide. And shame is like that need to hide, the need to not expose and, and like she is shameless in a way, you know. She's just right there. She's just totally, totally open and vulnerable and, and it's like she doesn't know the world yet. The world hasn't imposed itself on her yet at all.

I feel like, like there was a time when I felt like this. Like there was a time when I felt, you know, totally, like I could be totally vulnerable . . . it's, you know, earlier than I can remember. It's when I was tiny. But she's given me that feeling that I can grow to be more and more vulnerable and I can grow to be more and more open and less and less encumbered by the desires of the world and the expectations of the world and, you know, so to be more and more this perfect creature that God created. This perfect Nell that God created. She's like given me that, um, that knowledge sort of.

I feel very, um, caring for her and very . . . it's like I need to take care of her. That's really true. I do need to take care of her, need to take care of her and I need to take care of her within me, you know. That, um, she is fragile. She is fragile. And she's been, you know, manipulated out of herself, out of necessity, but now it's like she can, she can, I can be more her again, growing toward her. . . .

I've been learning to assert myself with my mom and things that, um, and to claim my own person even though, I once I told my mom, "Mom, I'm just as selfish as every other daughter" and she didn't want to hear that! Surprised me that she didn't want to hear it. I mean, you know, in a way it did, in a way it didn't. We're all selfish, for goodness sake! But see, I mean I couldn't, I couldn't, that wasn't part of who she wanted me to be is selfish, so, it's embracing all of this.

## Nell says that embracing herself is recovery, is her spiritual journey.

. . . the more I can be who God created me, God created me and He knew what he was doing, you know, and my call is just to be more and more who that real Nell is. . . . You know, I can't see the two [Nell's recovery and spiritual journey] as being different from each other.

## Nell explains why making the baby has been important to her.

I know that she is, you know. I mean, I can hold her. I can look at her, you know. . . . The making is really powerful. The making. The act of making, you know. It's something, I don't know. I can't describe it . . . she holds power.

## Before Nell made the baby, she felt

just like she was in me wanting to come out. It's like, I felt, again, compelled sort of. I felt, um, oh, I'm excited about this, um, I'm energized by this, um, you know. It felt just like a real compulsion to do it, to get it, to let her, birth her, it's like a birthing or something. It is.

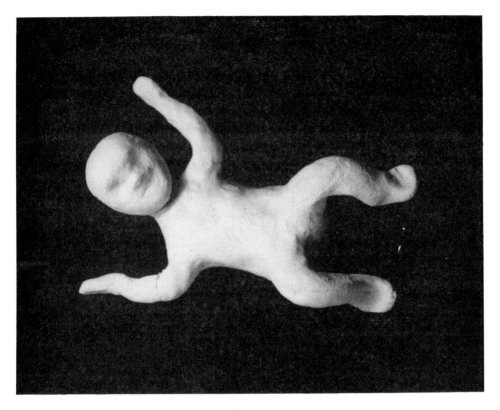

Figure 11-4

Nell compares the making of the baby to the dove and pinch pots.

And the most . . . more with the pinch pots than her. With the dove I crafted it some, you know. These things aren't crafted the way I saw them. They didn't have any bit of, so little of my thought in them. The dove had some because I finally had to look at a picture of a dove to see exactly how it sat. . . .

Nell tells of a clay cradle, Picture 5 (not shown). She made it to fit the baby, although it is similar to her pinch pots.

And then I made her this cradle sort of, or whatever this represents. This is something to hold her in. And this I just made very, very fast that day in class, you know. And it's like she needed something, for there's something about this that makes for wholeness also. . . . For the shape . . . it's sort of circular and a little bit oblong. I mean, in a way it's almost womb-shaped . . . I mean, like she just fits. She just fits in there! . . . I was securing her sort of. . . . Yeah, giving her a place and, uh, and making this life secure, safe for her somehow. That she can be in here and maybe it's protecting a little bit of her vulnerability or something, you know?

Again answering "Who am I?", Nell makes "I am" statements for the baby.

> I am myself. I am Nell. And I am perfect, you know. I am who God created me to be. I am vulnerable. I am okay, you know. Yeah, I'm perfect. I am perfect is what it comes to, you know. I am perfect. Something, there's something. I love her. I do love her. She's just real. She's just herself. She really takes on a, you know, humanness to me or something, human—alive, she comes alive practically to me. She's very much alive. . . . To me, you know, it makes me think that, yeah, she's alive in me and I love her in me, you know.

Nell ponders why it is hard to call herself an artist or a creator.

> It's like, uh, it's not I am a creator. I am Creator. I am, it's like the Creator within me is coming. It's something, it's not, I don't know . . . I don't want to call myself a creator because that then almost becomes a role or something. It's like I want to be.

Next Nell shares the clay mother and baby, Picture 6 (Figure 11-5).

> Here's this mother and little girl and they came out of me, too, and I don't even remember how it was. Something about the need to hold her, to mother this little girl. . . . Well, yeah, sure, it's the same little girl but at a different age. And she broke and I glued her and I don't know if she's gonna stay glued or not. She's pretty grotesque, but isn't she wonderful? . . . I think that . . . and it's me mothering me.
>
> I'm trying to be a pretty caring and loving and accepting mom, you know. I'm trying to let me, um, take, I'm trying to let me do what wasn't done for me when I was little. So, I'm trying to parent my own child, really. Just to hold her. Just to hold her and to know that she's okay, you know. And I want to give her what she didn't get.
>
> It's, it's sort of strange to me. I mean, it's a mother, it's a figure holding a little figure and for me, it's a mother, although it's really, um, sort of, um, androgynous or something, isn't it? And so is the child.
>
> They're two and one, both . . . the feeling . . . It's mixed . . . I can't say what it is. Something is grotesque about it to me, you know. And I don't know what it is. . . . I don't mind it being grotesque . . . but it does have sort of a grotesqueness, you know. Something is depressed about it. You know, like I can almost see this, um, remember what's his name? Northern European—this guy who does this shocked look on people's faces? I mean in a way it's almost that. It's like this, it's a depressed, it's not horrified, but it's a depressed.
>
> Could be a grief, yeah. A grief and like a need here to grieve, to, um, I really feel a need to allow myself that grieving and that, that being depressed. . . . And it's a sadness about the adult, you know, to me. And the child doesn't really have much expression at all. . . . It's that depression and then the comfort both.
>
> I have a feeling that in some counseling that I've gotten that I have been sort of depressed off and on my whole life, although I don't come across as being

that depressed . . . abandonment from very early on has been an issue and that, um, this figure is saying to me, the adult figure here is [saying], "Do the grieving you need to do. Do the mourning you need to do." And allow it to come.

I mean, that's, that's and yet it's interesting, see to me now that I would say grotesque because I'm sure to my mom, depression was grotesque and so, you know, yeah, and she's been depressed her whole life. She's depressed now, you know. . . . No, no, she wouldn't even look at it. No.

It's where I'm at. It's like it's where I'm at, so it's okay. I don't know what it means. I don't know where it's gonna take me, you know. I mean, I guess I trust it. I know I trust it . . . because it came from inside of me and I really believe that's true, that's who I am.

Reflecting on art and spirituality in her recovery, Nell says:

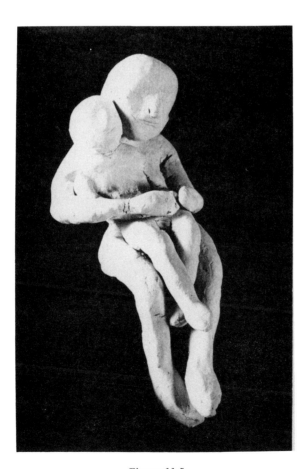

Figure 11-5

It's, um, and through the years like with the music, too, and the writing and this [all of her clay pieces] they've been a way, it's almost as though they've been a way that God has drawn Nell out of me, to make me aware of who Nell really is. It's like, um, I didn't know rationally, consciously and so each step along the way, He's given me a part, as I've been ready, He's drawn a part out of me that then I can look at and I can study more and I can, it's concretized, um, you know, it's out there.

I mean both in the music and the poetry and in the clay that, um, it's like God's way of saying, "This is who you are, Nell," you know. This is who you are. Each step of the way and so it's different, you know, it'll continue to be different, but it's, that's really neat 'cause I'd not really thought about that in this way before. It's like, you know, "Nell, this is where you"... it's almost as though I like to analyze and be in my head and it's like God is, you know saying, um, you don't need to figure yourself out, you know, rationally, as much as just look at yourself and here you are, you know, and once you're out there, it's almost like once it's out there it's easier to embrace, you know. Once it's concretized in some way it's almost as though, I don't know, that that putting it out makes it okay or something.

Nell says as she honors the image, the image honors who she is.

It's available and then I guess it's like once, when it comes out of me, that tells that I am ready to have that known about me to the outside world even though I couldn't have told you I was ready to whatever. Each one of these pieces before I did them, before they came out, you know, I couldn't say, yeah, now I'm ready for me to remember this dove and so I'm gonna make this dove. You know, it was the reverse... it's almost like the image honors me or something.

And the image has honored me before it's even been expressed, you know. 'Cause it's there, I don't know. And then I honor it. I like it more that the image honors me. Just because, I mean, that comes from within sort of. And this is secondary to the images in me in a way, but it's just so helpful. If I didn't have these concrete things, yeah, I mean, it is circular, you can't say where it starts and where it ends. It just keeps on going.

Nell believes that art will continue to be a part of her life journey. She doesn't even like to say she will be "making" art because even this sounds contrived to her. Nell says, "the art will come out from within me."

## SUMMATION AND REFLECTION

### Addiction History

The rules in Nell's family about certain feelings being unacceptable caused Nell to deny and be ashamed of much of who she truly was. Her role in the family was that of the stable "good girl." Nell's desire to fit in and be "sophisticated" had much to do with her early drinking. She received maternal nurture from her grandmother, but felt the severe lack of nurture and, rather, enmeshment with her own mother.

There was very little drinking in Nell's family while she was growing up, and she did not start drinking until she was 17 or 18 years old. Her mother's own addictive behaviors support a possible genetic tie to Nell's alcoholism. Nell has also been an emotional caretaker for both her mother and her own son who is a recovering chemical dependent.

Nell's alcoholism developed slowly, but by the time she quit drinking seven years ago, she was drinking a quart of wine a day and more than that when she went out socially.

### Spiritual History

Nell's higher power is God. Nell remembers, as a small child, feeling a conscious awareness of God's presence. Through her experience of nature and her senses, she was aware of a "personal and loving" God. She later questioned her childhood beliefs and eventually came to her continuously growing adult faith in God.

Spiritual journey and recovery mean the same thing to Nell. The question she has asked herself in her life and recovery is "Who am I?" and as the answers continue to unfold, she is becoming more connected with herself. She believes that the more fully she becomes who God created her to be, the closer she comes to God.

### Art and Spirituality Experience

Nell experienced her spirituality and spiritual growth through writing and music earlier in her life. She hesitated to do graphic art because she felt that if there was a product coming out of her being, it would be taken from her. When she does clay pieces, they feel like a part of herself.

Over the last several years, Nell has created a number of clay pieces.

Each one of them has been a richly rewarding part of her spiritual journey, helping her to answer yet more of her "Who am I?" question. Her "Scabby God," Picture 1 (Figure 11-1) enabled her to love and embrace the "shadow" part of herself she had found so frightening years earlier when she was trying to be a totally good co-dependent. The repetitious circular motion of the pinch pots, Picture 2 (Figure 11-2), gave her an image of wholeness through the roundness, and yet she finds herself thoroughly enjoying an acceptance of their unfinishedness. All of Nell's clay work is a wonderful tactile adventure for her. Both Nell and the clay pieces seem to give life to each other as she caresses and touches them. That is interesting because Nell says that spirituality is anything life-giving, as God is the giver of life.

Nell said the dove in Picture 3 (Figure 11-3) involved conscious cognitive activity while she was making it. She says the other pieces are more entirely emotional, almost being birthed out of her. The dove in her childhood memory represents her first conscious sensing of God's presence in her childhood. She handles it gently.

Picture 4 (Figure 11-4), the clay model of her baby self, gave Nell an opportunity to love and caress and hold her child self. She even put herself in the vulnerable position of the baby to see how that felt. It has enabled her to imagine and desire even a greater vulnerability for herself. She created the "womb"-like cradle, Picture 5 (not shown), to hold and care for this baby self in yet another way. She likes to see the oval circular top of this piece because it is reminiscent for her of the roundness of the pinch pots.

Picture 6 (Figure 11-5) shows a mom and little girl whom Nell calls "grotesque." She accepts the fact of this appearance and believes the piece is honoring the depression she has experienced. Depression was not allowed by Nell's mother, and Nell sees this piece of art as "me mothering me," accepting even the depression which her mother would have found grotesque.

When Nell's images come out in concrete form, she says she accepts more fully all of who she is as she continues to answer the question, "Who am I?"

# Chapter 12

## NANCY'S STORY

### INTRODUCTION AND HISTORY

C reative expression provided a healing and nurturing place for me to be me before I knew about either art or therapy. As a child, I spent untold days tucked in the branches of my backyard fruit tree experiencing the light and shadows cast by the sun through the leaves, aware of the movement and sound of the breeze. I was acutely aware of the colors, textures, forms, lines, and fragrances provided by nature. My creative tendencies were also used as means for coping when problems arose in my family.

Out of my early childhood also came many creative "survival" techniques. I was the second and last child born into a family "crisp" with tension that escalated during the first years of my life and eventually ended in the divorce of my parents.

As the battle raged inside my home, I learned to appreciate the places of quiet and solitude I found in nature and in my imagination. I now recognize my "artist self" as well as my "spiritual self" in that little girl who survived and was nurtured through her total involvement in the lacy shadows cast by leaves or the sunbeams pouring into the cozy pantry.

In a much less positive vein, my co-dependent coping included becoming a pleasing, almost totally "good girl," believing in my child's mind that I could solve my family's problems that way. I followed the rules, but found that no matter how good I was, the family still was not fixed. Inside I felt I was bad because things didn't get better in spite of my manipulations. I hid "my bad self" under shame and tried harder to be good.

My mother moved my brother and me across the country when she left my dad, and within months I got sick in this faraway city. A long hospitalization with rheumatic fever at age eight increased my feelings of powerlessness and loneliness. My mother had to work. My dad was far away. I thought that my job was to be good and cause no trouble.

The situation in our family worsened, and I was sent back to the Midwest at the end of a year to live with my favorite aunt until our family could reorganize. Living for a year as a guest in my aunt's home sealed my constant effort to cause no trouble and be as perfect as possible.

After my parents finally divorced, I completed my childhood by being popular, liked by all, and known by none, not even myself. I did not see my father again for eighteen years after the divorce. I continued to try to make my mom happy. I thought that was my job, and I had no awareness of or belief in God, although I went to church.

Loneliness, an interior emptiness, was a constant for me. I felt better when I was with other people or making other people laugh. I could focus on them and temporarily forget my empty feeling. I thought that I was bad, because I couldn't make everyone happy. When I was with them, I tried to be who I perceived they needed me to be which left me feeling invisible, as if I didn't exist. With the denial of my true self, I felt lost and lonely.

I had lost the connection with the creative sensate child I had been because my focus had turned to the exterior with pleasing people and "fitting in." In moments of honesty, I felt chaos and a lack of trust under my perfectionist's shell.

After college I got married, and my husband and I renovated houses and raised two children. This proved to be a safe environment for me to be more than "the good girl," and my creative side started gradually to kindle again. However, in a sense, I continued the role I had adapted to with my efforts to create the perfect home and family.

Sixteen years ago at age thirty, I found myself happy but a little bored with the suburban, materially oriented "empire" that my husband and I had created. I was an atheist, but began to read about and consider the possibility of God's reality over a several-month period.

One night, by myself, I decided to pray. After this prayer, the room I was in was filled with a luminous light, and I felt an incomprehensibly loving presence. I was overwhelmed. I felt no fear during the experience. The reality of that experience changed me at my deepest core and was the beginning of my conscious journey with God.

## NANCY'S ART EXPERIENCE

Being reconnected with my Creator has caused my own creativity to further blossom. The worlds of painting, writing, and living my life as a process rather than a goal have opened to me. Feeling the love of the One who knows me to the depths of my being eventually has helped me to let go of my good girl image in favor of being all that I have been created to be. Spirituality for me has meant growing more whole within myself through experiencing the love and life of God who helps me increasingly to give up more fear and to risk more life. The process has been, at times, very difficult as the freedom and creativity growing from my faith have collided with my rigidly fear-based co-dependence.

For example, I had always wanted to paint and considered myself an artist, but I never painted. I said I couldn't use my drafting table because I didn't have a skylight! I was afraid to paint because I never tried anything in which I could imagine a possibility for failure. I was well-insulated from the chaos of my childhood, and I wanted to remain in rigid control and not feel that frightening sense of powerlessness again.

However, as my faith in a powerful and loving God grew, it occurred to me one day that if God wanted something to happen in my life and if I were willing to cooperate, then it would happen. I realized that if God wanted me to be a painter, then I needed to be willing to paint and reveal that part of myself. If, on the other hand, painting was not my gift, then my effort at painting would also surely reveal that. In effect, I could not fail. I could only be a willing cooperator in the revelation of God's will.

That same day, I painted a watercolor landscape in two hours which was clear and rich and definitely of far better quality than anything I had previously painted. I felt free and energetic and full of praise for my creator who had "encouraged" me to do this. The painting process had felt like a wonderful transcendent prayer to me. I was lost in joy. The resulting painting was like a thank-you note to God. After that, I began to pray and paint every day. Eventually I had a stack of work which I framed and sold. Within one and one half years of that time, I was selling and renting watercolors through the Chicago Art Institute.

As I grew in my realization of how much God was active in the events of my life, my gratitude increased. I decided, at one point, that I wanted to paint a picture which would glorify this amazing God who made a dwelling place in me. The resulting painting is Picture 1 (Figure 12-1). All I could come up with was an interior of my kitchen floor and butcher block with several plants, one in an earthenware pot. I saw the living plant as the life of Christ growing in me, an earthenware pot. I worked hard on this painting and felt very discouraged by the finish. It looked just like my other paintings and didn't seem special.

Figure 12-1

I put away a stack of work and forgot it for several months. I pulled it out one day when I was heading for the frame store and unconsciously finished up the shadows in the few minutes before leaving the house. Several months later, a visitor looked at this painting on the wall and remarked that the face of Christ with the crown of thorns was in the shadow. I was shocked because I saw this. I had genuinely wanted and tried to glorify God, but it had not happened until I released my control and, in a few moments of unself-conscious freedom, God became visible through the last-minute shadow.

Although I knew my painting and spiritual walk were woven together, I also need to admit that painting quality watercolors enhanced my position as a socially acceptable person in my prestigious suburb. This, in effect, also allowed me to continue to wear my pleaser mask.

Eight years ago what was left of my "good girl, people-pleaser" self collided with my developing spirituality, uncovering my remaining addictive behaviors. I had tried unsuccessfully to please and/or repair my family of origin, never quite giving up the idea that I had that kind of control. I always came away feeling lost and worn out even after "one more try" to make things work better when we were together. And still I would try again. I had learned that one could try to control the destiny of oneself and others by watching family members desperately try to do so during my childhood.

Over the years, I had come to depend on God in many ways. However, at this time when I was confronted with a friend "victimized" by multiple problems, instead of allowing her Higher Power to deal with her, I was only too happy to step in and play "god" myself. In my effort to solve this woman's problems, I found that I made a very poor "god" and only became totally weary, solving nothing! My sympathetic ear caused her to stay "stuck" or come up with bigger problems. My "good girl" played her strongest "savior" card. I admitted failure and this was a very traumatic experience for me.

I knew that I was not responsible for the events of my childhood, but now I was a "responsible" adult causing chaos for myself, my family, and the person I was trying to be a controlling "god" to. I realized through this experience that the painful events of my childhood were still controlling parts of my behavior in unhealthy ways. I had felt very out of control in my family situation as a child, and my reaction was to take responsibility for everything and everyone to regain a sense of control.

The hole I still felt at the center of my being caused me to scramble around trying to meet the needs of others and in this way attempt to meet my own needs. However, I could not admit my own needs. That was far too frightening. Unaware of my needs and God's ability to be a companion, I often experienced chronic loneliness which lifted when I focused on others.

In response to the horror I was feeling over my behavior, I went to God and begged to have my needs met. I finally knew that I could not meet my own needs or the needs of others. I was not God. During this period, I learned to receive and live in the comfort of the companionship of Jesus. I learned to depend on God for the peace and serenity that only God provides. Actually, I would describe this time as a love affair with God. I have experienced loneliness very rarely during the years since. The hole I used to feel in my chest has been filled with God. The fit works.

Through the above situation, I saw how limited my power over others was. I learned about the addictive process and my own co-dependence. The situation in my family of origin had caused me to deny a large part of my real self. As I learned about the addictive process and co-dependence, I could clearly see how my life had been affected by it and how unhealthy that had been for me and my growth. It also marked the beginning of my profound interest in the field of addictions. The last eight years has been a growing and integrating time for me, bringing together my interests in art, spirituality, and addiction recovery. Art has been like a gentle quiet force which reveals and binds together the various parts of my life. Art has been a significant part of my recovery.

As I started believing and behaving as though God was actually a power greater than myself, the pace of my life and growth seemed to pick up. I had an interest in combining art and spirituality at a professional level. It no longer seemed like enough for me to sell paintings for a good deal of money, leaving God who was in the middle of it, out of it. I began work on a master's degree in religious studies which included many classes combining spirituality and creativity. One of my first classes was about writing and spirituality.

My writing teacher said that the artist is merely the servant of the work of God, that creativity is born of God. I believed her and started to write, although I was afraid of writing and thought I could not. I wrote and wrote. Another piece of me was mine and another bit of fear was gone. She played a song about love's likeness to a daffodil as it breaks through the bleak snow of late winter.

A painting, Picture 2 (Figure 12-2), came to my mind as I reveled in the joy of new life and less fear. The picture in my mind was of a giant yellow daffodil with green leaves, which had burst from the dirty last snow of winter. The yellow meant light and life to me, and the green meant growth. The circle of the trumpet was my symbol for the perfect circle of God. The deeper purple color within the trumpet symbolized spirituality.

Figure 12-2

There are three faces superimposed over the daffodil. For me the baby represents the pure, almost perfect, but transparent way we come into the world. It seems as though we have a certain wholeness, but it has not been tried by the challenges of living. The small girl has interfaced with the pain of our broken planet, and her face is over the death and darkness of the snow. The woman has chosen the light and life of the yellow and the green of growth and with this choice has come resurrection.

This painting made concrete for me my early learnings about addiction and recovery. In innocence we are born, and often our space is not treated as sacred. The world in its broken state invades, and the struggle to survive begins. We forget who we truly are and become who we need to be to get along. Through the loving mercy of a power greater than ourselves, we can choose the journey back into the light.

What was left of my bound-little-child side came to me through a meditation in another class a short time later, and this story was described in an unpublished paper I wrote.

> I was caught up short with an image that came to me in a prayer meditation during an art class. The meditation dealt with finding and knowing various parts of ourselves. I visualized a tiny black creature shut in the basement as one of my parts. This meditation caused me a great deal of anxiety, fear, and stress, since I had not admitted consciously that anything so apparently broken was left in me. I really spent some time trying to forget about it and, finding myself unable to do that, I decided to deal with it "my way."
>
> After a couple of frustrated weeks of trying to "prayerfully" force this little black image to become healthy and normal in every way I could think of, I finally stopped. I decided to take this problem to Jesus in prayer and ask Him where it came from and what to do. I instinctively gave the creature's hand to Jesus in the prayer image that came to me. He took it, while lovingly peeling the little black layer from the rest of her. A normal child who looked very nice and not the least unusual emerged. Feeling incredible relief, I gave her to Jesus to hold and, in this prayer image, He reached out and pulled me in also, holding us together.
>
> I then asked Him where she came from, and my childhood house immediately appeared in my mind, the scene of the angry situation which resulted in the divorce of my parents.... I could feel the little girl's fear, pain, and loneliness, caused by the situation in her home and her frightened feelings of fault. Her hatred for herself and her inability to stop her family's problems caused her to finally disappear into the protected little creature rather than break completely. I had cut this little child out of my life after about the age of five, playing instead the role of a responsible person who tried to please everyone. Now, at age thirty-eight, my child side was back in my conscious life (*A Woman's Journey,* pp. 65–66).

One day soon after, a picture of a little girl came into my mind's eye. The creation of the resulting painting, Picture 3 (Figure 12-3), was a healing balm to me in my recovery.

> She seemed like a nice, healthy, comfortable girl of about ten or eleven years. I filed her with a thumbnail sketch and returned home at the end of the weekend ravenous to paint her.... As I worked on her, I became more and more filled with a sense of love for her. I began to identify the child in the painting more and more as my child-self who was being re-created in God's wholeness, which he had wanted for her from the beginning. Finally, as I looked at her one day when she was almost finished, the love I felt for her was so great that I said aloud, "I love you." It was like the final point in the circle of God's loving re-creation within me. He had redeemed my lost child-self and

He had transformed her. Now He, in His perfect love, had created in me a wonderfully loving acceptance of her (*A Woman's Journey,* pp. 67–68).

Figure 12-3

The *Little Nanc* painting is of a daydreaming girl painted in peaches and purples. She looks as though she is about to burst into the fullness of life like the budding amaryllis which is next to her. The jacks and ball in front of her are forgotten as she occupies a space which seems to hold her as if she were suspended between childhood and womanhood.

An even greater healing came for me when I was able to paint Picture 4 (Figure 12-4). It is a mask of the "tiny black creature" from the meditation. Accepting the beauty of my healthy child side was a joy. Loving the broken and bound creature she had become so long ago was one of the great gifts of my life. This little black tempera mask is one of the dearest pieces of art I have. Covered and protected with the black wrapping with only a slit for one eye showing, it looks like a mummy.

As I contemplated the space within me after the first year of my recovery, I felt peace inside where there had been painful emptiness. I

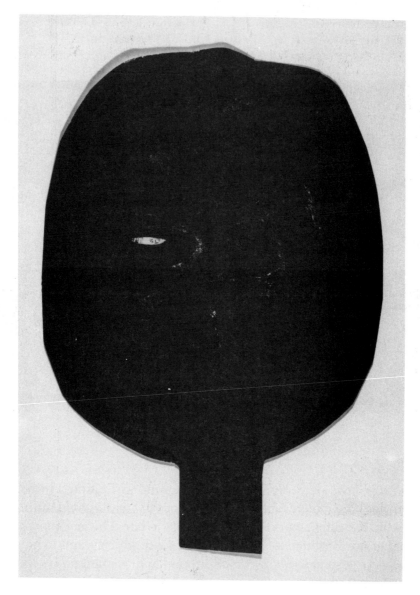

Figure 12-4

wanted to pinch myself because it was as though someone different was living in my body. It felt too good. I considered walking quietly so it wouldn't go away. One day I was describing this quiet place inside of me to a friend, telling her that it was the sacred place where God lives, and she asked what it looked like. Into my mind came a painting, Picture 5 (Figure 12-5).

Figure 12-5

It was a wonderful kinesthetic experience painting this picture. The great oval shape is colored with peaches and purples, and this large part of the painting was done with a single watercolor wash. I was feeling continually bolder, and doing this expansive wash made my boldness fluidly available. There is a quiet luminous feeling about the painting and the altar in the center.

In each of the corners is a symbol for a part of my life. The upper left corner contains the bud for Little Nanc. The upper right has a symbol for marriage. The lower left shows a symbol of a mother and baby and the lower right contains a chambered nautilus shell as a symbol for the whole journey. The symbols radiate around but do not intrude upon the sacred space. In my recovery at this time, my space with God was allowing me to have people and things in my life without infringing too much on the serenity at my center.

About a year and one half into my recovery, I was feeling strong and able to reach out to others in a healthy way. The idea of a colorful butterfly came to me for the painting which is Picture 6 (Figure 12-6).

Figure 12-6

As I studied what butterflies looked like, I realized that they have dark ugly little bodies and snout-like "noses." My still-alive desire for unblemished beauty and perfection caused me to place the butterfly on a geranium leaf and try to cover the ugly parts with the part of the leaf in the forefront. I could not cover it all without ruining the balance in the painting.

After I finished this painting, I learned two important things from it. First, I noticed that the butterfly appeared to be in harmony with its environment. The leaf was in colors which were harmonious with the colors of the butterfly, and the veins of the leaf picked up the lines in the butterfly's wings. I also no longer felt a struggle with my environment. Secondly, I became very glad that I had left in the butterfly body. I, too, carried the scars of my past life, and they were a part of and valuable to the whole of me. Scar tissue is stronger than original tissue, and my recovery was allowing me to fly with a depth of compassion I believed would have been impossible had I not been wounded. I know all of this is possible because of God's grace. I found out around that time that my name, Nancy, means grace.

The last several years, I have continued to grow, and art has been my signpost companion along the path. All along the way, I have reflected the beauty I find in nature with paintings whose freedom, scale and color vibrance has increased with the journey. I will share some of my recent images from a year or so ago which have continued to guide the spiritual part of my recovery. They will be shared in the order in which they were drawn. For me, recovery is an ongoing process of continued growth into wholeness.

Picture 7 (Figure 12-7) is a wax crayon drawing of a chasm. The black chasm with black cracks reaching out into dry brown dirt looks quite unpleasant. I drew it during a time when I was taking a big risk and doing something new and challenging. These are the notes I wrote about it at the time.

> My chasm is knurled, filled with energy and pain, reaching out, trying to grow, cracking new ground ... painful, grinding, pushing, opening, frightening ... dark, necessary, growing, energy filled, alive ... pulling, pushing. My chasm is filled with energy. I am surprised that I am not afraid of it. It is so dark and foreboding. I like it. I feel curious and energized by it. I feel proud of its energy and have the desire to push the cracks and growth further.
>
> I'm almost always on the cutting edge of living and growing. It is sometimes scary to me, and I'm afraid to look down and not be able to see. I consistently choose to be bold and to stretch out and grow into new territory, cracking open, being vulnerable, being sometimes a bit raw as a result. I realize that my life is filled with choice and that I choose to live the way I do.

I am very aware of the fact that my willingness to risk comes out of the faith that I have in God. I would never have been able to admit to a chasm like this one if I didn't believe that God could get me through it. I am aware now that fear is what makes this chasm feel so dangerous to me. I drew another chasm recently, and it was far gentler. I was more centered on God's ability to get me across than on my fear about the difficulty. Recovery continues.

I drew Picture 8 (Figure 12-8) which is of an early memory. I drew it during a time when I was struggling with my perfectionism and recognizing my actual lack of control in many circumstances. Perfectionism and

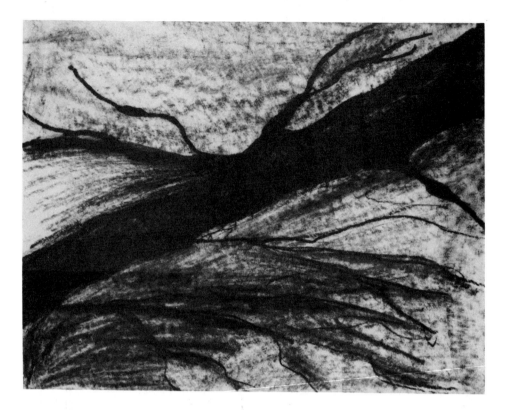

Figure 12-7

control are characteristics of addiction, and learning to let go of these behaviors has been an ongoing part of my spiritual walk. Following are some reflections about this early memory drawing which I wrote at the time I did the drawing.

> I drew the hollyhock-covered side of the Wisconsin house where I lived until I was eight years old. I am in the foreground of the picture, head to waist from the back, wearing a white blouse with a ruffled top, pulled down a bit and exposing my neck and shoulders. The driveway is ahead of me, going down the hill to the square, blackened space of the open garage door. In the memory, but not apparent in the picture, is the fact that I was running home from school and had just wet my pants at that moment.
>
> The picture is idyllic, light, fluffy, and pastel. The black open door presents quite a contrast to the rest of the picture and is most prominent for me. The "perfect" scene, interrupted by the painful "unpretty" wetting of my pants . . . or the open gaping black space of the garage door.
>
> It is still painful to me that the imperfections are there. I am open, I am

willing to see, but it hurts. Jesus said, "Blessed are those who mourn, for they shall be comforted." I have been going through the mourning process of my lost perfect, fantasy world of all pastels, and I feel ready to accept God's comfort in my imperfection much of the time now. This memory of then certainly speaks to me of my life process now.

Figure 12-8

Several months and much growth later I looked back at the drawings of the early memory and the chasm drawings, Pictures 8 and 7. I include the following notes from this later date which show a gentler, more compassionate view than previously. I had this to say about the same early memory.

> She is so lightly drawn and looks so fragile to me that I could weep as I see her bravely facing the dark door of the garage, i.e., the unknown. She is ready to face the monster, but she is afraid. Her shoulders are bare, and she is very still, frozen in time. I admire her and love her. My heart aches for the willingness she has to enter into the frightening unknown. She is flanked by the safe comfort of those hollyhocks which boundary both the girl and the picture. I feel pride for her, for me for entering into the choice of facing more of my darkness. I say with the fellow in the Bible, "Once I was blind and now I can see."

And this to say about the chasm.

> The chasm holds the same darkness as the garage door, and the brown earth around it is the color of the girl's hair. The earth is cracking into the chasm, in a sense, entering into it just as the girl is entering into the black of the open door. The darkness of the chasm has a great clarity to it.

Through art, the path appears to be opening up before me. I continue walking the path because I believe it contains messages and signposts from God along the way.

Picture 9 (Figure 12-9) appeared a couple of months later as a picture drawn by me in a dream I had. We were having financial difficulties in our family at this time, and this is an area in which I experience particular fear and chaos because my family of origin was destroyed because of financial instability. The desire for everything to be orderly and under my control are co-dependent traits of mine, and sometimes it is hard for me to believe that God can create order out of my life as well as I can. I am speaking about the areas over which I have no control after I have done my best. I believe God's best for me is to be willing to let go and trust Him when I can do no more. The following reflections were noted at the time I did the artwork.

> The dream symbol I sketched was of a tangle of branches going to the outside of the paper and enclosing at the center a fetus surrounded by several concentric shapes with the words "In the midst of all this chaos there is a baby growing" written in one of the concentric circles. I had felt comforted thinking about the dream's message that in the midst chaos, there was life. It also allowed me to face the chaos instead of ignore or run from it.
>
> As a former pleaser, charmer, make-no-trouble kind of person, it is very

hard to be honest about not being totally happy and together. I guess this was a place for me to practice honesty, living my own process rather than denying it.

After drawing the dream image above, birthing symbols began to appear in my mind's eye. As a result of the following process of journaling and drawing whatever came into my mind, another painting emerged, Picture 10 (Figure 12-10). It is a landmark for the spiritual part of my recovery. I would like to allow the reader to experience the process with me that led to this painting. At the time I wrote the following, I was beginning to believe that God could bring new life and order out of the chaotic situation I was in. However, I still felt the chaos. I experienced what is recorded in the following notes during the course of an art therapy class where I had an opportunity to practice my recovery.

Figure 12-9

I decided to journal after a period of quiet away from the group and ask God what He had for me. These words came to my mind: "As you give birth to Me, I give birth to you."

I went back to the group feeling quieted, at peace, and a little sad. Then the group focus turned to me. I suppose it was because I did not look happy. I got the feeling they were desiring to fix me, to take the "blame" for my feelings, to explain what they perceived as their contribution to my feelings, or to do anything so that they would not have to deal with the fact that I was not my usual smiling self.

I told them that people sometimes expect me to be happy all the time. People expect that of me because it is a large part of who I am. It is not all that I am. I am at a place right now where I have a desire to honor the other parts of myself and not just stuff them so everyone does not have to deal with my less comfortable parts. I explained, as well as I could, that I would like to be responsible for my own chaos and just live in it until I moved to the next place.

Then I did a series of five drawings which evolved into the painting, Picture 10 (Figure 12-10). I had this prayer entry in my journal previous to doing this work.

Figure 12-10

I feel quiet, spent, open. My last drawing from yesterday feels that way also. New . . . something feels new and more simple. Lord, please give me the images to draw today which will bring me closer to your image. I love you. Thank you for drawing me in. How will you be born in me today?

In my journal I told about the five drawings which led to the painting. This is a description of the final steps in the evolution of "As You Give Birth to Me, I Give Birth to You" which is Picture 10 (Figure 12-10).

As I looked at the birth symbol [the third drawing in the series] the small circle began to look like a baby's head, and the large circle like a halo. The two thighs fanned out to take the shape of wings. The blue and yellow lines at the top looked like light fanning out. I decided to draw a little angel, Christ child, combination image. As I drew the little head, with the halo and the light radiating from it, the wings and the vulnerable neck and shoulders, I was reminded of the same vulnerable neck and shoulders, of the little Nancy picture of the early memory. The picture started to flip back and forth from Baby Jesus, to an angel, to me, etc. I remembered God's words to me when I was journaling at the beach, "As you give birth to Me, I give birth to you." I inserted the words between the light beams on the halo.

The birth felt finished. I am proud of myself for having the courage to stick with and live through my chaotic feelings while I in my powerlessness waited for God's order. Looking back at my journal prayer from the beginning of the morning, I see God's clear answer to me through my art. I wonder how many of these answers I miss in the busyness of my life. . . .

Several weeks later I made the following entry in my journal.

I did a watercolor painting of Jesus as a boy which came out of the paintings of the last weekend. This painting has sustained me over the Christmas holiday, reminding me of Christ's words for me, "As you give birth to Me, I give birth to you."

I have been told several times after doing this painting that the boy Jesus looks like me. I think maybe we don't know what Jesus looks like so that any individual can identify with Him. This painting is framed and in my house. It is a constant reminder to me that as I allow God to be more fully birthed into my life, I am also more fully birthed onto who I have been created to be.

Sometime after, I was engaging in media exploration using a cyclamen plant in all cases because I wanted my concentration on the particular medium rather than the subject. I tried painting it in watercolor, Picture 11 (Figure 12-11) for my last medium. Even in this simple process, my learning was rich and I moved along in my spiritual journey, recovering more of my true self.

I decided to paint the cyclamen in watercolor, which is my most familiar medium, because I wanted to see how the same forms felt in this medium after the experience of four others. I was aware of being separated from the medium of watercolor by the tool, i.e., the brush. I do not really like getting dirty and it never occurred to me that this is one reason I like watercolor so much. Because of the mastery I have with watercolor, I loved seeing the forms glide onto the paper. With this piece of work came two interesting differences from what I usually do with watercolor. I left a large amount of empty space, and I used two distinctly different styles in the same piece. I will address that more in the next section.

When I looked at the large watercolor of the cyclamen with all of the white of the paper surrounding it, my sense was that the white of the paper was really representing my darkness or the part of me that I keep hidden. I have never had the guts to leave that kind of emptiness before, other than one time, and then I consciously felt the need to allow it. The one exception was a painting of rocks and driftwood which I consciously painted as a symbol of my acceptance of death and letting go. This painting, with empty space combined with the painted, is paradoxically more symbolic of an acceptance of life. The flower, standing gracefully amidst the empty space, felt sturdy and brave to me, like the little girl standing in front of the darkened garage door in the early memory.

The flower and the space coming together felt like pieces meeting to make a whole. It reminded me of the vulnerability of my childlike side joined with the certain surety of my adult self. I had a very solid feeling as I studied the painting. A friend said it looked to her like complete innocence joined with complete sophistication. That defined it for me perfectly. I have found out that I can choose to be myself without needing the others around me to be positive, negative, or neutral. That is very freeing for me.

I realize that I do not need to be trapped into the role of rambunctious child or stuffy adult as a result of the people with whom I find myself. The various complex components that make up my person can work together to form a whole, and I don't need anyone's permission to be fully myself. I realize it is my choice, and that I need to take responsibility for that.

It has been very difficult. It has caused me to come to a place where I have had to decide whether or not I was willing to risk the exposure of being who I am and just be. I made the choice to be me . . . approval or no. I feel very good about it. . . . A friend talked to me about a coming together of all the elements with no loss of energy. I believe that is what is happening to me.

I continue to learn, and occasionally I have moments where I feel like I am right back at the start. Mostly, I am grateful to feel alive and growing.

Figure 12-11

## SUMMATION AND REFLECTION

### Addiction History

A sensitive child, growing up in a troubled family, I learned early to hide many feelings in an effort to be more pleasing. I tried very hard to "save" my family from pain and lost much of myself in the process, developing the fearful, perfectionistic, controlling traits of co-dependent behavior.

### Spiritual History

I had no belief in God as a child, although I went to church. Because I did not have a higher power, I thought that I needed to save and fix other people, in effect acting like I was the higher power. Coming to believe in God as an adult was enabled first through experiencing the love and acceptance of others. The experience of having God as a higher power has been liberating, allowing me to take more chances, let go of control and fear, and learn to live more fully in the moment.

## Art and Spirituality Experience

I always considered myself an artist, although I did little artwork and was afraid of failure until after coming to believe in my higher power. I eventually had the courage to paint, and the making of art has been a growthful, freedom-producing, life-filled spiritual experience for me. Through making art, I have recovered many parts of myself which had been lost.

The shadow in the painting, Picture 1 (Figure 12-1) helped me to know that God is with me even when I cannot see that this is true. Painting the daffodil pushing through the snow, Picture 2 (Figure 12-2) allowed me to make concrete my philosophy of life and God's way of working. Visualizing the painting in Picture 3 (Figure 12-3) helped me to love and bring back to life my lost child self. The painting in Picture 4 (Figure 12-4) allowed me to honor the part of my lost child self that I had judged and denied. Picture 5 (Figure 12-5) shows a painting which permitted me to make concrete the holy place inside of me where the I believe the Holy Spirit resides. The butterfly in Picture 6 (Figure 12-6) respected me as whole, valuing both the "dark and light" sides. The chasm of Picture 7 (Figure 12-7) gave me the knowledge that I am willing to face and walk through what life brings me. The little girl of the early memory drawing in Picture 8 (Figure 12-8) showed me that I have the courage to face life's difficulties and my imperfections. Working with the dream image in Picture 9 (Figure 12-9) helped me to trust life's process in the midst of chaos and look for new life. The series of drawings which resulted in the painting of the boy Jesus in Picture 10 (Figure 12-10) enabled me to welcome the newly birthed idea that as I let go and allow myself to be transformed by God, I become more fully myself. The last painting in Picture 11 (Figure 12-11) gave me the knowledge that acceptance of myself and life as it is, is a grace-filled activity.

# Part III
# THEMES, LITERATURE
# AND REALIZATIONS

# Chapter 13

# INDIVIDUAL STORIES
# WEAVING COMMON THEMES

As I sorted through the individual stories of recovery, many themes started to become clear and parts of the stories seemed to echo one another. This chapter begins with a "portrait" which presents a holistic picture of the experience of spirituality through art in recovery that incorporates the themes which are common to all of the co-researchers. The chapter ends by presenting the themes of the co-researchers which were gleaned from the data.

## A PORTRAIT OF THE EXPERIENCE

### The Experience of Spirituality Through Art in Recovery from Addiction

The experience of spirituality through art in the process of recovery from addiction is a positive energetic affair engaging the recovering person on both affective and cognitive levels. What is normally considered complex from a merely cognitive point of view is often clarified and even appears "simple" to the person during the course of making the art or processing it afterward.

The conscious experience of spirituality through art was usually preceded, for the people in this study, by a conscious sense of spirituality outside of the art experience. The art experience enhanced the spiritual experience, affirming it and facilitating growth.

Ordinarily "difficult"-to-express feelings such as anger or sadness are encouraged through the art process, thus allowing the recovering person to more easily access and recover these parts of himself or herself. The co-researcher's found, through art and the art-making process, that the fluid, invisible nature of spirituality became visible and physically available and thus more possible to understand and accept.

Transcending oneself in the act of imagination or fantasy allows images and ideas to come into the conscious mind to facilitate change. Rejected parts of oneself can be projected into the artwork, examined, and released or reclaimed. Powerful images of pain and darkness can bring deeper realizations of powerlessness during the recovery process.

Because of the transcendent nature of a higher power or power greater than oneself, the transcendent nature of art allows an intersection, making, in effect, the invisible visible. The open attitude which often results from the childlike sense of playfulness while using art materials allows greater openness to communication with a higher power. As this openness to the transcendent allows the recovering person to continue stretching his or her horizons, spiritual growth occurs with greater acceptance of self, others, and the higher power. A sense of newness accompanies transcendence, while memories and parts of oneself that have been lost through the addictive process are allowed back and recovered by the conscious mind. Although the artwork often encourages transcendence, it is grounded inside of the person where the image was accessed, giving it very personal meaning and bringing balance to the experience.

The moment-by-moment process of being a living, feeling human being is reinforced through the process of making and being with the art. Being with the art allows one to be with oneself in a concrete way which also enables acceptance of self. The acceptance of not only oneself but others and a higher power brings a sense of peace and unity. The unity and openness of a peaceful interior allows greater transcendence and knowledge of a loving higher power. A greater personal knowledge of an accepting higher power brings more openness to acceptance and thus recovery of self. The empty, lonely feelings of the addicts who feel lost without a sense of acceptance for themselves or a higher power gradually fills, through the acceptance of their true selves and their higher power. The experience of spirituality through art is warm and full and facilitates further growth, bringing the recovering people home to themselves and their higher power.

## THE ELEVEN THEMES MENTIONED BY ALL THE CO-RESEARCHERS

Each theme came from direct quotes from the co-researchers illustrating the particular theme. The 16 themes which emerged from the data are shown on the matrix in Figure 13-1. There were eleven themes cited by all ten co-researchers and they will be presented with a description of each in this chapter. Accompanying sample quotes relating to particular themes are included with the themes. The discussion will begin with the first six of the most cited themes. The first theme was cited many more times than any other. The second through the sixth are all cited nearly the same number of times.

After the first six themes, there is a large drop in the number of times a theme is mentioned for the second grouping of three themes. There is another drop in the number of times a theme is mentioned before the third group of two more themes complete the eleven themes mentioned by all co-researchers. These themes will be named in the following sections.

Five other significant themes cited by only part of the co-researcher group will be addressed more briefly after the first eleven. One theme was mentioned by nine co-researchers. Of the themes not mentioned by everyone, two appear only in the data for the co-researchers new in recovery while two appear only in the data of the long-term recovering co-researchers.

## A DESCRIPTION OF THE THEMES

A brief description of each theme harvested from the stories of the co-researchers will follow along with a couple of sample quotes from the co-researchers. The eleven themes mentioned by all of the co-researchers will be mentioned first.

### Identification and Acceptance of Self

The theme cited most frequently was the experience of finding and accepting oneself through art as a component of the spiritual part of recovery. Art was described as a way to facilitate this experience by reducing fear and defenses, opening the way to see more honestly and accept and claim the parts of oneself.

> Letting go of my emotions and today's picture, you know, I have that warmth and I can see it when I look at the pictures. I can see how I've graduated . . . I see me. I really do. I see myself growing and learning and loving. (Marcus)

> [I] sort of saw inside myself and saw that it wasn't evil and dark, but bright and full of dreams and hopes. (Mel)

**FIGURE 13-1, THEME MATRIX**

**HOW HAS ART CONTRIBUTED TO THE SPIRITUAL PART OF YOUR RECOVERY?**

| CO-RESEARCHER | KATE | SAM | MARCUS | DANA | BETTY | MEL | NELL | ANN | DAVE | NANCY |
|---|---|---|---|---|---|---|---|---|---|---|
| *THEMES*<br>THEMES MENTIONED BY ALL CO-RESEARCHERS | | | | | | | | | | |
| 1. IDENTIFICATION & ACCEPTANCE OF SELF 57 | *** | * | ****** | **** | *** | *** | ***** | ****** | **** | ***** |
| 2. ADMISSION OF POWERLESSNESS 41 | *** | ** | * | *** | *** | ***** | ***** | ****** | **** | ***** |
| 3. PERSONAL MEANINGS IN ART ELEMENTS 41 | **** | ** | *** | *** | ** | ** | ** | * | | ****** |
| 4. LIFE AND FEELING IN PROCESS 41 | * | ** | ***** | ***** | ** | **** | **** | *** | | **** |
| 5. GOD'S COMMUNICATING THROUGH ART 41 | ** | ** | **** | ***** | *** | ***** | ***** | *** | | ***** |
| 6. GROWING SPIRITUALITY 37 | ** | * | **** | **** | *** | *** | ***** | **** | ** | ***** |
| 7. CHILDLIKE NEWNESS 26 | ** | ** | **** | *** | *** | ** | ** | ** | ** | ***** |
| 8. CLARITY THROUGH MAKING AND/OR PROCESSING ART 26 | * | * | ** | * | * | * | **** | ***** | *** | ****** |

| Theme | | | | | | | | | | | |
|---|---|---|---|---|---|---|---|---|---|---|---|
| 9. KNOWLEDGE OF GOD AND KNOWLEDGE OF SELF 22 | ** | * | * | * | ** | *** | ** | * | ** | * | ***** |
| 10. HOPE IN THE MIDST OF DARKNESS 16 | * | * | * | ** | ** | * | *** | ** | *** | * | * |
| 11. PEACE 15 | ** | * | * | ** | ** | ** | * | ** | ** | * | ** |
| THEME MENTIONED BY 9 CO-RESEARCHERS | | | | | | | | | | | |
| 1. LONELINESS AND/OR EMPTINESS 20 | *** | * | ** | ** | *** | *** | * | ** | *** | * | |
| THEMES, NEWLY RECOVERING CO-RESEARCHERS | | | | | | | | | | | |
| 1. IMAGERY OF A HIGHER POWER 18 | ** | ****** | * | **** | ** | ** | ** | | | | |
| 2. WARMTH OF SPIRITUAL FEELINGS 9 | * | *** | *** | ** | *** | | | | | | |
| THEMES, LONG-TERM CO-RESEARCHERS | | | | | | | | | | | |
| 1. POWERFUL AND TRANSCENDENT ART 10 | | | | | | | | * | **** | * | **** |
| 2. ART AS REVELATION 10 | | | | | | | | ** | * | ** | **** |

## Admission of Powerlessness

The theme of powerlessness was cited by all of the co-researchers. The long-term recovering researchers mentioned it much more frequently than did the newly recovering people. The newly recovering people appeared to approach the admission of powerlessness tentatively and painfully, but necessarily. It seemed as though the long-term people were more willing to enter into an admission of powerlessness and they had an easy familiarity with the concept. Admission of powerlessness seemed to be thought of as a way to facilitate movement on a spiritual path among the long-term people. Powerlessness, for the co-researchers, involved admission of loss, isolation, confusion, emptiness, pain, and self-judgment. The co-researchers addressed the theme of admitting powerlessness as experienced through the metaphors of art.

> I feel like I run into a snag like a balloon [that] is caught on a dead branch and it just can't float free. (Betty)

> Okay, the image I think was an expression of the intertwining of good and evil in me, and that the evil was this inescapable—consequences of this fall which the more I try to suppress, the more it came out in my fears and, uh, doing things that I told myself I would never do, and uh, the more I try to squash it, the more it popped out, and I guess basically the fact that I couldn't control it—there was no way I could control myself, how I acted, or how other people acted and yet I also knew that there was the possibility of good in me. (Dave)

## Personal Meanings in Art Elements

Color and shape were the two elements of art mentioned as having personal meaning by the co-researchers. Hues of color were mentioned by eight of the co-researchers. Values of color were very significant to one co-researcher. One of the co-researchers who did not mention color worked exclusively in clay, which might explain her lack of mention. She expressed strong personal meaning when she spoke in the tactile terms of the elements of shape and form. She physically handled the art throughout the interview. Most of the other co-researchers did not mention shape. They all chose to work mostly or exclusively in two-dimensional media, which could perhaps account for this.

I have divided the quotes about color into two sections. The first includes general quotes about color hues and values. The second is about the color yellow which had strong spiritual meaning for all of the newly recovering co-researchers. I used a separate section for the color yellow because it was mentioned in a similar way by so many co-researchers. A separate section was used for shape because it is a different element of art.

Most of the comments about the personal meanings of shape and color were definite and clear. They usually involved either an expression of affect or symbolism. Here is some of what the co-researchers had to say about these art elements:

## Color

white is the open space . . . orange is just that, it's just a slight barrier between me and my higher power [the yellow space]. . . . The black is my anger. . . . The red is my depression. . . . (Dana)

I just drew me which was red and I wanted me warm and then I drew the blue for cold around me in my red. I have my little squiggly line reaching out and I'm trying, I'm trying to reach out into the coldness and black which was the world because it was dark, cold, too. It was colder than the blue. The blue was more or less the people, the places. Black to me means empty. It means nothing, like an empty black room. No fear, no nothing, just empty, emptiness. (Kate)

## Yellow as Symbolic for a Higher Power

Yellow was mentioned as a symbol for the higher power by every newly recovering co-researcher. Yellow was not directly mentioned in this context by any of the long-term recovering co-researchers. There was usually a great deal of happy energetic affect as well as a definitive certainty expressed by the co-researchers who talked about yellow being used in this way. It appeared to be both important and affirming to all of them.

There isn't any emptiness. . . . Oh, gee, it must be all of that crayon yellow! It's definitely my higher power, um, if you were to paint me a color it would be yellow. (Betty)

My higher power was providing both sides of this picture. . . . Because it's right here with me—it's yellow, bright yellow, and it's bright yellow over here, too. . . . (Dana)

## Shape

I had all these pinch pots inside of myself that had to come out. And so, I went out and I searched and I searched until I found clay . . . it was like I was compelled to do this and I honestly don't know why, but there was something in the making of these pinch pots that, that was a statement of my wholeness somehow and I made all variations of an expression of my wholeness because, you know, you make them by starting with the blob and then keep going around and turning them around and around and around and around and around. . . . The shape, definitely, yeah. (Nell)

The circle of the trumpet was my symbol for the perfect circle of God. (Nancy)

## Life and Feeling in Process

In this theme, process living is differentiated from goal-oriented living. One can focus one's energy on possible goals or one can learn to live moment by moment in the midst of the process of life. All of the co-researchers mentioned art as a way to help them live in the process of life or a way to facilitate the processing of their feelings. For example, process living might help one to enjoy or be present to what is actually happening in the moment rather than wishing something else was happening. Process living might help one enter into and move through hard-to-experience feelings rather than trying to avoid them.

This theme was mentioned in terms of simplifying and enabling changes in life. Difficult feelings seemed filled with discovery as the co-researchers entered into them and worked through them. The co-researchers explain what this experience of living in process through art means for them:

> turning my will and life over . . . what I didn't realize was that I could do that every day. So, that space was empty till after I drew this picture and got the message that it's time to make your third step. . . . So I did my third step and I turned my will and my life over and I feel good. And I can do that everyday and I can know that, so this made me take my third step which I was procrasti-nating it for a long time. (Kate)

> But the thing that really strikes me here is, uh, in the earlier picture in order to get to that peaceful natural setting . . . I had to do it through this convoluted way through a book and through some mystical vortex to get there whereas in the later one, all I do is walk through a door and there I was. . . . Yeah, why make it hard? . . . "knock and it shall be opened." (Dave)

## God's Communicating through Art

All of the co-researchers identified God as their higher power. Each of them had the experience of God communicating with them through their artwork. These experiences are variously described as feeling God's presence, or seeing and/or finding God's revelation through the art. The co-researchers tell about these experiences with God in their own words:

> I feel like He's [God has] broken the chains and opened the walls 'cause I couldn't have done that by myself.... He broke it open for me.... With the help of my higher power I've gotten on the road to recovery.... That's about it, simple. (Mel)

> I mean both in the music and the poetry and in the clay ... it's like God's way of saying, This is who you are, Nell, you know. This is who you are. (Nell)

## Growing Spiritually

Growing spiritually was the sixth and last theme in the first grouping of most cited themes. Spiritual growth was described as feelings of closeness with or trust in the higher power and is visible in the artwork through changes in the actual size and color of the higher power on the paper. The ability to make changes and choices, or even the appreciation of where one has already journeyed, were also used as evidence of spiritual growth and seen in the artwork. The co-researchers tell about what spiritual growth through art means to them:

> Ever since Thanksgiving, He's [God via the sun] been in every one of my pictures. He's always there now. Um, it's really strange. He's getting bigger and bigger, too. (Marcus)

> It was a very ugly picture, but then you have this beautiful white pure clean beam [God] just like slowing everything down, kind of pulling me back up. (Sam)

## Childlike Newness

Feelings of childlike newness begins the second grouping of themes mentioned by all ten co-researchers in connection with their artwork in the spiritual part of their recovery. This is variously expressed by the co-researchers in such terms as being complete, another chance, increased vulnerability, new peace, transcendence, and birthing. To some, it seemed exciting and to others frightening. The co-researchers made these remarks about this experience:

> I really felt like I was reaching out, picking my little self up and holding it, and as I was cuddling it, it became me that I'm holding.... This one had a smile. This one was havin' a chance to come, come back and live it all again.... (Dana)

When I'm really with Him, like when, you know, I'm, just like my little girl
[self] with Him [God] and we're playing . . . everything is full . . . it's like I go
beyond myself. (Ann)

## Clarity through Making and/or Processing Art

All of the co-researchers talked about increased understanding or
clarity about themselves or their lives coming with the making or
processing of their artwork. Clarity is used here for their insights involving increasing consciousness of themselves, finding that they were more
clearly seen by others through their work, recognizing their own symbolism, having their questions answered through their art, recognizing
their own growth, and so on. The following are comments by the
co-researchers addressing this issue:

> I think the main thing that helps me through my journey is meditation and,
> uh, then putting your meditation out on paper with the art and it just really
> makes things a lot clearer, 'cause when it's in your mind, or when it's in my
> mind, I'm not exactly so sure of what it was until it comes out on the paper and
> once it's on the paper it's really defined. . . . It's so clear to make out, you know.
> In your head it may be a clear picture, but you don't totally understand it and
> it helps a lot. (Sam)

> I was tearing away from my mom and like I felt so horrible about it and so
> guilty and I mean all these pictures are about, about what that was like, but I
> think a lot of the impact was just visually to see how connected we are and it's
> like siamese twins . . . it makes me feel sick. (Ann)

## Knowledge of God and Knowledge of Self

Each co-researcher indicated that as they got to know God, they also
got to know themselves, and/or as they got to know themselves, they got
to know God. They grasped this knowledge through the art elements,
through their feelings, through their developing beliefs and thoughts.
They described this phenomenon in various ways including the following descriptions:

> It means to let God totally come into my life and help me figure out what to do
> when I don't know what to do. And I may not know consciously that He's
> working through me . . . I just know He's here. I know He's in me. I know He's
> with me. I don't know how I know, I just know. I feel it. (Kate)

> I just think He's [God], He's on the other side of it. I went through this
> really—my bottom. When I hit my bottom, I hit it spiritually, too. And I said

before that you can't be close to yourself and not be close to God, you know. It all goes in line and I hit a bottom in every dimension of my life. . . . I had felt like eternally far away from Him. . . . (Ann)

### Hope in the Midst of Darkness

The idea of having hope in the midst of darkness was expressed by all ten of the co-researchers through their artwork. They talk about this in terms of image, color, determination, and knowledge. This experience is addressed by the co-researchers with the following quotes:

me in my using world, knowing what was out there 'cause there's a little yellow, hint of life. . . . (Mel)

God trying to get me to change . . . [giving me] some insight into me, starting to come together enough to a whole, enough so I could start to develop my spirituality. And it was a sign, I guess. . . . Yeah, it was very powerful [at the time he made it] . . . but I knew that it had said something. In a way, it gave me some hope. (Dave)

### Peace

A sense of peace as a part of their art experience was mentioned by each co-researcher. This was described in terms of affect and cognition. The co-researchers tell about this experience:

And then the final one in that series is just me feeling at peace . . . spent, exhausted, cool, calm. . . . (Mel)

The symbols radiate around but do not intrude upon the sacred space. In my recovery at this time, my space with God was allowing me to have people and things in my life without infringing too much on the serenity at my center. (Nancy)

### FIVE ADDITIONAL THEMES MENTIONED BY SOME OF THE CO-RESEARCHERS

Five additional themes were mentioned by from four to nine of the co-researchers. One theme was mentioned by all but one co-researcher, two themes were mentioned by only newly recovering people, and the remaining two themes were cited only by long-term recovering people. These five themes will be addressed next.

## Loneliness and/or Emptiness

The theme of being and/or feeling alone and/or empty was mentioned by nine of the co-researchers. This was usually referred to in terms such as a sense, a fact, a feeling and/or a pattern. It was usually mentioned as an early recovery issue, even by the long-term recovering co-researchers. They describe this experience in their own words:

> The hole was like the empty space I felt. And when it was gone, even though I knew God was there, I still felt like there [points to the picture of the hole]. I had something ripped right out of me, an emptiness. (Mel)

> I'm the huge whirlpool spinning in fear and emptiness—reaching out for clarity and purity for myself. (Sam)

## Imagery of a Higher Power

All six of the newly recovering co-researchers and only these six co-researchers described their higher power in terms such as light, bright, clean and/or the sun. The language of this imagery was often used for the higher power when these co-researchers described their artwork. Their words in this imagery follow:

> [YELLOW SUN] that's my higher power. Gosh. When I look at the picture, yeah, I become a child again. (Betty)

> Uh, you have a picture of my higher power which is the sun as I draw Him, okay, I draw Him as a sun. (Marcus)

## Warmth of Spiritual Feelings

Four of the six newly recovering co-researchers and only these co-researchers mentioned the word *warm* in connection with their feelings about their higher power. Here are their words about this experience:

> I just felt really warm, it was like that bright light in my dream. (Dana)

> I feel that He [God] is by, through this picture, He takes my coldness which is the blue and the black and He warms me from inside, me, the warmth, the red in the middle. (Kate)

## Powerful and Transcendent Art

All four of the long-term recovering co-researchers and none of the newly recovering researchers articulated the idea that art is a powerful and/or transcendent experience in our lives. This is described as part of the making, the looking over of and the sharing of the art. They tell about this experience of power and/or transcendence in the ensuing words:

> When I did it, there was something powerful about art, there was something transcendent—I would never have known what that word meant, you know, I could never put my finger on it—but there was something about art that always drew me ... something that always seemed to promise more, or to promise a path. ... (Ann)

> I felt free and energetic and full of praise for my creator who had "encouraged" me to do this. The painting process had felt like a wonderful transcendent prayer to me. I was lost in joy. The resulting painting was like a thank-you note to God. (Nancy)

## Art as Revelation

All of the long-term recovering co-researchers articulated the experience of the image just coming to them. It was as though they had received it inside of them and needed to then let it out. (None of the newly recovering people mentioned this experience.) They describe this experience in the following ways:

> This was the first one and starting to see that even though it was a two-dimensional image, it did come out of me, and there was something stirring in there that was trying to express itself. (Dave)

> Just like she was in me wanting to come out. It's like, I felt, again, compelled sort of. I felt, um, oh, I'm excited about this, um, I'm energized by this, um, you know. (Nell)

The next chapter reviews previous literature which interfaces art, spirituality, and addiction. This study's relationship to the previous literature is also examined.

# Chapter 14

# LITERATURE INTERFACES OF ART, SPIRITUALITY, AND ADDICTION

T his chapter is a review of both historical and recent schools of
thought on the interface of the areas of art, spirituality, and addiction.
I have reviewed the literature on art combined with spirituality, on the
theology of play (which places creative play in a theological framework),
on art therapy used with addictive behaviors, and on spirituality with art
therapy and/or psychology. The end of the chapter interfaces the stories
in this book with the previous literature.

## ART AND SPIRITUALITY REVIEW

### The History of Visualization, Art Making, and Spirituality

It is important to consider the history of the intersection between art
and spirituality in order to establish its central place in the life of human
beings. Art making often begins with a vision or visualization which is
then made concrete in the art and so we will begin with a history of
visualization.

In their comprehensive book, *Seeing with the Mind's Eye: The History,
Techniques and Uses of Visualization,* Samuels and Samuels (1984) report on
the long history of visualization and spirituality. Primitive people related
to the world through dreams and fantasy in the pre-verbal world. The
Lascaux cave paintings are believed to have functioned both spiritually
and ritually for the cave dwellers.

Reports of visions, dreams, illuminations and revelations are recorded
throughout the Bible. Both Judaism and Christianity have mystical
traditions which report deliberate visualizations (Samuels & Samuels,
1984). The spiritual exercises of St. Ignatius involve a series of visualizations. During biblical times, the Kabbalah movement was formed out of
the Jewish mystical tradition and practiced visualization techniques dur-

ing which they reported experiencing God or being surrounded by light according to Samuels and Samuels. They report that mystical spiritual practices aim at a liberated union with God. They also relate that immersion in light and a vision involving the meaning of the universe are often visual characteristics of this union. The recounting of such manifestations is important to this book because the experience of spirituality is being examined.

Matthew Fox made an important contribution to the historical literature on the art and spirituality interface by editing and publishing *Illuminations of Hildegard of Bingen* (1985) which records the experience of a twelfth century woman. Hildegard was a Christian from the Rhineland valley in Germany who experienced her spiritual journey via vision, art, and writing. She was the abbess of a Benedictine abbey, as well as a renowned preacher, doctor, scientist, poet, composer, writer, and artist. At the age of 42, Hildegard reported having a vision during which a bright light from heaven entered her mind and heart. God told her to write and to bring people to salvation.

In describing her visions, Hildegard says she was not asleep or enraptured, but saw and heard through her inner eye and ear while awake (Ed., Fox, 1987). Hildegard believed that the Holy Spirit illuminated her (Fox, 1985), and that her job was to light up the darkness for others. Her story is of historical significance to this art and spirituality review.

Visualizations are expressed in a symbolic imagery. A symbol is defined in *The American Heritage Dictionary* (Ed. Morris, 1976) as, "Something that represents something else by association, resemblance, or convention: especially a material object used to represent something invisible." Carl Jung (1968) contributed greatly to our knowledge of symbol language with his book, *Man and His Symbols,* which expressed his theory that symbols are the language of the unconscious from which we can gain understanding about ourselves. He supports this theory with citing empirical experiences involving himself, his clients, and other people. Jung concluded that imagination was an important part of human beings and deserved serious attention. The wide scope of his work on symbols and its contribution to our present knowledge of symbol is helpful in understanding symbol as used in art from earliest times.

For all of recorded history, for some groups of people, the symbolic meaning of sun and moon have been considered as the elemental revelation of the sacred (Lathrop, 1988). Symbols are material things that help us to see what is real, bear our tension and bring us closer to wholeness (Reeder, 1988). I see symbols as metaphorical translators between the ego self and the unconscious and therefore important to psychological study. For example, the use of the sun as a symbol of God allowed some co-researchers to begin to relate to God on a conscious level as warm, loving, and life-giving.

## RECENT CONTRIBUTIONS TO THE ART
## AND SPIRITUALITY INTERFACE

The well-known twentieth century artist, Wassily Kandinsky (1977), said in his book, *Concerning the Spiritual in Art,* that he valued only artists whose work expressed their inner life. This description of his own hypothesis for what makes art valuable, along with his call for a spiritual revolution in art away from the material world, heavily influenced modern art. He theorized about various of the art elements and their meanings for the artist. Kandinsky believed that one must consider only inner meaning when looking for spiritual relationships in art and that real art is nourishing to the spirit. From my experience, art without the spirit of the inner life might be technically precise, but lacks vision and vitality.

In her book, *The Inner Rainbow: The Imagination in Christian Life,* Kathleen Fischer (1983) sights examples to support her claim that faith expresses itself first through the creative arts. She claims that art confronts us with powerful truths about ourselves and humility is a necessary part of receiving the message it brings, using examples of well-known work to prove her point.

Samuels and Samuels (1984) say that the spiritual life is a process of visualizing. They report that visualization gives people a spiritual, non-material model to describe their association with the world resulting in less ego involvement and more openness.

The well-known Christian writer, Madeleine L'Engle, reports in her book, *Walking on Water: Reflections on Faith and Art* (1980), that her feelings about God and art cannot be separated. Her theories about art and spirituality come out of her own experience as a writer and resonate with my experience as a graphic artist. L'Engle believes that artists need to listen with openness to the kind of imagination and vision our society reserves for children and that the true artist is really the servant of the work which transcends conscious knowing and comes from God. She says that freedom and timelessness are available to the creator of art who lets go of control and enters into faith.

Frederick Franck (1973) says in *The Zen of Seeing: Seeing/Drawing as Meditation,* that the artist "is the unspoiled core of everyman, before he is choked by schooling, training, conditioning until the artist within shrivels up and is forgotten" (p. x). His theory, which states that art used as meditation facilitates awareness and clarity of sight, has evolved out of personal experience and teaching others. The inclusion of everyone as "artist within" is an important contribution from Franck.

Peter Rogers (1987) chronicles his thirty-year quest for and finding of enlightenment through writing and painting in *A Painter's Quest: Art as a Way of Revelation.* Rogers believes that graphic art begins as vision. His work contributes a lengthy and complex personal spiritual journey via art to the art and spirituality literature. Lauck and Koff-Chapin (1989) and Needleman (1986) have also contributed to the literature by sharing their personal experiences of the art and spirituality journey.

Much examination of the combined areas of art and spirituality has risen from the "grass roots" level of individual experience. Jung's (1968) work on symbols, and Kandinsky's (1977) work on the spiritual in art, and Burke's (1985) study on art therapy, spirituality, and chemical dependency provide a more formal ground from which to work. These works provide a foundation which supports the value of the art and spirituality interface.

## THE THEOLOGY OF PLAY

The theology of play concerns the study of play in the nature of God and human beings. God is considered as creator whose "creation artwork" is God's serious play. I have included this subject for review because creating and making art are actions involving play and they also interface with spirituality. I wish to examine the effect that play has on the spiritual life, keeping in mind the playful qualities of art making.

Johan Huizinga (1955) set the stage for a serious discussion of play with his classic book, *Homo Ludens: A Study of the Play Element in Culture* which was originally published in 1944 in German. He states that play is older than any culture. The social relationships of people in society create culture, and play is therefore described as primary and foundational.

Huizinga (1955) defines play as free, bounded and orderly, not rational, inviting to social interaction and completely absorbing, with no material goal in mind. All that is really ritual involves play according to Huizinga. His theoretical work is the important beginning of discussion on the subject of play.

In his theology of play called *Man at Play,* Hugo Rahner (1967) describes play as not having another goal but being enough in itself. He was a Christian theologian who felt that addressing play was a necessity for the Western culture because of materialism and our tendency to take ourselves too seriously.

Rahner said that true play is beyond description, requiring both the body and the soul and an expression of spiritual skill, bringing humans to a balance intended by God. God is presented by Rahner as artist player in the act of creation, expressing freedom, skill, spontaneity, and joy as well as tremendous seriousness and involvement through His play. We can see the order, wisdom, and goodness of God through the creation resulting from this play, according to Rahner. He says that humankind, created in the image of God, is able through God to take itself less seriously and to transcend to the balance of play which is neither grave nor silly. Through the play of God, we can come to a balance which helps us transcend ourselves and, in our own resulting play, heaven and earth can be joined for that moment. Rahner believes that art gives humans the ability to take life seriously and still play.

When a person has faith in and love for God, there is an ability to play and an eternal childlikeness which comes with the light heart of transcendence, says Rahner. His work is a theoretical contribution of great value, thoughtfully bringing together theology and play. Rahner's work was followed by the work of several others who have addressed this area of study.

Harvey Cox considered the loss of true play in our empirical culture in his 1969 book, *The Feast of Fools.* He says that the deep joy of true festivity and fantasy which once had an important place in the Christian church, no longer do. With our unwillingness to transcend ourselves, we have lost our childlike unity within ourselves and have become focused on our own egos, according to Cox. His work is based on the empirical fact of what has happened to true festivity within the church along with his theories about what needs to change. This book contributes a hard and prophetic look at the effect of the loss of festive joyful play in human beings.

Robert Neale wrote a book called *In Praise of Play: Toward a Psychology of Religion* in 1969. Neale defines a play self as being in harmony within oneself and a work self as being conflicted within oneself. He says that work is the attempt to resolve the conflict. People who experience themselves as being at play in their world have an inner harmony, according to Neale. True play is refreshing and leaves the player with gratitude and greater acceptance of future conflicts, states Neale. The fullness of play in an adult has greater range than that of a child and can be found in mature religion, according to Neale. He believes that, in our culture, adults often play at the level of children, substituting recreational activities for religion and never coming to the full play intended for adults. Neale says of the adult experience of full play, "To be filled with harmony and power is to experience the elements of peace, freedom, delight, and illusion" (1969, p. 122). This allows people to accept and live in and through conflict, according to Neale. He believes that full play is the response to what is sacred and enables the work of reaching out to others.

David Miller (1970) wrote *Gods and Games: Toward a Theology of Play* in which he discusses the difficulty for an adult of returning to the state of original freedom of living in the present moment that is enjoyed by a small child. As children grow up, they find out the rules of adult life and doubt entering into true play because they no longer trust themselves and become concerned about getting the rules of the games right according to Miller. Miller's contribution is also theoretical, and the important piece he adds is his emphasis of the possibility for an adult to become once again childlike and trusting.

*Jesus the Peacemaker,* written by Carol Frances Jegen (1986), has a chapter devoted to play and the making of peace. She states that a theology of play could help Christians to become peacemakers, as they follow Jesus the peacemaker who has been revealed as joyous and playful in the Gospel stories. In a 1989 article on play, Jegen says playing is necessary to Sabbath rest. Jegen's recent theory about play as facilitator of peace brings us back full circle to the idea of God as player and giver of the only peace that results in true Sabbath rest.

The theology of play was opened up by the theories of Huizinga on play and has been built on with the work of Rahner, Cox, Neale, Miller, Jegen and others. This book provides experiential data about this theoretical framework as the playful quality of art is considered as facilitator of spirituality in recovering addicts.

## ART THERAPY AND ADDICTION RECOVERY

There is scanty literature on the use of art therapy with recovering chemical dependents and almost none when spirituality is included, with the exception of Sister Kathleen Burke's study. Burke (1985) found evidence of mental, emotional, and spiritual growth through studying the artwork of chemically dependent adolescents in recovery during treatment. This section considers contributions of other previously published works, most of which report empirical data that has been gathered on what has been found effective (or ineffective) about using art therapy as a treatment mode with recovering addicts.

Confrontation of the denial of addiction and learning to take responsibility for oneself are necessary parts of the early recovery from addiction. Group therapy is the therapy of choice because it opens the opportunity for peer and counselor confrontation of both denial and irresponsibility.

The following phenomena have been reported by art therapists working with recovering chemical dependents. I have found similar phenomena in my group art therapy work with addicts and so affirm the following as true.

### Art and Denial of a Problem

Donnenberg (1978) found through working with addicts that a visible statement in art is hard to deny when a client's verbal statement is incongruent with it. Art therapy initiates changes in behavior by helping clients "see," by being actually confronted with their own art according to Albert-Puleo and Osha (1976–77).

Marinow (1980) found that art can be used as a form of communication between the conscious and unconscious mind, in effect breaking denial. Art can help integrate unconscious thought and conscious behavior in what is often a playful way. According to Foulke and Keller (1976), fun is an important part of recovery from the desperation of addiction and art can provide it. Art therapy also provides a place to express explosive feelings without being judged or stopped (Albert-Puleo, 1980).

Kaufman (1981) found that art helps clients who are defensive or have difficulty expressing themselves verbally, so that insight can often be gained much more rapidly than with verbal therapy. The time factor is important in a short-term program. According to Virshup (1985), drug abusers are often non-verbal and more difficult to treat with verbal therapy than with art therapy.

## Art and Self-Responsibility

Tyszkiewicz (1975) said that art making can lead clients through their own healing process causing them to take responsibility for themselves. In art therapy, clients draw the symbols and then verbalize their own interpretations and in this way the therapist may better understand clients and help them understand themselves (Naitove, 1978).

An important task during early recovery is facilitating clients' healthy connection with emotions, or affect. Through the art experience, addicts, who usually express their emotions only indirectly through destructive behavior, are given a way to express and see their feelings through the images. This brings together feeling and cognition, and helps them "own" or take responsibility for their own feelings state Foulke and Keller (1976). Devine (1970) found that as recovery from chemical dependency progresses, client artwork often changes from a controlled style to a more feeling-oriented style, indicating a decrease in the denial of feelings associated with addiction.

## Group Work in Art Therapy

Group art therapy is recommended in an inpatient setting because group confrontation of addictive characteristics in the artwork is effective in cutting through denial according to Albert-Puleo and Osha (1976–77). Kaufman (1981) found that group art therapy provides a place where similar problems are recognized and can be seen through the artwork of another, thus bringing help to oneself.

A structured group art therapy program integrates the overall inpatient treatment approach according to Allen (1985). Donnenberg (1978) found that structured group therapy provides both support and pressure from peers and staff where a client can confront problems and behavior while being drug-free.

Art therapy permits group members to express themselves, at the same time giving each person a more equal amount of time for expression. Landgarten (1975) describes how a person's feelings are often spontaneously apparent on the paper with little room for intellectualization.

## SPIRITUALITY AND PSYCHOLOGY/ART THERAPY REVIEW

Most of psychology has traditionally ignored the transcendent or spiritual aspect of human beings, however, throughout history human beings have become aware of their limitations and searched for the transcendent. Carl Jung studied and recommended the spiritual element as part of health for an individual (Alcoholics Anonymous, 1976). According to Jung, integration of the personality is partially controlled by what he calls the transcendent function. The goal of this function is wholeness (Hall and Nordby, 1973).

More recently, M. Scott Peck (1978) has written a good deal about psychology and spiritual growth. He says that in the occurrence of real love there is a contribution to the spiritual growth of another. He describes the spiritual path as a difficult one, but a possible one which leads to growth.

The question of whether spiritual issues belong in psychological practice is answered by Robb (1986) with the suggestion that, if they must be addressed, it must be within the logical-empirical philosophy of psychology. Because of the elusive nature of spirituality, I would suggest that the most helpful studies would gather empirical data in a qualitative way which honors the essence of an experience without imposing the logic of the material world.

Small (1987) says moving on a transformational path requires the leap of dying to old ways, which requires a belief in something beyond the ego, allowing for new life. The spiritual path is other than the path of ego and so does not abide by the laws which the ego demands. Deep spiritual metamorphosis requires a willingness to let go and transcend past known self.

Fear, the cause of much pathology, can be overcome with faith motivated by the power of love, which then makes movement possible, according to Causey (1987). She says there is a loss of self associated with faith development that requires courage in order for the person to allow it.

In my opinion, control issues pit transcendence (which cannot be captured) against the ego self (which desires dominance). It does require courage to enter into more than one can logically understand in hopes of greater mental health.

Gerald May (1988) proposed that addiction makes us slaves of our idols. The process of addiction involves attachment and dependence on something which eventually proves to be unhealthy. Once this happens, the addict has already developed an idolatrous dependence and which makes extrication seem impossible.

The literature on the treatment of alcoholism shows that traditional psychotherapy brings about little emotional or psychological improvement according to White (1979); however, the experience of transcendence does cause a personality restructuring with the result that the world looks less chaotic and more meaningful. Addressing the transcendent element is absolutely crucial in the recovery process.

High rates of relapse for chemically dependent clients who have been through hospital treatment programs are partially due to the lack of interest in the inner person and the spiritual nature of the recovery process, in the opinion of Small (1987). I have noticed that as counseling techniques for the treatment of addiction have developed, the emphasis on spirituality has often lessened and the dependence on technique has increased. Addiction counseling professionals need to address the crucial issue of spirituality.

I have often heard concern expressed about the possibility of the transfer of addiction to a higher power when people consider the spiritual part of recovery. Gerald May (1988) says there can be addiction to a religious system, but there cannot be addiction to what is truly God, because God declines being an object.

Van Kaam (1987) believes that addiction is a counterfeit of true religious presence. I have found that addiction promotes a non-living condition, whereas true spirituality is life-giving and growth producing. The world of the addict is passive according to Van Kaam (1987), with little balance between receptivity and work.

White (1979) says that chemical dependence may be an attempt to see one's inner self, but it actually protects one from the pain of one's inner self. The choice other than addictive attachment, according to Fournier (1987), is to live through pain and learn to depend on God.

The 12-step recovery process is experienced as the single most powerful transformative force in the lives of many addicts, according to Buxton, Smith, and Seymour (1987). The 12-step model often effectively addresses a personal spirituality and has been researched more than any other model for recovery.

During the addictive process, complete dependence on self has brought destruction, and a 12-step program begins with an admission of powerlessness and unmanageability. As people work through the 12 steps they go back continuously to work on all of the steps and thus learn to function at all levels at the same time, giving special attention to what is currently needing attention state Buxton, Smith and Seymour (1987). I have found that the 12 steps can provide a flexible framework which allows for continuous individual growth during the recovery process.

### *Art Therapy and Spirituality*

Gardner (1982) assesses that in neuropsychological research, the skills required for artistic expression are most often performed by the right hemisphere of the brain. I would agree with Beit-Hallahmi (1986) when he says that the psychological processes involved in doing art are the most similar to religious process of any activity. Both provide comfort, order, and beauty. Art and spirituality processes are natural companions.

The arts are signs of the psyche's efforts to become transcendent and enter into an experience of the sacred, says Johnson (1985). I see both art making and spiritual journeying as transcending oneself to find oneself.

Religion, art, and play help structure our healing forces and means of transformation in a society which is capable of self-destruction, asserts Johnson (1985). In a society where the assertion of self has brought us to the brink of ultimate destruction, the need for healing transformation becomes paramount. Prezioso (1987) states that every area of an inpatient treatment program needs to address spirituality. Bill Wilson, one of the founders of Alcoholics Anonymous, began his sobriety with a transcendent spiritual experience. Many other alcoholics would describe a similar path to recovery.

## THIS STUDY'S RELATIONSHIP TO THE PREVIOUS LITERATURE

The experiences of the co-researchers in this book are usually compatible with the available literature, while adding to it. Much of the literature is theoretical and this study adds the empirical data of lived experience.

Visualization and spirituality share a long combined history which began with the cave paintings and continues through the art in this study. The experience of seeing light or immersion in light as a sign of union with God reported back in biblical times (Samuels and Samuels, 1984) has occurred in the contemporary lives of Dana and Nancy of this study. Betty, Marcus, and Dana have drawn the sun as symbol for God in their artwork, not knowing that the sun has been used as a symbol of the sacred for all of recorded history (Lathrop, 1988). Kandinsky's (1977) beliefs that art nourishes the spirit and that the inner meaning of the art reveals spirituality have been birthed into truth through the stories of the co-researchers.

L'Engle's (1980) ideas about the necessity for childlike openness to imagination which allows transcendence was also acted out in the lives of the co-researchers who honored their childlike images and found their higher power. The co-researchers, many of whom began by saying that they were not artists and then found out they were, affirm Franck's (1973) proposition that everyone is an artist.

The serious, deep, and often spiritual knowledge resulting from the seemingly playful artwork of the co-researchers leads me to the body of literature on the theology of play which is largely theoretical. Huizinga (1955) described play as having no goal in mind. When the co-researchers allowed themselves to enter into the "play" of making art and honored the images which came through drawing them, often the rewards in self-knowledge and a deepening spirituality were astounding.

Rahner (1967) says when we allow true play, we take ourselves less seriously and thus are able to transcend ourselves. This principle was proven out again and again as the co-researchers in the study played at making and processing the art and, often with an element of humor, came to accept themselves as they truly were and admit their need for a higher power. The deep joy of recovery found through art by many of the co-researchers reminds me of the lost art of true festivity that Cox (1969) talks about.

Neale's (1969) definition of the self at play as being at harmony within makes me think of the harmonious clarity the co-researchers reported through making and processing the artwork. The meditations that the newly recovering co-researchers experienced in art therapy also promoted an inner harmony which was less conflicted. Miller's (1970) claim that adults can once again become childlike and trusting was borne out in the way the co-researchers openly and willingly shared their stories and images. Many of the themes reflect a growing inner peace which supports Jegen's (1986) idea that play is a facilitator of peace.

The literature on the art therapy and addiction interface was also affirmed by the results of this study. The art not only confronted denial in general as reported by Donnenberg (1978) and Albert-Puleo and Osha (1976–77), but also confronted denial on a spiritual level, helping the co-researchers open to a deeper spirituality, as in the stories of Kate and Sam. Albert-Puleos's (1980) statement that art provides a way to confront explosive feelings was shown powerfully through the work of Mel who drew out his anger and found even this as a way to grow more deeply into his relationship with God.

The responsibility for self which is gained as clients are led through their own healing process via their art (Tyszkiewicz, 1975) was affirmed by all the co-researchers as they got to know and accept themselves and their higher power through their art. In the co-dependency literature review, Smalley and Coleman (1987) report that co-dependents look for external validation and so the internal affirmation through the art is very important. Taking responsibility for and accepting feelings through art, as reported by Foulke and Keller (1976), was extended by this study to feelings about the transcendent.

In the literature review on psychology and spirituality, Causey (1987) reports that pathological fear can be overcome with faith. The results of this study show the "faith" of entering into the art process and drawing helped the co-researchers confront their fears. For example, Marcus confronted his fear of "hating" his adult self and Betty drew her fearful repeating pattern of co-dependency with men. Art, for the co-researchers in this study, has enabled the leap of dying to old ways which Small (1987) says is required for transformation.

The results of this study also add to the literature about 12-step programs. More alcoholics have been rehabilitated through AA than through other means (Arnold, 1977; Madsen, 1974), and it is therefore important for treatment professionals to understand and cooperate with 12-step programs. In this study, some of the co-researcher's themes of art's contributions to their spiritual recovery, not only cooperate with the steps of AA, but parallel them. For example, acceptance of self, one theme, allows one to admit powerlessness which is another theme and parallel to step 1. The theme of growing spiritually is surely a part of 12-step work. The hope in the midst of darkness theme reminds me of step 2, where one enters into belief that there is a restoring higher power. Other themes, such as imagery of a higher power, the warmth of spiritual feelings, and yellow as a higher-power color, all made the idea of step 3, where one turns one life over, seem more real to the newly recovering co-researchers.

This study affirmed much of the literature and in many cases presented empirical data where there was only theory. It also contributed practical ways of aiding recovery from addiction, including the spiritual dimension. It tied together the "new" idea of making spirituality concrete through art with the relatively new 12-step model of spirituality. Reflecting on the new images of this study, which were appropriately visible in the material world we are accustomed to seeing and living in, I realized they were coloring an ancient paradigm which brings us to the realizations in the last chapter.

# Chapter 15

# NEW IMAGES, ANCIENT PARADIGM

The primary task of this chapter is to leap past what is known and clear away the veil to see the experience being studied in a new way. A synthesis which realizes the essence of experiencing spirituality through the imagery of art in recovery builds on the depiction or portrait in Chapter 13.

The experience of spirituality in recovery revealed via imagery is not new. The following was written by Bill W., one of the founders of Alcoholics Anonymous, about an experience which happened prior to the beginning of his recovery from alcoholism and the founding of the AA fellowship in 1935:

> My depression deepened unbearably, and finally it seemed to me as though I were at the very bottom of the pit. For the moment, the last vestige of my proud obstinacy was crushed. All at once I found myself crying out, "If there is a God, let Him show Himself! I am ready to do anything, anything!"
> Suddenly the room lit up with a great white light. It seemed to me, in the mind's eye, that I was on a mountain and that a wind not of air but of spirit was blowing. And then it burst upon me that I was a free man. Slowly the ecstasy subsided. I lay on the bed, but now for a time I was in another world, a new world of consciousness. All about me and through me there was a wonderful feeling of Presence, and I thought to myself, "So this is the God of the preachers!" (*As Bill Sees It,* 1980, p. 2)

The above quote relates the story of Bill W. in which he ties together his admission of powerlessness, the visual imagery of "the great white light" of his spiritual awakening and the visual picture which followed in his mind's eye, leading to "wonderful feeling" of the presence of God. Bill's story of recovery from alcoholism which includes a spiritual dimension has been a testimony to the twentieth century world through the blossoming of the AA program.

In the book *Alcoholics Anonymous* (1976) there is a story of a client of the famous psychiatrist, Doctor Carl Jung. This client finished his treatment with Doctor Jung, felt relapse was unthinkable and proceeded to relapse. The client went back to Doctor Jung and begged the doctor for the whole truth about his case. Doctor Jung told him that in his opinion the client's disease was hopeless.

> The doctor said: "You have the mind of a chronic alcoholic. I have never seen one single case recover, where that state of mind existed to the extent that it does in you." Our friend felt as though the gates of hell had closed on him with a clang.
>
> He said to the doctor, "Is there no exception?"
>
> "Yes," replied the doctor, "there is. Exceptions to cases such as yours have been occurring since early times. Here and there, once in a while, alcoholics have had what are called vital spiritual experiences. To me these occurrences are phenomena. They appear to be in the nature of huge emotional displacements and rearrangements. Ideas, emotions, and attitudes which were once the guiding forces of the lives of these men are suddenly cast to one side, and a completely new set of conceptions and motives begin to dominate them. In fact, I have been trying to produce some such emotional rearrangement within you. With many individuals the methods which I employed are successful, but I have never been successful with an alcoholic of your description."
>
> Upon hearing this, our friend was somewhat relieved, for he reflected that, after all, he was a good church member. This hope, however, was destroyed by the doctor's telling him that while his religious convictions were very good, in his case they did not spell the necessary vital spiritual experience (*Alcoholics Anonymous*, 1976, p. 27).

The client whose story is recorded above was eventually able to enjoy the freedom of recovery from his alcoholism because of his opening to a personal spirituality. The necessity of genuine spirituality as a part of the recovery process from an addiction is not a new idea and has been affirmed by many others in addition to the eminent Doctor Carl Jung.

This book recounted ten stories which are similar to the above stories in terms of the recovery from addiction which includes a spiritual dimension. The stories in this study are current, many decades after Bill W.'s experience and Doctor Jung's client's experience. One difference in these stories is the fact that they have been recorded through art media and often lived through the art process.

## NEW IMAGES, A VISIBLE
## AND CONCRETE SPIRITUALITY FOR TODAY

Through the stories in this study, art emerged as a valuable facilitator of holism in the experience studied. Art can make spirituality not only visible during the recovery process but also concrete—in effect, connecting the physical world with the spiritual world. The spiritual world is translated through art into comprehensible terms making spirituality visible—sort of like spray painting a ghost. This simple image clarified, for me, the essence of what was occurring in the experience studied.

Someone who is not consciously aware of spirituality but would like to be, such as a newly recovering person, often doesn't know how to connect with a personal and conscious spirituality. A person who is newly conscious of spirituality often finds it difficult to understand when the material world has been the focus.

The co-researchers who had been dangerously involved in looking for "salvation" through the addictive behaviors of the physical world were given a chance to "see" their spirituality and spiritual growth materialize through art media and the making of art. A further look at the implications of what a visible spirituality might mean to the Western culture of our times follows.

All of the twentieth century co-researchers in this study found their personal spirituality was grounded and growing through the physical process of making and then seeing and being with their art. A clearer and deeper experience and understanding of the spiritual growth process was thus facilitated appropriately through concrete means, as spirituality is often hard to grasp in the Western culture because of the material focus. Even in a fast-paced, goal-oriented culture, art is a slow-paced, process-oriented activity.

If a higher power is truly greater than the person who is believing, then a willingness to live in a daily process of faith is necessary. A person balances his or her goals with living on the path laid out by the higher power, moment by moment. The visibility of art not only helped the co-researchers see where they were on the path of spirituality, but it helped each of them move along.

Making invisible spirituality visible is not a new idea, but rather a very old one. Hildegard of Bingen, a twelfth century mystic nun, said that she "received visions according to the will of God while I was awake and alert with a clear mind, with the innermost eyes and ears of a person" (Hozeski, 1986, p. 2). She had received visions from the time she was a child, but when she was forty-two years old in the year 1141 a "light coming from heaven poured" (Hozeski, 1986, p. 2) into her mind, and she was told by God to write down what she saw and heard.

Hildegard was at first very reticent to do this and decided to cover up her abilities because she was worried about the opinions of others. She proceeded to become ill and bedridden for a long while. When she finally decided to courageously share what she saw and heard, she quickly regained her health and eventually became a writer, artist, musician, and scientist. I could make a very good case for a diagnosis for Hildegard of what we currently refer to as co-dependency. She was concerned about disapproval from the hierarchy of her patriarchal church and the larger community and consequently kept herself locked inside herself until it made her sick. Only in reclaiming who she was, grounded in her spirituality, did she start to recover. After her recovery, she honored the images of her visions, wrote nine books, and did much other fruitful work during her lifetime. Interestingly, living her life fully and honoring what she knew and who she was did not bring the discredit she feared, but rather respect, even from the head of her patriarchal church.

Art provided a way for each of the co-researchers to "see" and grow in their spirituality. As they opened themselves to the images of their minds' eyes and made them concretely visible through their art, they grasped where they were and moved along their spiritual paths. This facilitated their entrance into early recovery as well as deepened their long-term journey.

I see a creation-centered spirituality unfolding for the co-researchers through their art process. The following excerpt is from an interview with Matthew Fox, where Fox describes creation spirituality:

> For starters, let's say that it's liberation theology for the First World, for the overdeveloped peoples. Unlike that of Third World peoples, our poverty is not so much material as it is spiritual and psychological. Our addictions to alcohol, drugs, sports, entertainment and work spring from our alienation from the earth and God and our effort to cover up both our pain and our joy. The mystical tradition that I am seeking to revive has a lot to say about freeing ourselves from addiction, getting high on the beauty of the created world and recreating our society. (Keen, 1989, p. 56)

I offer the powerful option of the physical presence of art and art making as path to spiritual liberation for the people of our materially overdeveloped, spiritually underdeveloped addiction-producing culture. This has proven to be a path and balm of healing to the co-researchers. Matthew Fox goes on to share his opinion that,

> Both therapists and politicians should join the mystics in leading us, gently but surely, into the wounds of our times, because if we did not live in such denial we could develop the collective imagination necessary to deal with our problems. But we are afraid to face the nothingness. The mystics tell us that

from the encounter with nothingness comes a breakthrough into imagination and creativity—the next step in the journey. Once you experience the awe and face the darkness, creativity is unleashed. (Keen, 1989, p. 58)

According to the findings of this study, art can facilitate recovery in many ways including the transcendent. If one is working as an art therapist, the theoretical framework of humanistic psychology with a transcendent element is a possible approach for enabling this kind of growth. The reverence and care for each individual that is promoted through humanistic psychology with a transcendent element can open a space which is safe enough for a person to re-member, re-claim, re-deem, and re-cover the parts of themselves that they have forgotten in the process of addiction.

The humanistic perspective views each person as unique and precious with great potential. The possibility exists for the self-actualization that Maslow (1978) talks about, including transcendence via grace. Being is essential and affirmation of the being is necessary in order not to lose it. Inner affirmation comes as people identify, feel, and name what they feel inside.

The practical principles of Adlerian Psychology can also be useful in the recovery process. For instance, the Adlerian framework promotes ideas such as taking responsibility for self, equality for human beings, and experiencing the logical consequences of behavior which are very helpful in the recovery process. Art is a way to help a person "see" and "own" these components of healthy living.

## ANCIENT PARADIGM

With art and spirituality's ancient intersected roots it is not surprising that the themes of this study echo at least one ancient model of spirituality. The paradigm of which I am thinking is just one ancient source which comes out of my own reflections and tradition. Perhaps there are others. It seems important to re-member and re-claim the ancient roots of these new images as this is a part of the recovery process.

As the themes of this study emerged, I kept feeling that I had heard this all before somewhere else. Some of the themes of spirituality which the co-researchers came up with, gradually began to connect with the words of the beatitudes in the *Bible*, an ancient model for spiritual growth.

For example, I was aware of the devastating losses which had brought the co-researchers to their humbling admissions of powerlessness. Instead of being met in their powerlessness with increased struggle, they kept telling me stories of how they finally felt and/or became aware of their higher power's presence. They appeared energized and delighted that their admission of powerlessness had somehow brought them closer to their higher power.

Then while sifting through data for this study, several of the co-researcher's themes kept running through my mind—such as the admission of powerlessness, warmth of spiritual feelings, and God's communicating through art. It seemed to me that following a humbling admission of powerlessness, God had become very real to the co-researchers. This was surely consistent with the 12-step model for spirituality where admission of powerlessness opens the door to the reality of a higher power.

One day a beatitude popped into my consciousness: "Blessed are the poor in spirit for theirs is the kingdom of heaven" (*The Holy Bible,* Revised Standard Version, Matthew 5:3, 1962). It seemed that the humility required by the admission of powerlessness had somehow indeed opened the co-researchers to the spiritual world, which in a sense connects one with "the kingdom of heaven." For instance, I remember the painful powerless dark picture of Marcus's using space followed by the bright open "sun" picture of his higher power after he had admitted his powerlessness and experienced his higher power.

The co-researchers became aware of God's communication, the warmth of spiritual feelings, and even their ability to "see" God through image, color, and shape. It occurred to me that the co-researchers' stories of search for their higher power shared a sincerity, single-mindedness, or purity of purpose and that continuous visual references to God showed up in the artwork. For instance, all of the newly recovering people connected God with the color yellow. Imagery words like *bright, light,* and *clean* had been used by every newly recovering co-researcher for their higher power. I recalled another beatitude that paralleled the information collected from the co-researchers. It was, "Blessed are the pure in heart, for they shall see God" (*The Holy Bible,* Revised Standard Version, Matthew 5:8, 1962). The co-researchers on their single-minded spiritual journey had, in fact, been seeing God through their art. This reminds me of Betty's picture of the muddy water in the beaker being made pure and the childlike picture of her higher power which followed.

There is tremendous grief work involved in the giving up of an addiction. Mourning the loss of what one has looked to for fulfillment is a very painful process. Pictures of this painful process of letting go run throughout the stories of the co-researchers. Processing feelings and living through the grief resulting from this loss was an important theme of the artwork. As these co-researchers allowed this mourning to occur, the signs of comfort are visible through their artwork. The themes of hope in the midst of darkness and feelings of childlike newness both support the idea of comfort after loss. The following beatitude seemed to me to reflect this process: "Blessed are those who mourn for they shall be comforted" (*The Holy Bible,* Revised Standard Version, Matthew 5:4, 1962). An example of this process is Dana's picture which mourned the various paraphernalia of her unhealthy repetitious addictive behaviors which were outlined in yellow. Later, she used the same yellow outlines to celebrate her spirituality and her higher power. She had been comforted.

Looking at the passage containing the beatitudes, I noticed the other themes seemed to dovetail in and out. Perhaps this synchronization is understandable in light of the fact that all of the co-researchers in the study chose God as their higher power. If God is timeless, then there is little surprise that the process revealed through the data in this study is consistent with an ancient paradigm. The most consequential part of this reflection in terms of this study is that this paradigm is available to these co-researchers currently, in a personal way, through art making.

## THIS STUDY'S MEANING, USEFULNESS AND SIGNIFICANCE FOR OUR CULTURE

In a culture which caters to the outer person and thus promotes addiction, a return to reverence for each human being's inner self could have great ramifications. The social implications of this study are important and consequential to a country plagued by addiction and spiritual poverty.

This study of the experience of people recovering from addiction shows personal encounters with dark "nothingness" resulting in the creative and healing journey toward wholeness and a growing spirituality. As long as we as a society remain in collective denial about our spiritual impoverishment as a materially "overdeveloped" people, the growing tide of addiction will continue.

This study provides a glimpse of another way and a creative path which makes this way available. Our fast-moving, technological, materially oriented society has pulled us out of balance, and we are forgetting our humanity, treating ourselves as a mechanized part of the society we have created. We have looked outside of ourselves for satisfaction in things, people, places, drugs for so long, and we have come up empty. The last frontier, the only area left unexplored to an exterior people, is their interior. Art making can facilitate this interior journey.

On the day after the San Francisco earthquake in 1989, there was an intelligent, young, upwardly-mobile-appearing newscaster telling about the scene, on the spot, in his hometown of San Francisco. He had very little to say and looked a little disoriented. Several of his words have been with me since: "We found out we are only little creatures after all." This was a powerful admission of his humanity. It implied need. It implied powerlessness.

In addiction recovery in general and in this study in particular, it has been found that an admission of powerlessness can open one to the possibility of a power greater than oneself. This allows the order of things to come back into balance. We can work and play and just be, knowing that we are wonderfully human and need the loving care of a higher power. We have promoted the idea in our culture that we are something other than what we are by surrounding ourselves with things, polishing our intellects to impress others, forgetting about our spirits. We have gazed at the boxy forms of our skyscrapers so long that our eyes have the same empty glaze of the skyscraper windows. We have forgotten that there is more to a human than what can be seen. We are a culture haunted by addiction, where people are desperately looking outside of themselves for answers.

Spirituality is the foundation of recovery. Creativity has proven to be fertile ground for spiritual growth to the co-researchers in this study. A grounded spirituality allows transcendence which both embraces and enlarges all of the possibilities for that person.

Addiction counseling professionals and art therapists working in the field of addiction need to take seriously a holistic approach to recovery that honors spirituality. Addiction is thought by many to be the number one problem in our society. The United States has spent billions of dollars on exterior methods for dealing with this disease, and it continues to grow. This study reveals art as a path out of this disease and into a continuing, process-oriented recovery.

The number of co-researchers involved in this study is small, as is appropriate with Heuristic Research, but the demographic range is wide to give a broad view of the experience studied. The age range is wide.

The co-researchers are both men and women. The length of recovery varies greatly. The addictions vary. Art facilitated of the spiritual part of recovery in each co-researcher even though they had many differences from one another. Look for *New Images, Ancient Paradigm* (Chickerneo, 1990) in the reference section for more specific procedures of conducting the study, limitations, etc.

## CONCLUSION

The data acquired from the co-researchers in this study are rich and powerful. The very fact that these people have been willing to admit their human powerlessness and need for a higher power has allowed transcendence to happen. The willingness of the co-researchers to be open has produced the abundant themes of their journeys. The art process has facilitated and enhanced their spiritual process.

Our country has spent billions of dollars to deal with the problem of addiction and has not found an effective solution. The results of this study indicate a path to health for the co-researchers, with art as the vehicle for change and growth. This could point the way to possibilities for others. Art as expeditor of the spiritual part of recovery is an individual and positive approach which proved very fruitful to the co-researchers in the study.

We have forgotten, as a culture, that true power for a human comes with an admission that we are not God so that we can be open to the real power available to us through a higher power. An admission like this is a way back to our human earthiness where we can once again enter into the freedom that is part of our inheritance as creatures with a loving creator. For the co-researchers of this study, art, which was accessed on the interior of their beings, has proven to be a way back home to them and their higher power.

# REFERENCES

Albert-Puleo, Nancy. (1980). Modern psychoanalytic art therapy and its application to drug abuse. *The Arts in Psychotherapy, 7*(1):43–52.

Albert-Puleo, Nancy and Osha, Valerie. (1976–77). Art therapy as an alcoholism treatment tool. *Alcohol Health and Research World, 1*(2):28–31.

*Alcoholics anonymous.* (1976). 3rd ed. New York City: Alcoholics Anonymous World Services, Inc.

Alford, Geary S. (1980). Alcoholics anonymous: an empirical outcome study. *Addictive Behaviors, 5*(4):359–370.

Allen, Pat B. (1985). An alcoholism treatment program. *American Journal of Art Therapy, 24*(1):10–12.

Arnold, Robert J. (1977). AA's 12 steps as a guide to ego integrity. *Journal of Contemporary Psychotherapy, 9*(1):62–77.

*As Bill sees it.* (1980). New York: Alcoholics Anonymous World Services, Inc.

Bean, Margaret. (1975). Alcoholics Anonymous. *Psychiatric Annals, 5*(2):45–72.

———. (1975). Alcoholics Anonymous: II. *Psychiatric Annals, 5*(3):83–117.

Bebbington, Paul E. (1976). The efficacy of Alcoholics Anonymous: the elusiveness of hard data. *British Journal of Psychiatry, 128:*572–580.

Beit-Hallahmi, Benjamin. (1986). Religion as art and identity. 91st Annual Convention of the American Psychological Association. *Religion, 16:*1–17.

Bissell, LeClair; King, Barbara L.; and O'Brien, Peter. (1979). Alcoholics Anonymous, alcoholism counseling, and social work treatment. *Health and Social Work, 4*(4):181–198.

Blumberg, Leonard. (1977). The ideology of a therapeutic social movement: Alcoholics Anonymous. *Journal of Studies on Alcohol, 38*(11):2122–2143.

Bogdaniak, Roman and Piercy, Fred. (1987). Therapeutic issues of adolescent children of alcoholics (AdCA) groups. *International Journal of Group Psychotherapy, 37*(4):569–588.

Bornet, Andrew and Ogborne, Alan C. (1982). Abstinence and abusive drinking among affiliates of Alcoholics Anonymous: are these the only alternatives? *Addictive Behaviors, 7*(2):199–202.

Buber, Martin. (1970). *I and thou.* New York: Charles Scribner's Sons.

Burke, Kathleen. (1985). When words aren't enough... a study of the use of art therapy in the treatment of chemically dependent adolescents with special focus upon the spiritual dimension. *Dissertation Abstracts International, 46,* 08-A, p. 2166 (University Microfilms No. AAD85-23, 669)

Buxton, Millicent; Smith, David; and Seymour, Richard. (1987). Spirituality and other points of resistance to the 12-step recovery process. *Journal of Psychoactive Drugs, 19*(3):275–286.

Caldwell, Jean. (1986). Preparing a family for intervention. special issue: drug dependency and the family. *Journal of Psychoactive Drugs, 18*(1):57–59.

Capaldi, N.; Kelly, E.; and Navia, L. (1981). *An invitation to philosophy.* Buffalo, NY: Prometheus Books.

Causey, Beth. (1987). Fear, faith, and movement. *Journal of Religion and Health, 26*(1):50–56.

Cermak, Timmen. (1986). Diagnostic criteria for codependency. special issue: drug dependency and the family. *Journal of Psychoactive Drugs, 18*(1):15–20.

Cermak, Timmen. (1986). *Diagnosing and treating co-dependence.* Minneapolis, Minnesota: Johnson Institute Books.

Chickerneo, Nancy Barrett. (1986). *A woman's journey.* Unpublished master's thesis, Mundelein College, Chicago.

Chickerneo, Nancy Barrett. (1990). New images, ancient paradigm: A study of the contribution of art to spirituality in addiction recovery. *Dissertation Abstracts International, 51,* 11-A, p. 3781. (University Microfilms No. AAD91-10801)

Clark, Jon. (1987). Duet: The experience of the psychologically androgynous male. *Dissertation Abstracts International, 49,* 01-B, p. 0235. (University Microfilms No. AAD88-04371)

Cleveland, Martha. (1987). Treatment of co-dependent women through the use of mental imagery. *Alcoholism Treatment Quarterly, 4*(1):27–41.

Cox, Harvey. (1969). *The feast of fools.* Cambridge, MA: Harvard University Press.

Devine, Diane. (1970). A preliminary investigation of paintings by alcoholic men. *American Journal of Art Therapy. 9*(3):115–128.

Donnenberg, Debra. (1978). Art therapy in a drug community. *Confinia Psychiatrica, 21*(1–3):37–44.

Douglass, Bruce and Moustakas, Clark. (1985). Heuristic inquiry: the internal search to know. *Journal of Humanistic Psychology, 25*(3):39–55.

Faltico, Gary J. and McElroen, Lawrence J. (1977). Reality therapy and Alcoholics Anonymous: a comparison of two approaches to behavior change. *Corrective and Social Psychiatry and Journal of Behavior Technology, Methods and Therapy, 23*(3):79–82.

Farris-Kurtz, Linda. (1981). Time in residential care and participation in Alcoholics Anonymous as predictors of continued sobriety. *Psychological Reports, 48*(2):633–634.

Fischer, Kathleen. (1983). *The inner rainbow: The imagination in Christian life.* New York: Paulist Press.

Foulke, William and Keller, Timothy. (1976). The art experience in addict rehabilitation. *American Journal of Art Therapy, 15*(3):75–80.

Fournier, Robert R. (1987). Suicidal movement: an addiction to death or an invitation to spiritual formation. *Studies in Formative Spirituality, 8*(2):175–185.

Franck, Frederick. (1973). *The zen of seeing.* New York: Vintage Books.

Friel, John and Friel, Linda. (1988). *Adult children: The secrets of dysfunctional families.* Deerfield Beach, FL: Health Communications, Inc.

Fox, Matthew. (1985). *Illuminations of Hildegard of Bingen.* Santa Fe, NM: Bear & Co.

Fox, Matthew. Ed. (1987). *Hildegard of Bingen's book of divine works.* Santa Fe, NM: Bear & Co.

Gardner, Howard. (1982). *Art, mind, and brain.* New York: Basic Books, Inc.

Gendlin, E. (1978). *Focusing.* New York: Everest House Publishers.

Gierymski, Tadeusz and Williams, Terence. (1986). Codependency. Special issue: Drug dependency and the family. *Journal of Psychoactive Drugs, 18*(1):7–13.

Hall, Calvin and Nordby, Vernon. (1973). *A primer of Jungian psychology.* New York: A Mentor Book.

Heidegger, Martin. (1972). *On time and being.* New York: Harper Torchbooks.

*Holy Bible.* (1962). Revised Standard Version, New York: Oxford University Press.

Hozeski, Bruce. Trans. (1986). *Hildegard of Bingen's scivias.* Santa Fe, NM: Bear & Co.

Huizinga, J. (1955). *A study of the play-element in culture.* Boston: The Beacon Press.

Jacobson, Steven B. (1987). The 12-step program and group therapy for adult children of alcoholics. *Journal of Psychoactive Drugs, 19*(3):253–255.

Jegen, Carol Francis. (1986). *Jesus, the peace maker.* Kansas City, MO: Sheed & Ward.

Jegen, Carol Frances. (1989). Space and time for the spirit. *Lutheran Woman Today,* 2:1.

Johnson, David R. (1985). Envisioning the link among the creative arts therapies. *Arts in Psychotherapy, 12*(4):233–238.

Johnson, Vernon E. (1980). *I'll quit tomorrow,* San Francisco: Harper & Row.

Jourard, S. (1968). *Disclosing man to himself.* New York: D. Van Nostrand Co.

Jung, Carl G. (1968). *Man and his symbols.* New York: Dell Publishing.

Kandinsky, Wassily. (1977). *Concerning the spiritual in art.* New York: Dover Publications, Inc.

Kaufman, Gail Hope. (1981). Art therapy with the addicted. *Journal of Psychoactive Drugs, 3*(4):353–360.

Keen, Sam. (1989, June). Original blessing, not original sin. *Psychology Today,* pp. 54–58.

Kinney, Jean and Leaton, Gwen. (1987). *Loosening the grip.* St. Louis: Times Mirror/Mosby College Publishing.

Knox, Wilma J. (1973). Attitudes of social workers and other professional groups toward alcoholism. *Quarterly Journal of Studies on Alcohol, 34:*4-A:1270–1278.

Kurtz, Ernest. (1982). Why A.A. works: the intellectual significance of Alcoholics Anonymous. *Journal of Studies on Alcohol, 43*(1):38–80.

Landgarten, Helen. (1975). Group art therapy for mothers and daughters. *American Journal of Art Therapy, 14*(2):31–35.

Lathrop, Gordon. (1988). How symbols speak. *Liturgy, 7*(1):9–14.

Lauck, Marcia and Koff-Chapin, Deborah. (1989). *At the pool of wonder: Dreams and visions of an awakening humanity.* Santa Fe, NM: Bear & Co.

L'Engle, Madeleine. (1980). *Walking on water: Reflections on faith and art.* Wheaton, IL: Harold Shaw Publishers.

Madsen, William. (1974, Spr Exp Issue). Alcoholics Anonymous as a crisis cult. *Alcohol Health and Research World,* pp. 37–30.

Marinow, Alexander. (1980). Symbolic self-expression in drug addiction. *Confinia Psychiatrica, 23:*103–108.

Maslow, A. (1978). *The farther reaches of human nature.* New York: Penguin Books.

May, Gerald. (1988). *Addiction and grace.* San Francisco: Harper & Row Publishers.

May, Rollo. (1967). *Psychology and the human dilemma.* Princeton, NJ: D. Van Nostrand Company, Inc.

———. (1985). *The courage to create.* New York: Bantam Books.

McNeil, Evadne. (1984). Art therapy: Birthing our proper creativity. *Dissertation Abstracts International, 45,* 10-A. (University Microfilms No. AAD85-00796.)

Miller, David. (1970). *Gods and games.* Cleveland, OH: The World Publishing Co.

Morris, William, Ed. (1976). *The American heritage dictionary of the English language.* Boston: Houghton Mifflin Company.

Moustakas, Clark E. (1961). *Loneliness.* New York: Prentice-Hall, Inc.

Naitove, Connie E. (1978). Symbolic patterns in drawings by habitual users of street drugs. *Confinia Psychiatrica, 21*(1–3):112–118.

Neale, Robert. (1969). *In praise of play: Toward a psychology of religion.* New York: Harper & Row.

Needleman, Carla. (1986). *The work of craft: An inquiry into the nature of crafts and craftsmanship.* New York: Arkana.

Peck, M. Scott. (1978). *The road less traveled: A new psychology of love, traditional values and spiritual growth.* New York: Simon and Schuster, Inc.

Polanyi, M. (1967). *The tacit dimension.* Garden City, NY: Doubleday.

Prezioso, Fredrick A. (1987). Spirituality in the recovery process. *Journal of Substance Abuse Treatment, 4*(3–4):233–238.

Prosch, Harry. (1986). *Michael Polanyi: A critical exposition.* Albany, NY: State University of New York Press.

Rahner, Hugo. (1967). *Man at play.* New York: Herder and Herder.

Reeder, Rachel. (1988). Images for life. *Liturgy, 7*(1):5–8.

Robb, Harold B. (1986). Ninety-third annual convention of the American Psychological Association: spiritual issues: do they belong in psychological practice? *Psychotherapy in Private Practice, 4*(4):85–91.

Rogers, Peter. (1987). *A painter's quest: Art as a way of revelation.* Santa Fe, NM: Bear & Company.

Rubin, Judith. (1984). *The art of art therapy.* New York: Brunner/Mazel.

Samuels, Mike and Samuels, Nancy. (1984). *Seeing with the mind's eye: The history, techniques and uses of visualization.* New York: Random House.

Schaef, Anne Wilson. (1986). *Co-Dependence: Misunderstood-mistreated.* Minneapolis, MN: Winston Press, Inc.

Schaef, Anne Wilson. (1987). *When society becomes an addict.* San Francisco: Harper & Row.

Schaffer, Ulrich. (1980). *Surprised by light.* San Francisco: Harper & Row.

Small, Jacquelyn. (1987). Spiritual emergence and addiction: a transpersonal approach to alcoholism and drug abuse counseling. *Revision, 10*(2):23–36.

Smalley, Sondra. (1987). Dependency issues in lesbian relationships. special issue: psychotherapy with homosexual men and women: integrated identity approaches for clinical practice. *Journal of Homosexuality, 14*(1–2):125–135.

Smalley, Sondra and Coleman, Eli. (1987). Treating intimacy dysfunctions in dyadic relationships among chemically dependent and codependent clients. *Journal of Chemical Dependency Treatment, 1*(1):229–243.

Subby, R. (1984). "Inside the chemically dependent marriage: Denial and manipulation," chap. in *Co-Dependency—an emerging issue.* Deerfield Beach, FL: Health Communications, Inc.

Subby, R. and Friel, J. (1984). "Co-dependency: A paradoxical Dependency," chap. in *Co-Dependency—an emerging issue.* Deerfield Beach, FL: Health Communications, Inc.

Tyszkiewicz, Magdalena. (1975). A trial of comparison of pathological creative production of a drug-addicted alcoholic patient with the art of famous artists. *Materia Medica Polona. The Polish Journal of Medicine and Pharmacy, 7*(1):53–57.

Van Kaam, Adrian. (1987). Addiction: counterfeit of religious presence. *Studies in Formative Spirituality, 8*(2):243–255.

Virshup, Evelyn. (1978). *Right brained people in a left brained world.* Los Angeles: Guild of Tutors Press.

Virshup, Evelyn. (1985). Group art therapy in a methadone clinic lobby. *Journal of Substance Abuse Treatment, 2:*153–158.

Wadeson, Harriet. (1980). *Art psychotherapy.* New York: John Wiley & Sons, Inc.

Wegscheider-Cruse, Sharon. (1985). *Choice making: For co-dependents adult children and spirituality seekers.* Pompano Beach, FL: Health Communications, Inc.

White, Lynn Ward. (1979). Recovery from alcoholism: transpersonal dimensions. *Journal of Transpersonal Psychology, 11*(2):117–128.

Whitfield, C. (1984). "Co-Dependency: An emerging problem among professionals," chap. in *Co-Dependency—an emerging issue.* Deerfield Beach, FL: Health Communications, Inc.

Whitfield, C. (1987). *Healing the child within.* Pompano Beach, FL: Health Communications, Inc.

Woititz, J. (1984). "The co-dependent spouse: What happens to you when your husband is an alcoholic," chap. in *Co-Dependency—an emerging issue.* Deerfield Beach, FL: Health Communications, Inc.